Paving Tobacco Road

A Century of Progress by the North Carolina Department of Transportation

Paving Tobacco Road

A Century of Progress by the
North Carolina Department of Transportation

Walter R. Turner

Office of Archives and History
North Carolina Department of Cultural Resources
Raleigh, North Carolina

North Carolina Transportation Museum Foundation
Spencer, North Carolina

NORTH CAROLINA DEPARTMENT OF CULTURAL RESOURCES

Lisbeth C. Evans, *Secretary*

OFFICE OF ARCHIVES AND HISTORY

Jeffrey J. Crow, *Deputy Secretary*

HISTORICAL PUBLICATIONS SECTION

Donna E. Kelly, *Administrator*

NORTH CAROLINA HISTORICAL COMMISSION

Jerry C. Cashion (2007), *Chairman*	Paul D. Escott (2007)	Gail W. O'Brien (2005)
Alan D. Watson (2009), *Vice-Chairman*	Mary Hayes Holmes (2005)	Freddie L. Parker (2007)
Millie M. Barbee (2009)	B. Perry Morrison Jr. (2005)	Margaret Supplee Smith (2007)
Kemp P. Burpeau (2009)	Janet N. Norton (2005)	

Emeriti:
N. J. Crawford
H. G. Jones
William S. Powell
Max R. Williams

NORTH CAROLINA TRANSPORTATION MUSEUM FOUNDATION

Sturges Bryan, *President*
State Alexander, *Vice-President*
David S. Clay, *Vice-President*
Jim Wrinn, *Vice-President*
Steve Surratt, *Secretary*
Tracey McLaughlin, *Treasurer*
Elmer Lam, *Past President*

©2003 by the North Carolina Office of Archives and History
All rights reserved
ISBN 0-86526-305-1

Photo courtesy Southern Historical Collection, UNC-Chapel Hill

*To Frank Page, Chairman,
North Carolina Highway Commission, 1919-1929*

*And certainly if it may be said of many men in the modern world
it may be said as it was of Sir Christopher Wren:
"If you would see his monument, look about you."*

—*Editorial,* News and Observer *(Raleigh), December 21, 1934*

Contents

Foreword ix

Acknowledgments xi

Introduction xv

1 Setting the Stage: 1915-1920 1

2 An Impressive Beginning: 1921-1929 11

3 Growth and Expansion of Responsibilities: 1930-1948 29

4 Becoming a Modern Agency: 1949-1972 51

5 Broadening the Focus from Highways to Transportation: 1973-2003 81

6 Exploring Alternatives into the Future 113

Epilogue: Looking Back and Ahead 147

Appendixes 149

Selected Bibliography 153

Index 167

Foreword

North Carolina has had two paramount needs throughout its 350-year history as a colony and a state: better education and better transportation. The neglect of those public services for too long kept its people in economic and social poverty. Efforts made to address those dual needs afford both the most heartening examples of public leadership and too-frequent instances of the unwillingness of the state's leaders and its people to respond to those challenges.

When North Carolina's perceptive state leaders have set forth the prospective benefits from better schools and transportation, their messages often have been overcome by a combination of opposition to taxation, excessive localism, and resistance to change. Yet, advocates whose causes were both timely and pressed with political skill and power prevailed.

Complaints that poor transportation handicapped the economic and social advancement of North Carolina date from the mid-1600s, the earliest decades of European settlement within the state's present boundaries. State senator Archibald Debow Murphey (1777-1832), in a series of state reports published between 1815 and 1818, projected a visionary plan for improved waterborne transportation for the state, but to little avail. North Carolina, lacking a means to convey produce to its own ports at Beaufort and Wilmington, was obliged to rely upon seaports in neighboring Virginia and South Carolina. The completion of the 223-mile North Carolina Railroad from Charlotte to Goldsboro in 1856 and its eastern extension to Morehead City in 1858 marked a major advance, for it enabled many of the state's farmers to get their produce to distant markets profitably for the first time. North Carolina's short-lived and disappointing romance with plank roads and its more productive venture in turnpike building (especially in the western counties) in the mid-nineteenth century, which complemented the railroad, began to provide the state with an additional but still only partial answer to its transportation needs.

Those ventures, undertaken as private enterprises and typically with state financial underwriting, met only a limited part of North Carolina's need for efficient transportation of goods and people.

At the beginning of the twentieth century, most of the state's roads were little better than those of a century earlier. Road planning, construction, and maintenance were county responsibilities, dependent upon local taxation, as well as upon labor required by law to be contributed by all able-bodied men. Roads were laid out with only local convenience in mind; there was no concept of a true statewide road system, much less one designed to connect with the roads of adjoining states.

Late in the nineteenth century, a few far-seeing citizens began to advocate statewide road improvements. Initiatives came slowly and haltingly, chiefly in the form of limited state advice on and assistance with road engineering to counties that requested it. A weak and short-lived North Carolina Highway Commission was created in 1901 to give the counties advice and assistance, but control of the roads and the responsibility for funding them remained with the counties. The North Carolina Good Roads Association, formed in 1902, became the chief advocate for better roads. It gained legislative reestablishment of an advisory State Highway Commission in 1915, just in time to enable North Carolina to benefit from federal highway-building funds authorized in 1916 for distribution to the respective states.

The effective work of the association and the commission, strengthened by growing public desire for better roads to accommodate the rapidly increasing numbers of automobiles and trucks, paved the way for the State Highway Act of 1921. By that statute, the state took over from the counties full planning, construction, maintenance, and financial responsibilities for 5,500 (mostly unpaved) miles of highways connecting the county seats and other principal towns and institutions of the state. To finance the construction of all-weather roads, the General Assembly authorized—on its own authority, without a referendum—the issuance of $50 million in state bonds in 1921 and another $65 million before the end of the 1920s. (The state's operating budget for 1920-1921 was only about $16 million; the comparable figure at present is more than $14 billion.)

By 1921, state road costs were met by user charges in the form of motor fuel taxes and vehicle registration fees, as well as increasing federal aid. A decade later, responding to the crisis the Great Depression created for local governments, the General Assembly of 1931 assumed for the state responsibility for the remainder of the road system, relieving the counties of those burdens. The bold legislative actions in 1921 and 1931 thrust North Carolina ahead of all but a few states in the extent and quality of its road system at that time and earned for it the title of the "Good Roads State."

The changes in road policy that transpired in the early twentieth century did not come easily. Many citizens, including some who considered themselves good-roads advocates, favored continued county responsibility for secondary roads. Others were content to cope with mud and dust in lieu of better roads if the alternative were to be higher taxes and loss of local road control to some distant engineer in Raleigh. It is a high tribute to the good-roads promoters, including Governors Cameron Morrison (1921-1925), O. Max Gardner (1929-1933), and W. Kerr Scott (1949-1953—a generation later) that their longer vision and wiser leadership prevailed.

In this book, Walter R. Turner recounts in a richly detailed and engrossing narrative how North Carolina's present state highway system has evolved since 1915. His account comprehends not only North Carolina's current highway system—the second-longest state-maintained road system in the nation (after Texas)—but also other forms of transportation that are assuming increasing importance: air travel, the revival of rail travel (both regional and long distance), bus systems, bicycling, and even mass-transit systems. Turner identifies many of the leaders, political and professional, who helped to create the entire transportation system.

North Carolina's present state transportation system, like its public education system at every level, is the product of a major policy commitment made during the first third of the twentieth century. That commitment holds that the people of North Carolina should finance governmental services of comparable quality to everyone, regardless of place of residence, by taxing the resources of the entire state and spending the resulting revenue to serve the needs of all the people.

John L. Sanders,
professor emeritus,
public law and government,
University of North Carolina at Chapel Hill
December 2002

Acknowledgments

As historian at the North Carolina Transportation Museum at Spencer, North Carolina, my first assignment was to compile a detailed report on the history of the North Carolina Department of Transportation (NCDOT) to guide designers in creating exhibits for the museum's spectacular new Back Shop exhibit hall. As I delved into the NCDOT's early years, I realized the vital role the agency played in the state's twentieth-century development and that its story needed to be available to a wider audience. With encouragement and support from many special individuals and organizations, that realization developed into this book.

My acknowledgments begin with Elmer Lam, the longtime, visionary past president of the North Carolina Transportation Museum Foundation. Under his leadership, the foundation created the Back Shop project and funded my historian position, even during a time of tight state budgets. Elmer's enthusiasm for the book always lifted my spirits.

I value the contributions of Richard Knapp from North Carolina Historic Sites, my colleague, who was indispensable throughout the writing process. His involvement included teaching me the virtues of outlining, giving me tips on research, providing ongoing editing (as we sent chapters and segments back and forth via e-mail), and organizing the team that transformed the manuscript into a published book.

Additional persons read the entire text and made comments for improvements. Ed Rankin, a constant source of encouragement, offered suggestions for including the role of private-sector companies in this story. Michael Hill added historical details and dates. I am grateful to John Sanders, a family friend, who volunteered to read the manuscript, clarifying details and references to state government, and then agreed to write the book's perceptive foreword.

Robert Ireland reviewed drafts of chapters two and three and offered interpretation of the use of prisoners for road building and the link between roads and education. Richard Weingroff was invaluable in providing material from the Federal Highway Administration, clarifying federal highway actions, and offering commentary on the history of interstate highways. Sherri Johnson suggested improvements to chapter five and assisted with updating coverage of the current NCDOT administration. David King (and his division directors) and Larry Sams reviewed chapter six. Others who read selected chapters and provided commentary include Jack Murdock, Charles Young, Elizabeth Smith, Sid Bradsher, and Sturges Bryan.

NCDOT employees (in addition to those listed in the bibliography) who provided information included Secretary Lyndo Tippett, as well as Ted Alman, Al Avant, Gail Baines, Diane Berger, Edward Davis, Mary Pope Furr, Charles Glover, Ivonne Grady, Bob Hall, Linda Harrison, Julia Hegele, Kathi Johnson, Bill Jones, Mike Kozak, Calvin Leggett, Sharon Lipscomb, Chris McAdams, Mary Meletiou, Sandy Nance, Brian Padfield, Allan Paul, Miriam Perry, Charlene Phillips, Frances Pittman, Jim Rand, David Ritchie, Anthony Roper, Len Sanderson, Topsy Skinner, Wayne Stallings, Charles Tomlinson, Charlie Utz, Steve Varnedoe, and Denise Whitehead. Former NCDOT workers, including Bob Grabarek, John Watkins, Whit Webb, Jean Boyd, and Poe Cox, offered assistance. Information supplied by Crissty Martin enabled me to complete the revenue tables in the appendixes. One of the highlights of my research was spending a half-day in Raleigh talking and eating lunch with Billy Rose, who shared his knowledge of urban and interstate roads and his memories of working with Bill Babcock.

My colleagues at the North Carolina Transportation Museum were supportive—among them Alane Mills (an expert with the English language), Elizabeth Smith, Kelly Alexander, and Karen Nilsen, as well as board members Sturges Bryan (new foundation president) and Steve Surratt. Candice Boyd and John Mercer were always available to solve computer problems.

Libraries were essential to this project—beginning with the day Portia Jordan entrusted me with the NCDOT library's collection of agency annual reports, which occupied a shelf in my office cubicle for a year. The University of North Carolina (UNC)-Greensboro's Jackson Library, with its vast resources, quiet corners, and friendly reference staff, became my home library. My thanks go to Phil Kirk for giving me access to the library of North Carolina Citizens for Business and Industry, whose magazine provided an independent voice on highway and transportation issues. Other libraries that provided information include the State Library of North Carolina (especially Cheryl McLean), the North Carolina Collection at UNC-Chapel Hill, the Pack Memorial Library (Asheville), the Wake County Public Libraries (Raleigh), the Greensboro Public Library, the New Hanover County Public Library (Wilmington), the Shepard-Pruden Memorial Library (Edenton), the Public Library of Charlotte and Mecklenburg County, the North Carolina State University Library, and the Cumberland County Public Library (Fayetteville).

A critical turning point in the process of transforming my manuscript into a publishable book came during the summer of 2002 when museum board member Knox Bridges, motivated by his curiosity and love of North Carolina history, offered a generous contribution toward publication. Jim and Carolyn Turner, Trent Ragland Jr., and Parsons Transportation Group at the request of William Marley likewise made generous contributions; also contributing were Dillard Teer, Robb Teer, and Roy Teer. The North Carolina Transportation Museum Foundation supported the book as co-publisher with the Historical Publications Section of the North Carolina Office of Archives and History.

In preparing the book for publication, I was fortunate to work with very talented professionals in the Raleigh area. Donna Kelly of Historical Publications helped to arrange necessary contracts and to choose a printer and also arranged for the book's storage and distribution; Lisa Bailey from that office was the book's proofreader. Robert Topkins, who gave the text clarity, was an ideal editor. I especially thank him for his willingness to spend many hours on the telephone and for his toleration of all my follow-up calls and last-minute updates. Mark Moore and Brian Padfield created special maps to illustrate this transportation story. Ellen Holding generously shared the NCDOT's excellent collection of photographs from earlier decades, and Steve Massengill went out of his way to find appropriate photographs from the Archives and History collection. Charlie Jones spent countless hours searching for NCDOT photographs from recent decades and also made and supplied new photos specifically for this publication. Jim Willard printed several photographs and helped me organize illustrations.

For furnishing requested photographs and illustrations, I am grateful to Richard Weingroff of the Federal Highway Administration, Washington, D.C.; Beverly Tetterton of the New Hanover County Public Library, Wilmington; Ann Wright of Pack Memorial Library, Asheville; Pat Ryckman of the J. Murrey Atkins Library, UNC-Charlotte; Stephen Catlett of the Greensboro Historical Museum; Hugh Morton of Grandfather Mountain; Dennis Lawson of the Duke Energy Archives, Charlotte; Michael Southern of the North Carolina State Historic Preservation Office; and Kim Taylor of the Charlotte Area Transit System. I thank Sharon Dean for her assistance in designing an attractive book.

Most of the photographs (all uncredited) in the book are reproduced courtesy of the NCDOT but do not include identification of the respective photographers. Such photos in the first three chapters should be credited to H. K. Witherspoon and those in chapters five and six to Charlie Jones. Witherspoon was an engineer with the State Highway Commission from 1919 to the 1950s but is best remembered for his photographic record of the agency's early growth. Jones is an award-winning photographer who has spent three decades at the NCDOT. Because of the quality of his work, he also served as the unofficial photographer of the state's governors.

My lifelong infatuation with history began during childhood, while listening to family and political stories from my father, and continued with college courses under Bruce Pulliam at Methodist College in Fayetteville and Alan Keith-Lucas at UNC-Chapel Hill. But before I was ready to occupy the position of full-time historian, which led to this book, I went through a lengthy personal and professional transition in the late 1990s—moving from an established career in social work to an untested focus on transportation history. My longtime writing mentor, journalist Charles Young, encouraged that transition and introduced me to potential publishers. Editor Mary Best gave me the opportunity of producing articles for *Our State* magazine. In the meantime, my extended family—wife, Pamela Huntley Turner; in-laws, Henry and Ruby Huntley; and brothers, Jim, Wilfred, and Terry—provided moral support in so many ways. Those family members and friends went above and beyond the call of duty, and for that I shall always be grateful.

Walter R. Turner

Introduction

Growing up in Winston-Salem, North Carolina, during the 1950s, I always looked forward to our family's out-of-town trips. My parents, brothers, and I would pile into our 1948 Kaiser and head west on U.S. 158 and south on N.C. 801 to Mount Ulla to visit my great-aunt. Aunt Brooke, the only surviving member of a large family, lived alone in a rambling old family house without a car or electricity, though she did have a party-line wall telephone in the hall. She was slender, with white hair and rimless glasses and always wore dresses, regardless of the work she was doing. She cooked on a wood stove, lighted kerosene lamps at night, hauled water from a nearby spring, and used an outhouse. During visits to my aunt's house, whenever we boys heard the Southern Railway train coming, we'd run across a grassy field to wave at the engineer and watch the train pass through the cut below. When I was at my Aunt Brooke's in the summer, we would play board games, listen to her portable radio, and walk to visit neighbors. She told me stories about the relatives whose large, imposing pictures hung on the walls in the main room of the house.

On other occasions, our family would drive to Statesville, looking for the Burma Shave signs along the way. From there, we might take Buffalo Shoals Road (the route of the old east-west Central Highway) and cross the Catawba River to visit Turner family aunts and uncles at Monbo (near Sherrill's Ford), where my father was reared, or travel on U.S. 70 beyond Hickory to the village of Rutherford College, home of Uncle Walter and Aunt Freddie and their kids.

Pulling our pop-up trailer, we spent many summer weekends on the Blue Ridge Parkway, camping at Crabtree Meadows. It was a delightful place, where a trail through the woods led to a huge mountain waterfall. Riding through Parkway tunnels and looking down on mountains and valleys below the road were unforgettable experiences. Visiting another section of the state, we'd head for a summer vacation at Carolina Beach, starting the trip on N.C. 109. Stopping in the peach country at a roadside stand in Biscoe or Candor, my mother would find peaches for the pies she would later bake. My father surveyed the watermelons, thumping several to test their ripeness before picking the right one.

After my parents retired to Kure Beach (between Carolina Beach and Fort Fisher) in the 1960s, we seemed to use U.S. 421 for at least part of every trip upstate to Raleigh, Chapel Hill, or points west. It became such a familiar highway that dad called it "the old beaten path." When I entered Fayetteville's Methodist College, I hitchhiked home and back on N.C. 87, rarely getting stranded. After college, I lived in Salisbury, Carrboro, Cary, and Wadesboro, where I married my wife, Pamela. We felt right at home on U.S. 74, which took us to Charlotte for eating out, shopping, or movies.

Those were years in which interstate highways sprouted and transformed the state. One early interstate trip for me was to Asheville on I-40—so much faster than the two-lane highways of my youth. When Pamela and I lived in Wilmington in the 1980s, we felt isolated from the rest of the state, but that changed with the completion of the Raleigh-Wilmington portion of I-40. Since we have been living in Greensboro for several years now, the interstates have become indispensable to me—whether I'm commuting to work on I-85 or going to Raleigh for the day via I-40.

This book describes the development of the agency responsible for all of these transportation wonders, and more—the North Carolina State Highway Commission, reorganized as the North Carolina Department of Transportation in the early 1970s. It is a story of men and women determined to make a difference, to provide services for citizens in all counties, day in and day out, year after year. And as Rick said to Elsa in *Casablanca*, "It's still a story without an ending."

Chapter 1

SETTING THE STAGE
1915-1920

After the opening of the North Carolina Railroad in the 1850s, railroads dominated the transportation picture in North Carolina and in the nation for several generations. In 1915, if someone were traveling more than a few miles, railroads still offered the best service. More than fifteen hundred communities in the state had railway stations.[1] Anson County, for example, had thirteen such stations to serve a population of only 28,000. Many of the state's railroad stations, such as those in Salisbury, Rocky Mount, and Hamlet, were impressive for their size or architectural style.[2]

By 1915 vast rail companies served the state with extensive passenger and freight services and employed large numbers of workers. Southern Railway (with headquarters in Washington, D.C.) dominated the Piedmont and western areas of the state. The firm operated a maintenance facility in Spencer that employed up to 2,500 people. The Seaboard Air Line Railway (based in Portsmouth, Virginia) had a modest maintenance facility in Hamlet, which was upgraded in the 1950s. The Atlantic Coast Line Railroad (ACL), with headquarters in Wilmington until 1960, had a large maintenance facility in Rocky Mount. In 1916 Southern operated 108 daily passenger trains in or through the state, the ACL had 64, and the Seaboard ran 36.[3] In addition, about 50 short-line railroads served the state.

The condition of the state's roads, on the other hand, was generally poor. Responsibility for building and maintaining roads had always resided with the local governments, primarily the counties. Mecklenburg County (Charlotte) led the way in locally financed improvements, beginning in 1885, followed at the turn of the century by Buncombe (Asheville), Guilford (Greensboro), and New Hanover (Wilmington) Counties. Between 1885 and 1910, many county roads were constructed with macadam, a combination of crushed rock and a bituminous (asphalt or tar) binder.[4] Sand-clay, topsoil, and gravel roads, cheaper but less durable than macadam, were likewise built. Though such roads were popular and relatively inexpensive to build, they required constant maintenance and proved unable to hold up to the rapidly increasing number of cars and trucks in the state in the decade after 1910. The newer vehicles, with greater weight and speed than wagons and horses, were more damaging to the roads. By 1912 North Carolina had a total of some 48,000 miles of roads, nearly all of them composed of dirt and mud. Improved roads included 2,210 miles of sand-clay, 914 miles of gravel, and 1,232 miles of macadam.[5]

Because counties could scarcely afford machinery, road building and maintenance were largely achieved with manual labor. Prisoners, including chain-gang labor, were widely used.

Principal Railroads in North Carolina ca. 1925

By the 1920s, North Carolina's extensive rail network reached its peak. Map by Michael Southern, N.C. Office of Archives and History (A&H).

Efforts to involve all male citizens in contributing labor (based on laws dating to colonial days) were not successful. A number of counties voted to issue bonds to pay for roads and received engineering advice from the North Carolina Geological and Economic Survey, based at the University of North Carolina.

Cecil K. Brown, a professor of economics at Davidson College, characterized efforts by county governments to build roads as demonstrations of "incompetence, ignorance, even stupidity." Brown pointed out that the scale of county government efforts in independent road building was "too small in this day when the automobile demands long connected routes."[6] Indeed, the only county-sponsored road in North Carolina that benefited the long-distance traveler was the fourteen miles of macadam Guilford County had constructed from Greensboro to High Point. (As a result of a tour of automobiles sponsored by New York City and Atlanta newspapers, that road won a prize in 1909.)[7]

In 1901 the North Carolina General Assembly had created a feeble North Carolina State Highway Commission, composed of the commissioner of agriculture, the state geologist, and a secretary. The duties of the Highway Commission, which had virtually no funding, were to furnish an engineer to assist counties and towns (with the agriculture department furnishing one also), to establish rules for prison road crews, and to supply technical plans and advice. The legislation reiterated that county commissioners would have responsibility for the construction and maintenance of roads, bridges, and ferries in their respective counties. The Highway Commission disbanded two years later, with few results to show for its efforts.[8]

In 1915 the legislature again established a State Highway Commission and provided it with an annual appropriation of ten thousand dollars. (Gov. Locke Craig [1913-1917], a promoter of highway construction by the state, had been unable to convince legislators to provide additional funding to the agency, which a supporter described as "de-horned and denatured.")[9] Passage of this state legislation was largely attributable to persistent lobbying by the North Carolina Good

Members of N.C. Good Roads Association taking an excursion in 1911 at Mooresville (near Statesville). Postcard courtesy A&H.

Roads Association, a small group of civic leaders who advocated better roads. As state geologist with the North Carolina Geological and Economic Survey in Chapel Hill, Joseph Hyde Pratt was a key leader of the Good Roads Association. Pratt, a native of Connecticut and a graduate of Yale University, had taught at Yale and Harvard before coming to North Carolina to join the Geological and Economic Survey in 1897.[10] Continuing as head of that body, he also became the secretary of the new State Highway Commission. The commission initially consisted of three members appointed by the governor, who served as its chairman. The 1915 law, though a modest step, was a recognition of state responsibility for road building. The commission managed to survive, largely because the number of automobiles in the state, twenty thousand, was at least doubling every two years, and there was the expectation that federal moneys would soon be available to states with highway commissions.

W. S. Fallis, who had worked closely with Pratt as an engineer with the Geological and Economic Survey, became the state highway engineer. He and Pratt took offices on the ninth floor of Raleigh's Commercial National Bank building. In its first year, the commission provided services to sixty-seven counties, including lectures, advice, and engineering consultation. Fallis designed and supervised the building of several bridges. The U.S. Office of Public Roads furnished two engineers for improving the "Central Highway," which the 1911 legislature had authorized to follow existing rail routes that connected Beaufort and Asheville by way of Raleigh, Greensboro, and Salisbury.[11] The first person Pratt and Fallis hired in 1915 was O. F. Yount, a native of Catawba County. Yount, known as "Captain Jack," supervised construction of a bridge that crossed the Tar River in Edgecombe County, the first bridge built under the guidance of the Highway Commission.[12]

Typical of experiences in driving longer distances in the state in the early twentieth century was that of two brothers, Reginald and Rupert Turner, as they traveled from Carolina Beach to Clinton in their Oakland Six car in 1919. With no highway signs to guide them and country roads that often did not connect directly from one county to another, the brothers took several wrong turns. Near Harrells, thirty-five miles north of Wilmington, an overflowing stream covered a wooden bridge made of two-by-fours. Reginald changed to a swimsuit, offered a boy who came along fifty cents to help, and together they held down the ends of the bridge while Rupert drove the Oakland across. Taking fifteen hours to cover seventy-five miles, they arrived at a hotel in Clinton at midnight and had to awaken the clerk to obtain a room.[13]

To remedy such conditions, Congress in 1916 passed the Federal-Aid Road Act, which allocated a total of $75 million to the states over a five-year period. The main purpose of the legislation was to improve public roads, especially those that served farmers. One historian characterized the road act as "a milestone in American highway development, for it directly involved the federal government in highway building."[14] Each state was required to have a state highway commission and to arrange a 50 percent match for federal allotments. North Carolina's federal-aid allocation for the first fiscal year, 1916-1917, was $114,000, a figure that doubled the following year.

In July 1916 a severe flood that lasted several days destroyed roads, bridges, and property in the mountain and western Piedmont areas of the

While directing the N.C. Geological Survey at UNC, Joseph Hyde Pratt was a pioneer in road development and was active with the Good Roads Association. He was appointed to the N.C. State Highway Commission in 1915. Photo courtesy A&H.

Several persons and two mules help a stranded motorist in the mountains, early 1920s. This was a common occurrence in the early twentieth century.

state. Eighty people died. An eight-mile stretch of road through Hickory Nut Gap in Henderson County, a key link in the Asheville-Charlotte road, was destroyed. Rebuilding the road was the first major project of the fledgling commission, which supervised the work of sixty-six prisoners. The legislature matched federal-aid funding for the $33,000 project. The new road opened in 1918.[15]

The 1917 legislature expanded the authority of the commission to coordinate and maintain federal-aid-funded roads but provided little additional state funding beyond the annual allocation of ten thousand dollars. Thirty percent of progressive automobile registration taxes, which ranged from five to ten dollars, depending on a car's horsepower, was allocated to the commission for maintenance, with the remainder going to the counties in which the fees were collected. Since the legislature had refused to provide state funding for a portion of the 50 percent local match required to receive any federal-aid funds, counties continued to assume that obligation. That practice favored the wealthier and more populous counties, which could afford to build and maintain roads.

By 1918 the State Highway Commission had grown to thirty-five employees. The U.S. Bureau of Public Roads had assigned six "cooperating" engineers to assist with road building in North Carolina.[16] The commission divided the state into ten administrative divisions, primarily for coordinating road maintenance. William L. Craven, a native of Concord, became the commission's bridge engineer. After studying civil engineering and graduating from the North Carolina College of Agriculture and Mechanical Arts (now North Carolina State University at Raleigh), Craven had designed steel structures and bridges for companies in Pennsylvania, Virginia, and North Carolina.[17]

The United States' involvement in World War I during 1917-1918 caused material shortages and construction delays in domestic road building. In addition, there were differences of opinion in Congress on highway policy and in the U.S. Office of Public Roads (renamed the Bureau of Public Roads) on just how the agency should interact with the states. These federal issues began to be resolved when Thomas MacDonald became head of the Bureau of Public Roads (then part of the U.S. Department of Agriculture) in 1919. After earning a civil engineering degree from Iowa State College in 1904, MacDonald became an assistant professor of civil engineering at the college, where he specialized in highway construction. He was appointed state highway engineer three years later. When the Iowa State Highway Department was organized in 1913, he became its chief engineer. MacDonald's "experience at the state level gave him insights into federal-state relations that helped resolve many of the conflicts that had resulted from the Bureau of Public Roads' aggressive oversight of federal-aid highway projects."[18] MacDonald's effective leadership greatly benefited North Carolina and the nation for the next three decades until his retirement in 1953.[19]

When Joseph Hyde Pratt joined the U.S. Army overseas in 1917, Harriet Morehead Berry (1877-1940) took over direction of the North Carolina Good Roads Association. Berry was reared in Hillsborough and graduated from the State Normal and Industrial School (now the University of North Carolina at Greensboro). She joined the Geological and Economic Survey in Chapel Hill in 1901, beginning as a stenographer, working closely with Pratt, and becoming involved with road issues. She was promoted to assistant director of the Good Roads Association in 1912. Through her association with these two organizations, she became acquainted with the state's business, political, and newspaper leaders.[20]

Harriet Berry joined the N.C. Geological Survey in 1901 as a stenographer and worked her way up to acting director in 1917, while becoming increasingly involved with the Good Roads Association. Photo courtesy A&H.

One of 250 surplus trucks that the U.S. Army gave to the N.C. State Highway Commission following World War I. Note signage.

Berry and the Good Roads Association presented a comprehensive prospective bill to the 1919 General Assembly. Some called the proposal the "Chapel Hill Plan," because civil engineers, geologists, and economists from the university had contributed to the design. The plan envisioned a system of hard-surface, all-weather highways that would connect all of the state's county seats and principal towns. To finance that ambitious recommendation, the commission would receive the entire amount of vehicle registration fees, rather than the 30 percent allocation it was then receiving, and possibly additional revenue resulting from modest bond issues. While welcoming more federal aid, Gov. Thomas W. Bickett (1917-1921) told the legislature that counties, rather than the state, should build roads and that he opposed the issuance of state bonds for roads. The "good roads" bill was defeated in 1919, a bitter disappointment to the association. One historian subsequently concluded that the proposed bill had been defeated by "an attitude which distrusted centralized and professionalized authority and valued local, non-professional control."[21]

The 1919 General Assembly did enact a compromise bill that raised the annual license/registration fee to $10.00-$20.00 for cars (depending on horsepower) and to $12.50-$100.00 for trucks and levied additional charges for trailers (depending upon their carrying capacity). The bill also directed that these steep license taxes on vehicles be paid into a special "State Highway Fund," which was separate from the state's General Fund;[22] encouraged counties to furnish one-fourth of the cost of federal-aid roads within their respective boundaries (with the federal government paying one-half the cost and the state paying the remaining one-fourth); and suggested wider use of convicts for road construction.

Between 1915 and 1919, the governor had chaired the State Highway Commission. The 1919 legislature reorganized the commission so that it would have a full-time chairman. Many felt that Joseph Hyde Pratt, secretary of the commission and longtime leader both of the Geological and Economic Survey and the Good Roads Association, was the logical choice.[23] Another candidate was Henry Varner of Lexington, editor of a magazine published by the Good Roads Association. Governor Bickett's office received twenty-six hundred endorsements by letter or telegram recommending Varner. Not yet ready to make a decision, the governor asked his friend Leonard Tufts, whose father had created the resort of Pinehurst, to come to Raleigh for a talk. Tufts recommended Frank Page for the chairman's position. Governor Bickett had not met Page but knew three of his brothers. The governor later recalled: "Mr. Tufts asked me to send for Frank

Page and look him over. I did, and before he left my office, I'd offered him the job."[24]

What made the forty-four-year-old Page a strong candidate was his experience in transportation, business, and finance. His father, Allison Francis Page, who had founded the towns of Cary and Aberdeen, had also established short-line railroads, sawmills, and banks. After studying two years at the University of North Carolina, Frank Page moved to Aberdeen to enter the family businesses. While serving with the U.S. Army Corps of Engineers in France during World War I, he asked to be sent to the front lines. Attaining the rank of major, he worked with troop-train operations and built roads. His regiment presented him with a silver service in appreciation of his leadership. At that time, Page's brothers were better known than he was. Walter Hines Page, a scholar and editor, had served as U.S. ambassador to Great Britain during World War I. Robert Page had served several terms in Congress.[25] Between 1919 and 1921, as commission chairman, Frank Page employed the growing funds from registration fees and modestly increased federal funds to continue expanding the State Highway Commission's services to the counties. Entering into contracts with ninety-six counties, the commission employed 250 large trucks received as surplus war material to perform maintenance work on 5,200 miles of roadways.[26] Federal-aid projects coordinated by the commission included construction of several new bridges. On the Central Highway just outside Raleigh, a 1910 steel bridge with a wooden floor was replaced with a modern concrete bridge.[27]

Automobile tours, parades, car shows, and the booming sales of Model T Fords made cars increasingly popular. By 1920 a number of low-cost, mass-produced automobiles of various makes were available for sale in America. North Carolina was twentieth among states in total auto registrations, with 530 automobile dealers and 127,000 cars. A decade earlier, in 1910, the state had claimed only 3,220 registered autos, or one car for every 371.5 citizens, well behind the national ratio of one car for every 125 citizens. As historian Robert Ireland has observed, "Only one obstacle remained to be overcome before North Carolina could take full advantage of the auto age, and that was the enormous task of building a statewide system of highways and roads capable of handling the rapidly increasing automobile population."[28]

Workers use a dump truck and steam-powered roller to pave road near Asheville in 1920.

Notes

1. American Association of Passenger Traffic Officers, *Official Guide of the Railways and Steam Navigation Lines of the United States* (New York: National Railway Publication Company): 1916 issue, 1345-1599; 1930 issue, 1489-1757.

2. Railway Map of North Carolina, 1922 (New York: Rand McNally and Company, 1922), located at North Carolina Transportation Museum; U.S. Department of Commerce, Bureau of the Census, *Fourteenth Census of the United States Taken in the Year 1920*, 11 vols. (Washington: Government Printing Office, 1921), 1:120.

3. *Official Guide of the Railways and Steam Navigation Lines*, 1916 issue, 1246-1256, 1295-1303, 1309-1313.

4. Robert E. Ireland, *Entering the Auto Age: The Early Automobile in North Carolina, 1900-1930* (Raleigh: Division of Archives and History, North Carolina Department of Cultural Resources, 1990), 61-64; Capus Waynick, *North Carolina Roads and Their Builders* (Raleigh: Superior Stone Company, 1952), 28.

5. Hugh T. Lefler and Albert R. Newsome, *North Carolina: The History of a Southern State*, 3d ed. (Chapel Hill: University of North Carolina Press, 1973), 587; North Carolina Geological and Economic Survey, Economic Report 36 (Raleigh, 1914), 112-115, cited in Cecil K. Brown, *The State Highway System of North Carolina, Its Evolution and Status* (Chapel Hill: University of North Carolina Press, 1931).

6. Brown, *State Highway System*, 51, 52.

7. Harry Wilson McKown Jr., "Roads and Reform: The Good Roads Movement in North Carolina, 1885-1921" (master's thesis, University of North Carolina at Chapel Hill, 1972), 30-31.

8. McKown, "Roads and Reform," 18; *Guide to Research Materials in the North Carolina State Archives: State Agency Records* (Raleigh: Department of Cultural Resources, Division of Archives and History, Archives and Records Section, 1995), 689-690.

9. Ireland, *Entering the Auto Age*, 70-71.

10. McKown, "Roads and Reform," 26.

11. North Carolina State Highway Commission, *Biennial Report, 1915-1916* (Raleigh: State Printer, 1917), 5 (hereafter cited as *Biennial Report*, with appropriate dates); Brown, *State Highway System*, 57.

12. "Commission's First Bridge," *North Carolina Roadways* 1 (January-February 1951): 20.

13. Walter R. Turner, "The Good Roads State," *Our State* 68 (August 2000): 62-63.

14. Bruce E. Seely, *Building the American Highway System: Engineers as Policy Makers* (Philadelphia: Temple University Press, 1987), 73.

15. *Biennial Report, 1917-1918*, 8, 9; information about the flood of 1916 provided by Michael Hill, Research Branch, Office of Archives and History, Raleigh.

16. *Biennial Report, 1917-1918*, 4.

17. "William L. Craven, Bridge Engineer," *North Carolina Highway Bulletin* 2 (January 1922): 9.

18. Richard F. Weingroff, information liaison specialist, Federal Highway Administration, e-mail to author, August 9, 2002.

19. Seely, *Building the American Highway System*, 54-65; Richard F. Weingroff, "Man of the Century, Thomas H. MacDonald," *www.fhwa.dot.gov* (Federal Highway Administration website).

20. Billy Arthur, "The Mother of Good Roads," *The State* 57 (January 1990): 12, 13, 14. Berry's grandfather, Capt. John Berry, was a state legislator and an architect and builder who constructed the Playmakers Theatre at UNC-Chapel Hill and the Orange County Courthouse at Hillsborough. *Dictionary of North Carolina Biography*, s.v. "Berry, Harriet Morehead."

21. McKown, "Roads and Reform," 80. Sources for discussion of actions by the 1919 General Assembly are McKown, "Roads and Reform," 61-80, and Brown, *State Highway System*, 61-72.

22. *Biennial Report, 1919-1920*, 8-11. From 1919 to 1989 all revenues from vehicle, gasoline, and federal-aid taxes were processed through the State Highway Fund. Beginning in 1990, some revenues were processed through the separate Highway Trust Fund.

23. Because of injuries sustained in World War I, however, Pratt (1870-1942) was hospitalized for three years and by the mid-1920s had to resign as state geologist and teacher. He continued to publish articles on policy issues.

24. "Frank Page, North Carolina's Pioneer Road Builder," *North Carolina Roadways* 1 (July 1950): 9.

25. *Dictionary of North Carolina Biography*, s.v. "Page" (all entries); "Frank Page, Gentleman, Banker, Soldier, Road Builder," *North Carolina Highway Bulletin* 4 (June 1923): 5.

26. *Biennial Report, 1919-1920*, 6, 46.

27. *Biennial Report, 1919-1920*, 34, 44, 45.

28. Ireland, *Entering the Auto Age*, 58, 124-125.

Chapter 2

AN IMPRESSIVE BEGINNING
1921-1929

In the 1920s North Carolina created one of the best state highway departments in the nation, earning national and international recognition as "the Good Roads State." This chapter is the story of that accomplishment.

Although roads were not an issue of note in the gubernatorial campaign of 1920, the prospect of a new governor brought hope to those advocating roads. Cameron Morrison, age fifty, was of Scottish descent. He had grown up in Rockingham, completed high school, studied law with a judge, and was licensed to practice law. He served as mayor of Rockingham and represented his county (Richmond) for one term in the state senate. In 1905 he moved to Charlotte and became allied with the Democratic Party's conservative wing, headed by U.S. senator Furnifold Simmons.[1] The Simmons organization supported Morrison's bid for governor in 1920. Morrison's Democratic challengers were Lt. Gov. O. Max Gardner and former congressman Robert Page (brother of Frank Page). Two primaries were required; in the first, Morrison garnered 49,070 votes to Gardner's 48,983 and Page's 30,180. Morrison defeated Gardner in a runoff, 70,353 to 61,073.[2]

Speaking to a large outdoor crowd in Mooresville during the campaign, Morrison became distracted by the noise of a railroad freight yard nearby. He tried to ignore the constant clanging of rail cars but finally gestured with his arms in the air and exclaimed, "Do you see that? Those railroads, with their high freight rates, will do anything to oppose me and my program for better roads."[3] Morrison made his only substantive speech about roads during a campaign appearance in Wilkesboro. He declared that, if elected, "I will use every faculty I possess to help put a policy through the General Assembly which will result in the speedy construction of a great system of highways." But Morrison, Gardner, and Page were careful not to suggest specific methods of financing. Instead, they supported the Democratic platform, which called for a state system of roads connecting all county seats and principal towns, to be established "as rapidly as possible without undue burden on the taxpayers of the state."[4] With Morrison's election, the future of road building was still uncertain. Historian William S. Powell quotes a source stating that no one expected more than "unimaginative, routine leadership" from the new governor.[5]

In the meantime, Harriet Berry was busy reinvigorating the Good Roads Association. When the 1919 legislature turned down the "Chapel Hill Plan," the association had 272 active members and a cash balance of two thousand dollars. During the ensuing two years, Berry sent circular letters to more than 20,000 people, circulated 1,400 petitions, and spoke in 89 of the state's 100 counties.

Harriet Berry revitalized the N.C. Good Roads Association between 1917 and 1921 and played a major role in securing passage of the historic state Highway Act of 1921. She was likely the only woman in the nation so deeply involved in highway politics of the period. Photo courtesy North Carolina Collection, UNC-Chapel Hill.

Berry's influence was felt during a period in which the General Assembly refused to endorse women's suffrage, though the Nineteenth Amendment to the United States Constitution, which granted women the right to vote, was adopted in 1920.[6] One historian said of Harriet Berry: "Wherever she went her calm, quiet manner and her grasp of the practical details of road building left a favorable impression."[7] By 1921 the association had 5,500 members representing every county in the state. On the national level, men dominated the field of planning, financing, and creating highways, and women were limited to activities such as highway beautification. Berry was among a handful of women, possibly the only one, so deeply involved in state highway policy issues.[8] By 1921 only 135 miles of hard-surface (concrete or asphalt) roads had been built or were under contract to be built in the state. The counties had primarily built roads made of sand and clay, gravel, or macadam, all less durable than hard-surface roads.[9]

One of Governor Morrison's first decisions was to reappoint Frank Page as chairman of the State Highway Commission. Soon afterward the governor began lining up political support for good roads. The governor and legislative leaders held several meetings to design an acceptable highway bill, with Harriet Berry and Frank Page participating in the sessions. There soon emerged a consensus for a state system of roads to connect all the county seats and principal towns. Such a system would require the issuance of bonds, the levying of a tax of one cent per gallon of gasoline, and the allocation of the entire amount of revenue collected from auto registration fees to the state highway system. It is noteworthy that at that time only Oregon (in 1919) and four other states levied such a gasoline tax. A mere handful of states had issued highway bonds; examples included Pennsylvania ($50 million in 1918), Illinois ($60 million in 1919), and California ($40 million in 1919).[10] But there were several complicated issues for the General Assembly to resolve: the size of a bond issue; the types of roads to be built; whether the state or the counties should maintain the new roads; and whether a state property tax would be necessary to support the bonds.

Governor Morrison delivered a major address to the legislature on January 28, 1921, advocating a new highway system and large appropriations for education. He challenged those unwilling to borrow for the future. The *News and Observer* of Raleigh reported the "sweeping originality" of the governor's speech and his "undisguised challenge to old line leadership." The speech added to the momentum for a strong highway bill.

In February the historic and comprehensive state Highway Act of 1921, reflecting the energizing influence of Berry and the advocates of good roads, passed the house by a vote of 102 to 14 and the state senate by 32 to 6.[11] The bill (which became law on March 3) authorized a gasoline tax of one cent per gallon and the issuance of $50 million worth of bonds (both unprecedented in North Carolina) to finance construction of "hard

> **HOUSE PASSES ROAD MEASURE ON FINAL READING 102 TO 11**
>
> Proponents Bring It Through Without Vital Change to Provisions
>
> WOMAN REPRESENTATIVE CALLED TO CHAIR WHEN FINAL VOTE IS REACHED
>
> House Votes Down Templeton Amendments Giving Final Authority On Commission's Rulings To Governor; Twenty-Two Votes Polled By Opposition Wednesday Night Cut In Half On Final Reading; Matthews of Bertie, and Fountain Vote for Measure; Tumult of Shouting Greets Announcement of Victory for Doughton - Connor - Bowie Measure; Fight Now Goes To Senate

Raleigh News and Observer *headline concerning the 1921 state Highway Act, which authorized fifty million dollars' worth of road bonds and a one-cent-per-gallon tax on gasoline.*

surface and other dependable roads connecting by the most practical routes the various county seats and other principal towns of every county." (At that time, the North Carolina Constitution did not require that prospective bond issues be submitted to the voters for their approval; that practice would come later.) This bold step catapulted North Carolina into national leadership in the financing of highways. The projected network of roads was also intended to link important state facilities and to connect to national highways and major roads leading to and from adjacent states. The state assumed ownership and responsibility for maintaining a total of 5,500 miles of formerly county roads. The 1921 law again increased automobile registration fees substantially ($12.50-$40.00 per car, depending on horsepower, and $12.50-$300.00 for trucks, depending on carrying capacity).[12] The annual salary of the commission chairman, required to be a "practical business man," was set at $5,500.[13]

Meanwhile, at the federal level, Congress was debating new legislation in 1921 inasmuch as the five-year Federal-Aid Road Act of 1916 was nearing expiration. Although the legislation had funded many roads and encouraged states to organize highway departments, it had not achieved anticipated purposes. The biggest problem was that state highway agencies, including North Carolina's, had too often provided funding for short, isolated segments of roads rather than roads that served statewide purposes and connected to major roads in adjacent states. While everyone wanted more federal funding, the highway community was divided between those who favored emphasis on local roads and those who favored more federal control in requiring long-distance state-to-state roads.

Thomas MacDonald of the U.S. Bureau of Public Roads helped formulate a compromise that satisfied all parties. The Federal Highway Act of 1921 retained the federal-state partnership but required states to build a designated portion of interstate roads. The bill allocated $75 million for fiscal year 1922 alone (the 1916 bill had allocated only $75 million over five years), and subsequent sessions of Congress continued the more generous funding. The federal government eventually furnished 10 percent of the funds North Carolina spent on highways during the 1920s (see Appendix A). MacDonald and the Bureau of Public Roads furnished technical and engineering expertise to the states and enforced federal standards. At the same time, MacDonald sought to develop a working style of collaboration among the bureau, state highway officials, and the American Association of State Highway Officials, which had been organized in 1914 "for the purpose of providing mutual cooperation and assistance to the State highway departments and the several States and the Federal Government."[14]

With passage of the state's highway bill and a growing partnership with the federal government, Frank Page and the North Carolina State Highway Commission sprouted new wings. In April 1921 a reorganized board with nine commissioners, each one appointed by the governor

Gov. Cameron Morrison (1921-1925) meets with members of his 1921 State Highway Commission. Front row: Chairman Frank Page, Aberdeen; Governor Morrison; R. A. Doughton, Sparta. Back row: John Sprunt Hill, Durham; W. A. Hart, Tarboro; J. Elwood Cox, High Point; Word H. Wood, Charlotte; W. A. McGirt, Wilmington; J. G. Stikeleather, Asheville; J. C. McBee, Bakersville; and J. E. Cameron, Kinston.

to represent a specific geographic division, was seated. One of Page's first challenges was to expand his staff to meet the commission's vastly increased responsibilities. Charles Upham, accomplished chief engineer for the Delaware Highway Commission, went to Raleigh to ask Page to hire some experienced engineers who had previously worked for him in Delaware. Upham, a native of Massachusetts, had worked as a highway engineer since graduating from Tufts College in Boston. But Page instead recruited Upham as his chief engineer (replacing W. S. Fallis, who entered private practice). Years afterward, Page said of his meeting with Upham, "He intended to go back on the night train, but he hasn't gone yet."[15]

In October 1921 the State Highway Commission moved into a handsome four-story building on Morgan Street in Raleigh located one-half block from the Capitol. By that time, the commission's staff had grown to three thousand from

Thomas MacDonald, who worked cooperatively with N.C. officials, headed the federal highway program from 1919 to 1953. Photo courtesy Federal Highway Administration, Washington, D.C.

five hundred the previous year, and the number of roads under contract or completed had doubled.[16] A twelve-acre equipment depot was opened outside Raleigh. Each of the nine divisions

The new 36,000-square-foot State Highway Commission headquarters opened in 1921 a half-block from the State Capitol in Raleigh. The building housed the North Carolina Museum of Art from 1954 to 1983, when the Department of Transportation reoccupied it.

had a headquarters building for staff and equipment. All of the road-building equipment and vehicles owned by the counties were turned over to the commission for redistribution to the various division offices. The commission began publishing a monthly magazine titled the *North Carolina Highway Bulletin*.

In addition to building new or re-routed highways, the commission maintained 5,500 miles of roads and numerous bridges formerly owned by the counties. The roads in its charge generally included very little signage. The commission designed and installed uniform signs to designate highway numbers or routes, to inform motorists as to the specific distance in miles to towns and cities, and to impart basic information such as impending curves, schools, crossroads, and county lines. Maintaining various bridges required crews that specialized in timber trestlework, concrete work, bituminous surfacing, and structural steel erection.[17] The commission upgraded the Raleigh-Durham highway with funding from the state and federal governments. A new five-mile portion of

The Highway Commission's maintenance center outside Raleigh.

Frank Page, a visionary leader as chairman of the State Highway Commission during the 1920s, leads a tour of N.C. highways for visiting officials from Latin America in 1924.

that road eliminated three dangerous railroad crossings.[18]

Frank Page's reputation as a highway leader was growing. In 1923 the University of North Carolina, at which he had studied for two years, awarded him the honorary degree of LL.D. The legislature of 1924, not wanting to risk losing Page to a more lucrative job, stipulated that his annual salary be raised. The commission promptly did so—from $5,500 to the maximum allowed, $15,000, making Page's remuneration considerably higher than that of the governor, who made $6,500 a year during the 1920s. Page's peers in all the states elected him president of the American Association of State Highway Officials for 1925-1926.[19] Governor Morrison was consistently a strong supporter of Page and the State Highway Commission. When difficulties arose in attempting to sell the first North Carolina highway bonds, the governor traveled to New York to consult with influential bankers. He agreed to recommend that the 1923 General Assembly authorize the issuance of $15 million in additional bonds and increase the gas tax by two cents to a total of three cents per gallon, a measure that passed almost unanimously. The North Carolina General Assembly made the final decision in voting for and approving all state highway bonds issued during the 1920s (1921, 1923, 1925, 1927—a total of $115 million); none of them went to the voters.[20] During Morrison's term, 785 miles of paved highways were built in 66 of the 100 counties.

Governor Morrison developed a reputation as a man of vision. Known nationally as the "Good Roads Governor," he manifested equally impressive leadership in the realms of economic development; education (public schools and higher education); and strengthening insane asylums, reformatories, sanatoriums, and schools for the deaf, dumb, and blind. He and Frank Page shared a trusting working relationship.[21]

It is not surprising, therefore, that Frank Page faced a political dilemma in dealing with Governor Morrison's successor. At that time, the constitution of North Carolina limited the governorship to a single four-year term. When Angus Wilton McLean became governor in 1925, his stand on roads was unclear. McLean, a native of Robeson County, was an attorney who had represented the Atlantic Coast Line Railroad, founded three textile mills and a bank, and served as assistant secretary of the U.S. Treasury Department under President Woodrow Wilson. McLean expressed concern over the amount of the state's large debt caused by bonds for roads and education facilities. During Governor Morrison's four-year administration, the state had issued $90 million worth of bonds for highway, education, and other improvements. The debt of state and local governments in North Carolina totaled more than $300 million, more than any other state except New York and Massachusetts.[22]

Despite those circumstances, Governor McLean soon realized that Page and the commission could responsibly spend large sums of public funds to build the all-weather highways that citizens were demanding. The governor asked the General Assembly to issue $20 million more in bonds, to increase the gasoline tax by another penny to four cents a gallon in 1925, and to issue an additional $30 million worth of bonds two years later—all of which was approved. The number of vehicles registered in the state had more than doubled in four years—from 151,000 in 1921 to 341,000 in 1925. By 1924 the statewide ratio of cars to persons was one car for each 6.6 citizens, varying from 1 to 3.8 in urban Guilford County to 1 to 26.7 in rural Yancey County.[23]

Private companies played important roles in building highways in the state. The companies included contractors who built roads, firms that manufactured and/or sold equipment, and suppliers of materials such as rock, gravel, and sand. In the early 1920s, county commissioners frequently acted as prime contractors with the State Highway Commission, subletting construction work to individuals and companies with expertise in equipment and engineering. The commission increasingly worked directly with private contractors as the counties' responsibilities diminished. The commission staff clarified plans, coordinated any use of prisoners, and monitored overall progress.[24] The Beal Brothers of Chatham County used mules, steam shovels, and Caterpillar tractors to grade a roadway in 1926. Two years later, they used gasoline-powered shovels along with mules and tractors for a similar job.

Sometimes a company developed innovative ways of solving problems. The commission was having difficulty obtaining road-building materials for a project on Roanoke Island near Manteo. Arthur Hitch of Norfolk, Virginia, arranged to deliver the supplies by boat and then continued to do likewise for other projects in the eastern part of the state. The Seaboard Air Line Railway, seeking material for ballast (gravel or broken stone) for its construction of rail lines, discovered a gravel deposit in Anson County. The discovery led to the formation of the Bonsal Company, which subsequently furnished gravel and sand for highway building.[25]

By 1923 at least a dozen highway-construction contractors were coming to North Carolina from as far away as Pennsylvania, Illinois, Texas, and Louisiana. The fact that Page awarded substantial contracts for up to thirty-mile sections helped to attract such companies.[26] In that same year, the commission's magazine, the *North Carolina Highway Bulletin*, included twice as many advertisements from companies outside as inside the state.[27] North Carolina-based construction companies operating during the 1920s included:

Blythe Brothers Construction Company of Charlotte. F. J. (Joe) Blythe organized the company in 1921 with $2,500 and was later joined by his brother, Joseph (Jack) L. Blythe. They grew up in Huntersville. Jack served in the state senate.

Gilbert Engineering Company of Statesville. John N. Gilbert, an engineer, formed the company in 1926. The firm built U.S. 29 between Charlotte and Concord (in the 1930s).

Nello L. Teer Company in Durham. Teer, who had founded the firm in 1909 using mules, built roads for several counties, then began conducting grading work for the state in the early 1920s.[28]

The following North Carolina companies purchased full-page advertisements in the April 1925 issue of the *North Carolina Highway Bulletin*: Dixie Culvert and Metal Company of Asheville, Lakeview (near Southern Pines), and Atlanta, specializing in building culverts; J. C. Benjamin Company of Raleigh, selling Adams Adjustable Leaning Wheel Graders; and Motor & Equipment Company of Raleigh, selling Buda engines for construction machinery.[29] By the following decade, more North Carolina companies began providing services both inside and beyond the state boundaries.

Frank Page, while determined to be fair with the taxpayers, could be tough in negotiating with companies for the prices of materials and services. The Raleigh *News and Observer* related an incident involving a man named Rollo, who came to see the chairman as a representative of eleven manufacturers of cement. Rollo named a price for the cement those companies would sell to the commission, confident the chairman would quickly accept his proposal. Instead, Page calmly placed a telephone call to another vendor to

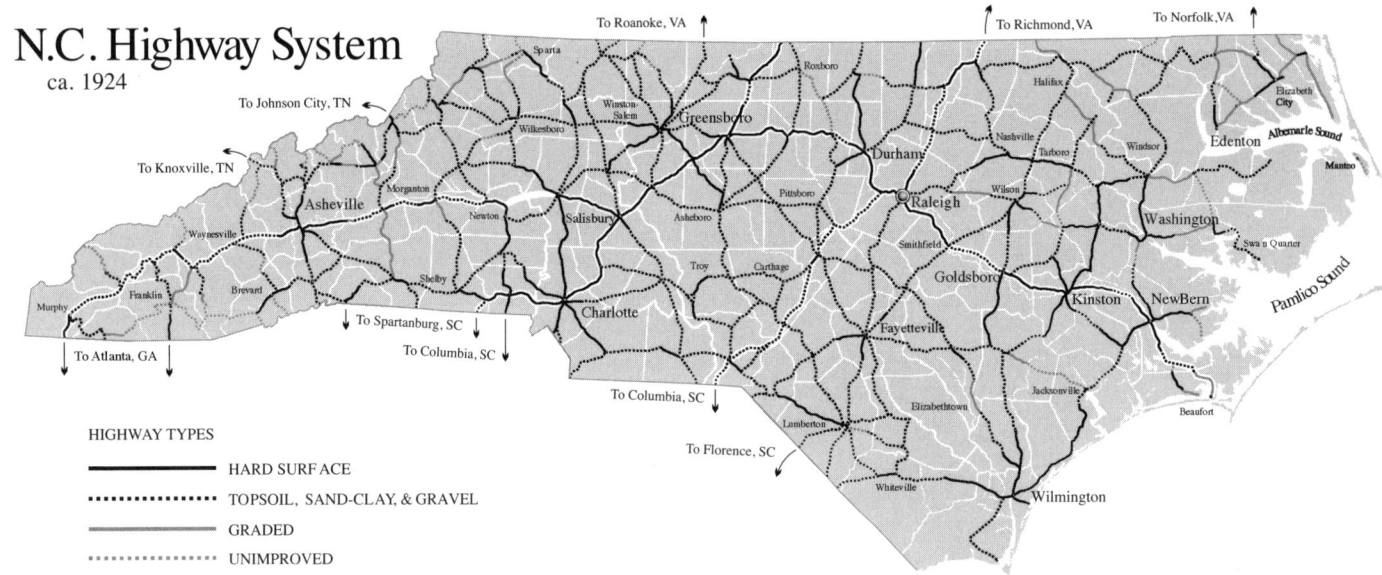

North Carolina highway map of 1924, showing main roads. By the mid-1920s, the State Highway Commission was making good progress in paving major highways. Map by Mark A. Moore, A&H.

instruct: "Radio your ship to put in at Wilmington. We can begin taking delivery on twelve thousand bags as soon as she has docked."[30] As in this incident, Page often drove other hard bargains to obtain the best prices for needed materials.

The presence of new private contractors notwithstanding, prisoners continued to be an attractive source of cheap manual labor and were widely used to build roads in North Carolina, often working in "chain gangs," teams of prisoners chained together to minimize opportunity for escape. Since the Civil War era, it had been common practice for inmates held by counties and the state to work on prison farms or to be leased to railway companies as construction laborers. By 1900 many counties used their prisoners for road building and competed with the railroads for use of state convicts. One-fourth of the counties still observed century-old laws requiring able-bodied men to spend time working on county roads, typically a few days annually. Adherence to what had become outdated statutes never produced much manpower, however, and provided another rationale for continuing to have road work performed by prisoners.[31]

Joseph Hyde Pratt feared that if chain gang labor were eliminated, it would curtail or cripple road-building progress. He concluded that it would be more practical to tighten state control over inmate labor while improving conditions in the realms of food, health, and work methods. But counties were reluctant to give up any control over their prisoners. When Harriet Berry was leading the Good Roads Association in the 1917-1921 period, she said little about prisoner issues but instead focused on gaining political support for financing the construction of highways.[32]

The use of prisoners and chain gangs for road building continued in the 1920s, with little change in the time-honored system. At mid-decade, there were 2,400 state prisoners, two-thirds of whom were nonwhite. Most of those prisoners of the state, joined by county prisoners who were serving at least sixty days, worked on roads.[33] Later in the decade, salaried workers for contracting companies played a larger role, operating machinery and equipment while prisoners provided most of the manual labor.

Over time, the technology of building highways changed. Macadam roads continued to be popular for a long period. During the years before World War I, however, they began to require heavy maintenance as traffic increased. Though more expensive than macadam, concrete roads were proving more durable. A basic eighteen-foot-wide concrete roadway was seven inches thick at the edges and eight inches at the center. To build one mile of concrete roadway in 1923, according to a bulletin from the U.S. Department of Agriculture, required 127 railroad cars to transport the basic materials—20 cars for cement, 42 cars for fine aggregate or sand, and 65 cars for coarse aggregate. (Obviously, it was more complicated to build such a road in an area not served by a railroad line.) Water was likewise required. These figures did not include material needed for drainage, grading, or bridge and culvert construction.

As an example, consider the challenge of building nineteen miles of concrete roadway as part of N.C. Highway 20 in Robeson County—from Maxton through Pembroke to within a few miles of Lumberton. That undertaking was summarized in a September 1923 article in the *North Carolina Highway Bulletin*, even though the project had not been completed when the article was written. Part of the existing roadway consisted of a sand-clay road built by the county years earlier. The total cost of the new road was nearly $600,000. The subcontractor was Robeson Construction Company of Lumberton, which poured an average of 800 feet of concrete per day. Fortunately, the highway paralleled part of the Seaboard Air Line Railway between Charlotte and Wilmington, which facilitated movement of construction materials. A material plant was erected in the middle portion of the mileage in Pembroke. The project commenced in July 1922. One year later, twelve miles of paving had been completed. The job was delayed by a shortage of material and by inclement weather during the winter and the following spring. Highway Commission engineers worked constantly to upgrade the quality of N.C.

Advertisement for road-building machinery in February 1924 issue of the North Carolina Highway Bulletin, *a monthly magazine published by the State Highway Commission.*

Highway 20 and all other modern concrete roads then under construction in the state. At that time, designing and building concrete highways was a still-evolving process.[34]

Motorists took an active role in creating better driving conditions throughout the state. When Coleman Roberts of Greensboro took an automobile trip in 1922, he was frustrated by terrible road conditions, poor maps, and the lack of road signs. He organized the Carolina Motor Club that year. By 1929 the club had 20,000 Tar Heel members, the sixth largest such organization affiliated with the American Automobile Association. (The club's membership rolls included 800,000 North Carolinians in 2000).[35] Members campaigned for several progressive measures, including the creation of a state police force (the North Carolina State Highway Patrol was established in 1929), driver education, and school crossing guards. The motor club even initiated court action to protect drivers caught in "irregular speed traps." Some of the measures sought by the organization took years to be implemented.[36]

By the mid-1920s, the state was promoting the building of new, larger, consolidated schools, which increased the percentage of children attending schools. New roads and school buses made that development possible, but only for a relatively few black students, especially in rural areas. New Deal programs furnished additional buses for blacks in rural counties during the 1930s. During the period from 1940 to 1952 in the South, there was a 20.6 percent increase in the number of white children transported to

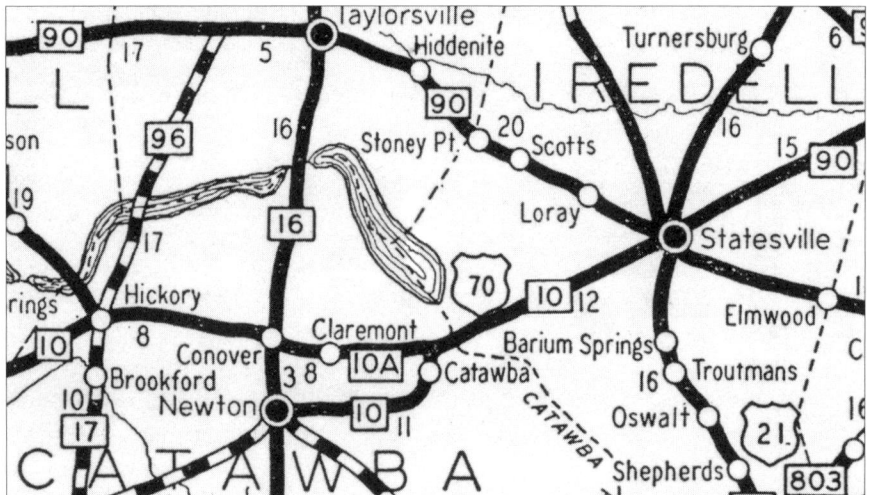

In the late 1920s, residents of Newton, county seat of Catawba County, insisted that the east-west N.C. Highway 10 pass through their town instead of following the state's plan to bypass it. The State Highway Commission built both the route through Newton and a more direct Statesville-Hickory route. Detail of map, "State Highway System of North Carolina" (1931), issued by the State Highway Commission.

For protection from hot asphalt used in paving roads, some highway laborers made shoes from discarded auto tires.

Opening of Wil-Cox Bridge across Yadkin River in 1924. The structure carried traffic on N.C. 10 (now U.S. 29/U.S. 70) between Lexington and Salisbury. It is one of six open-spandrel-style bridges surviving in the state. Photo courtesy A&H.

schools by bus and a 408 percent increase among black children.[37]

During the 1920s, controversies occasionally arose over the routing of new highways, including those between Tarboro and Halifax, Durham and Oxford, and Red Springs and Lumberton. One noteworthy dispute involved a portion of N.C. Highway 10, which crossed the center of the state between Beaufort and Murphy. Officials in Catawba County insisted that the portion of the highway between Statesville and Hickory be routed through Newton, their county seat. The Highway Commission recommended a more northerly route that was six miles shorter, avoided a ravine, and bypassed Newton. The town took the state to court and won. So the state, at a cost of an additional $250,000, built *both* routes. (Present-day travelers can observe the consequences of this conflict.)[38]

In a state with numerous rivers, creeks, and other waterways, constructing bridges was a major expense. The 1,300-foot bridge across the Yadkin River on N.C. 10 (now U.S. 29) between Lexington and Salisbury was built in 1924 at a cost of $212,000. In the eastern part of the state, the challenges of bridge building were even greater and more expensive because of the unique geography of the Outer Banks, huge sounds, and wide rivers. The legislature's solution was to authorize the issuance of special bonds to enable the Highway Commission to build drawbridges that would charge tolls. Since colonial times the six counties north of the Albemarle Sound and east of the Chowan River had been isolated, establishing an affinity with Norfolk rather than the rest of North Carolina. The 1925 General Assembly authorized the issuance of bonds in the amount of $600,000 to build a bridge across the Albemarle Sound on N.C. 342 (now U.S. 17). The 1 1/2-mile-long bridge near Edenton opened in 1927. The toll was 75 cents for cars, and an additional charge for trucks.

Wilmington, one of the state's largest cities for decades, had a different problem. Incoming traffic from the west (Charlotte) or south (Myrtle Beach and Shallotte) was obliged to use a ferry to cross the Cape Fear River into Wilmington. (The ferry ran from the present location of the USS *North*

Carolina to the city's Market Street.) The density of buildings in downtown Wilmington made constructing a bridge at or near the ferry location impractical. The solution was to locate the bridge on the northern edge of the city a mile upstream in an area of manufacturing and shipping industries. Because the river was divided at that point, two bridges were required—over both the Cape Fear (1,522 feet) and the Northeast Cape Fear (2,196 feet). The 1927 legislature authorized the sale of $1,250,000 worth of bonds to finance the two structures. The toll for the bridges, which opened in 1929, was 25 cents for each car.[39]

The durability of the bridges erected under the auspices of the Highway Commission was demonstrated by an unusual set of circumstances. In 1926 Carolina Power and Light Company and the commission reached an agreement for the com-pany to build a hydroelectric plant near the town of Norwood, on the Pee Dee River between Stanly and Montgomery Counties. Since the new dam and lake required elimination of the Swift Island Bridge, erected by the commission in 1922, CP&L agreed to pay for a new, higher bridge. Despite several attempts at demolition (including test aerial bombing) by the army, the old bridge stood. Engineers and newsreel cameramen from throughout the nation came to watch the drama. Finally, two thousand pounds of TNT, placed at the bridge's base, did the job.[40]

None of the roads on the state's highway map for 1920 is numbered. The commission inaugurated its "N.C." numbering system in 1921. The best-known state highway was N.C. 10 (now largely part of U.S. 70), formerly known as the Central Highway. Linking Beaufort, near the Atlantic Ocean, with Asheville and the Georgia mountains, it was one of the longest state highways in the nation. By 1926 the U.S. Bureau of Public Roads and the American Association of State Highway Officials formulated a plan for numbering highways that passed through more than one state. The plan, which applied to 96,626 miles of roadway in the nation, used odd numbers for north-to-south routes and even numbers for east-to-west routes.[41] A route from Maine to Key West, Florida, was designated U.S. Highway 1. In North Carolina, much of that highway was originally known as N.C. 50, which linked Henderson and Rockingham by way of Raleigh. The state's highway map for 1930 identifies several additional roads by both their state and federal numbers. Examples include:

Toll booth for Wilmington's twin bridges. Photo courtesy New Hanover County Public Library (Louis T. Moore Collection).

N.C. Highway 10—Beaufort to Murphy (now U.S. 70 as far west as Asheville)

N.C. Highway 20—Wilmington to Asheville and Marshall (now U.S. 74)

N.C. Highway 26—Sparta to Charlotte (now U.S. 21)

N.C. Highway 30—Virginia to South Carolina through New Bern and Wilmington (now U.S. 17, with a different route north of Windsor)

N.C. Highway 90—Columbia to Lenoir (now an extended U.S. 64)[42]

Meanwhile, Frank Page's career with the State Highway Commission and the frenzy of agency growth and road building during his tenure were about to end. During the 1920s the state authorized an astonishing total of more than $175 million to be spent on road construction, including four bond issues ($115 million) and federal aid ($13 million). Other major sources of income were the gasoline tax (increased to five cents per gallon by 1929) and a vehicle registration tax.[43] The total highway mileage for which the Highway Commission was responsible grew from 5,500 in 1921 to 7,444 by 1929, and the commission converted former county roads into a cohesive state system. The state constructed 3,425 miles of new hard-surface (concrete or asphalt) roadway in the process, including its first three-lane (connecting Greensboro and Thomasville) and four-lane (Charlotte-Gastonia) highways.[44]

O. Max Gardner was inaugurated governor on January 11, 1929. According to Gardner's biographer, Frank Page visited the governor the following day and "announced to an indignant Gardner that he wanted to retain his post (as commission chairman) and take on the vice presidency of the Wachovia Bank and Trust, and perform both duties."[45] Apparently Page also wrote a letter of resignation, perhaps following accepted protocol occasioned by the inauguration of a new governor. A few days later, Governor Gardner sent Page a letter that began: "Acknowledging receipt of your letter tendering your resignation as highway commissioner." The governor's letter flattered Page with praise and included this sentence: "If you were so situated as to remain on a full time basis, I would consider it a public duty to decline to accept your resignation."[46] It is likely that Page was committed to working for Wachovia but had mixed feelings about leaving the State Highway Commission. Though it is not known whether the circumstances of his departure were made public, it was nevertheless an unfortunate way for Page to end his distinguished career with the commission. He moved on to become executive vice-president of Wachovia Bank in Raleigh.

Frank Page died in 1934 and was buried in a family plot near Aberdeen. The *News and Observer* editorialized: "And certainly if it may be said of many men in the modern world it may be said as it was of Sir Christopher Wren: 'If you would see his monument, look about you.'"[47] Indeed, thanks in large part to Page, North Carolina by 1930 had well earned the reputation of being "the Good Roads State."

TABLE 1
Mileage of State-Maintained Road Types in North Carolina as of January 1, 1929

TYPE	MILEAGE
Concrete and asphalt	3,425
Macadam	313
Oil treated	1,101
Topsoil and sand-clay	1,151
Brick	30
Gravel	236
Shale	27
Unimproved dirt	747
Through towns	222
Not yet under state maintenance	192
TOTAL	7,444

Source: 1929 data compiled in Brown, *State Highway System*, 186-214.

Multiple highway signs in Raleigh. Photo courtesy A&H.

NOTES

1. *Dictionary of North Carolina Biography*, s.v. "Morrison, Cameron."

2. Hugh T. Lefler and Albert R. Newsome, *North Carolina: The History of a Southern State*, 3d ed. (Chapel Hill: University of North Carolina Press, 1973), 599-600.

3. Story told to the author by Reginald Turner (1898-1988), who heard it from a cousin who had attended the Morrison rally.

4. Cecil K. Brown, *The State Highway System of North Carolina, Its Evolution and Status* (Chapel Hill: University of North Carolina Press, 1931), 90-93.

5. William S. Powell, *North Carolina through Four Centuries* (Chapel Hill: University of North Carolina Press, 1989), 470.

6. The North Carolina General Assembly, meeting in special session in August 1920, rejected the proposed amendment to the U.S. Constitution, even though the state's Republican and Democratic Parties had endorsed the amendment. The amendment was adopted when three-fourths of the states ratified it. Women were able to vote in the general election of November 1920. Lefler and Newsome, *North Carolina*, 575.

7. Harry Wilson McKown Jr., "Roads and Reform: The Good Roads Movement in North Carolina, 1885-1921" (master's thesis, University of North Carolina at Chapel Hill, 1972), 94-95.

8. Richard F. Weingroff, information liaison specialist, Federal Highway Administration, e-mail to author, August 19, 2002.

9. Brown, *State Highway System*, 45.

10. James S. Burch, "Historical Outline of Road Administration in North Carolina" (unpublished paper written for the North Carolina State Highway Commission, Raleigh, April 1940), 7; Frederic L. Paxson, "The Highway Movement, 1916-1935," *American Historical Review* 51 (January 1946): 246, 249.

11. Harriet Berry left the Geological and Economic Survey in 1921. She worked for private and governmental agencies in the state, including two years as a reporter and editor with the *Greensboro Daily News*. From 1927 to 1937 she was state superintendent of savings and loan associations. Berry, never married, retired in Chapel Hill, where she died in 1940. A plaque in the lobby of the North Carolina Department of Transportation's headquarters in Raleigh honors her as "The Mother of Good Roads." *Dictionary of North Carolina Biography*, s.v. "Berry, Harriet Morehead."

12. North Carolina State Highway Commission, *Biennial Report, 1921-1922* (Raleigh: State Printer, 1922), 21, 22 (hereafter cited as *Biennial Report*, with appropriate dates).

13. Brown, *State Highway System*, 100-123. See *Public Laws of North Carolina, 1921*, c. 2, for the entire law. In 1936 the legislature and the voters of the state amended the constitution of North Carolina to require that all proposals to issue general purpose bonds, including road bonds, be submitted to the voters for their approval.

14. *America's Highways, 1776-1976: A History of the Federal-Aid Program* (Washington: Federal Highway Administration, U.S. Department of Transportation, 1976), 79, 106-109; Richard F. Weingroff, e-mail to author, August 9, 2002.

15. Brown, *State Highway System*, 148, 149.

16. "The First Birthday of the State Highway Commission," *North Carolina Highway Bulletin* 3 (April 1922): 5,

7. The primary road bill passed by the 1919 General Assembly included this statement: "The State Highway Commission shall furnish and provide suitable offices for itself in the city of Raleigh and shall provide itself with the necessary supplies, fixtures and stationery, and pay for the same out of the State highway funds." *Biennial Report, 1919-1920*, 11.

17. *Biennial Report, 1923-1924*, 66-67, 76-77.

18. C. O. Boyd, "Raleigh-Durham Highway Completed," *North Carolina Highway Bulletin* 4 (July 1923): 4.

19. Page also served as president of the American Road Builders Association, and President Herbert Hoover appointed him chairman of the National Highway Safety Council. *Dictionary of North Carolina Biography*, s.v. "Page, Frank"; Brown, *State Highway System*, 148; *North Carolina Manual, 1923*, 59; *North Carolina Manual, 1925*, 53; *North Carolina Manual, 1927*, 63; *North Carolina Manual, 1929*, 63.

20. If the question of whether to issue North Carolina's 1921 bonds in the amount of $50 million had been submitted to voters for their approval instead of being decided upon solely by the legislature, one can only speculate about the outcome.

21. After completing his term as governor, Cameron Morrison (1869-1953) lived in Charlotte except for brief periods of service in Congress. Gov. O. Max Gardner appointed Morrison to fill a vacant seat in the U.S. Senate in 1930, but Morrison lost the seat in the 1932 election. He served as U.S. representative from North Carolina's Tenth Congressional District from 1943 to 1945. *Dictionary of North Carolina Biography*, s.v. "Morrison, Cameron."

22. Lefler and Newsome, *North Carolina*, 603-605; Brown, *State Highway System*, 127-130.

23. Robert E. Ireland, *Entering the Auto Age: The Early Automobile In North Carolina, 1900-1930* (Raleigh: Division of Archives and History, North Carolina Department of Cultural Resources, 1990), 125. Motor vehicle registration figures from Frances Pittman, N.C. Division of Motor Vehicles, fax to author, December 2000.

24. Capus Waynick, *North Carolina Roads and Their Builders* (Raleigh: Superior Stone Company, 1952), 203.

25. Waynick, *North Carolina Roads*, 207, 219, 221-222.

26. Frank Page, "What North Carolina is Doing," *North Carolina Highway Bulletin* 4 (March 1923): 3.

27. Comparison of advertisements in *North Carolina Highway Bulletin* for March, June, and October 1923 issues.

28. Waynick, *North Carolina Roads*, 208, 209, 217, 236, 237.

29. *North Carolina Highway Bulletin* 6 (April 1925): 22, 29, 31.

30. Ben Dixon MacNeill, "Frank Page and the Man Called Rollo," reprinted from *News and Observer* (Raleigh), date unknown, as sidebar to article "Frank Page, North Carolina's Pioneer Road Builder," *North Carolina Roadways* 1 (July 1950): 8, 29.

31. Robert E. Ireland, "Prison Reform, Road Building, and Southern Progressivism: Joseph Hyde Pratt and the Campaign for 'Good Roads and Good Men,'" *North Carolina Historical Review* 68 (April 1991): 125-128.

32. Ireland, "Prison Reform," 136-153.

33. Ireland, "Prison Reform," 157.

34. The equipment used to construct the Robeson County highway included two cranes, a paver, a finishing machine, a gas roller, a sub-grader, 2,000 linear feet of forms, 6 locomotives, 10 miles of narrow-gauge track (perhaps similar to that used by temporary logging railroads), a pile driver, and a road machine. Articles utilized for discussion of concrete highways are from the *North Carolina Highway Bulletin*. They include W. E. Hawkins, "Developments in the Construction of Concrete Roads," 3 (March 1922): 8-10, 14-15; Charles M. Upham, "Recent Developments in Road Construction," 3 (March 1922): 11-12, 15; "What Goes into a Mile of Concrete Road," 4 (June 1923): 13; and C. V. Baker, "Building Concrete Road on a Large Scale," 4 (September 1923): 4, 23.

35. Tom Crosby, director of public affairs, Carolina Motor Club, Charlotte, telephone conversation with author, November 2, 2000.

36. Ireland, *Entering the Auto Age*, 84-85.

37. Robert Ireland, "Consolidation, Transportation and Educational Opportunity: The Paradox of the Early School Bus in North Carolina," *North Carolina Humanities* 3 (fall/winter 1995): 77-90.

38. A portion of U.S. 70 follows the northern route, and N.C. 10 dips southward through the towns of Catawba and Newton. Brown, *State Highway System*, 152-164.

39. Brown, *State Highway System*, 172-179.

40. Jack Riley, *Carolina Power & Light Company, 1908-1958* (Raleigh: Edwards and Broughton Company, 1958), 205-208.

41. *America's Highways*, 110; Bruce E. Seely, *Building the American Highway System: Engineers as Policy Makers* (Philadelphia: Temple University Press, 1987), 78-79.

42. North Carolina highway maps for 1920, 1921, 1925, 1930 (issued by the North Carolina State Highway Commission): map for 2000 (issued by the North Carolina Department of Transportation).

43. Brown, *State Highway System*, 224-226; *Biennial Report, 1929-1930*, 30, 34, 35. The author updated to June 30, 1929, a table titled "Construction Funds Available March 4, 1921, to June 30, 1928," summarized by Brown. Federal-aid allocations to North Carolina in the 1916-1921 period totaled $6 million.

44. Brown, *State Highway System*, 186-214. The road between Charlotte and Gaston County, the heart of the Piedmont textile industry, became known as Wilkinson Boulevard. It was named for William Cook Wilkinson, an influential Charlotte banker, millowner, and state highway commissioner who made the road a top state priority. Tom Hanchett, "When Wilkinson Made History," *Charlotte Observer*, November 20, 2000.

45. Joseph L. Morrison, *Governor O. Max Gardner* (Chapel Hill: University of North Carolina Press, 1971), 55, 56.

46. Letter of January 15, 1931, as reproduced in David L. Corbitt, ed., *Public Papers and Letters of Oliver Max Gardner* (Raleigh: North Carolina Council of State, 1937), 571, 572.

47. *News and Observer*, December 21, 1934.

Chapter 3

GROWTH AND EXPANSION OF RESPONSIBILITIES
1930-1948

Despite the Great Depression, the North Carolina Highway Commission in the 1930s and 1940s utilized increased revenues from gasoline taxes and emergency federal funding to further develop an expanded highway system. Much of the federal money came from New Deal relief programs designated to stimulate the economy and create jobs. Although highway construction slowed during World War II, heavy usage continued, and the pace of road construction and maintenance began to pick up after the conflict.

When O. Max Gardner became governor in January 1929, the nation's prosperity and stock market boom seemed unstoppable. Gardner grew up in Shelby and graduated from both the North Carolina College of Agriculture and Mechanical Arts (now North Carolina State University in Raleigh) and the University of North Carolina School of Law. After serving in the North Carolina Senate, he was elected lieutenant governor in 1916 at age thirty-four. He ran a creditable campaign for governor in 1920, losing to Cameron Morrison of Charlotte in a runoff primary. In a savvy political move, he decided against running in 1924, keeping in mind the tradition that governors tended to alternate between the eastern and western portions of the state. He stayed active in civic affairs in his home town of Shelby and throughout the state. In 1928 he was nominated in the Democratic primary and easily beat his Republican rival in the fall.[1]

The stock market crashed on October 29, 1929, leading the nation's financial system into collapse. Because lending organizations could not cover the difference between their loans and the value of their stock as collateral, 88 banks and 233 building and loan associations failed in North Carolina in 1930. Many people lost their homes, farms, and businesses. The following year, 100,000 Tar Heels lost their jobs, and nearly 1,000 died of malnutrition. Farmers were devastated, especially those dependent upon cotton and tobacco. The state's leading industries, including tobacco, furniture, and textiles, suffered. Labor unrest rose as wages were slashed, and tensions grew between owners and union organizers.[2]

Although North Carolina's debt had grown from $13 million in 1920 to $178 million by early 1929, greater than that of any other state except New York, the state's credit was good. But the counties were in worse shape, some because of poorly managed governments. They struggled to meet their obligations to maintain roads and carry out other services as falling prices for agricultural products reduced farmers' ability to pay property taxes.

In his inaugural address, Governor Gardner suggested that the state take over maintenance of the more important county roads so that county property taxes could be reduced. Early in 1929

After the stock market crash in October 1929, residents rushed to withdraw funds from Raleigh Banking and Trust Company in downtown Raleigh. Photo courtesy A&H.

the General Assembly enacted a biennial budget that included a one-cent addition to the gasoline tax. The legislature also established the State Highway Patrol as a division of the State Highway Commission to enforce motor vehicle laws and help the motoring public. Initially, patrolmen used Harley Davidson motorcycles, and lieutenants drove Ford coupes. Beginning in 1935, all patrolmen were issued Ford autos with powerful V-8 engines and bulletproof windshields. (The only surviving example, a 1935 Ford, can be seen at the North Carolina Transportation Museum in Spencer.) The State Highway Patrol remained a part of the Highway Commission until 1941.[3]

The governor, as director of the budget, was obliged to make cuts later in the year in an attempt to achieve a balanced budget. Gardner took additional action in the summer of 1930. He arranged for the Brookings Institution of Washington, D.C., to undertake a four-month study of how "more effectively to promote increased efficiency and economy in the conduct of the governmental affairs of the State."[4] The privately funded "think tank" took several months to complete the study and presented its recommendations to state officials at the end of 1930. The centerpiece of the report was a suggestion that the state consolidate agencies to operate more efficiently. The report also recommended that the state examine the benefits of uniting the University of North Carolina, North Carolina State College, and the Women's College (in Greensboro) into one statewide educational system.

The governor also organized a state-sponsored study of North Carolina's state and county roads. A committee made up of representatives of the State Tax Commission, the State Highway Commission, and the U.S. Bureau of Public Roads conducted a five-month-long (August-December 1930) inquiry concerning the state's roads and the way they were financed. Recognizing that counties could no longer pay sufficient property taxes to maintain the roads, the committee recommended that the state take over all public roads within the state and add an additional one cent per gallon to the gasoline tax.[5] By that time, the state highway system included nearly nine thousand miles of roads, mostly primary highways.

Taking into consideration the recommendations of both the Brookings Institution and the special committee he had created, the governor made a proposal to the 1931 General Assembly. He suggested that the State Highway Commission take responsibility for an additional 45,000 miles of existing county roads, county prisoners serving sixty days or more, and county-owned prison camps and road-building equipment. The plan would allow the commission to better utilize prisoners in constructing and maintaining the expanded state-sponsored road network. Six highway commissioners, each appointed by the governor to represent the entire state, would replace the nine sitting commissioners, who represented divisions. Another one cent per gallon would be added to the gasoline tax, taking it from five to six cents per gallon, in order to enable the state to maintain county roads.

Opposition was strong, particularly among county authorities, who did not wish to relinquish power; county workers afraid of losing their jobs; entrenched highway commissioners; and Col. T. L. Kirkpatrick of Charlotte (president of the United States Good Roads Association), who apparently were satisfied with the status quo. There had been little turnover of commissioners in the 1920s, even during the transition from Governor Morrison to Governor McLean in 1925. Even the state's leading academic expert on highways characterized a costly state takeover of so many roads as "the height of folly," pointing out that in North Carolina, the most heavily used 20 percent of the existing public roads (state and county) handled 90 percent of the traffic.[6]

Governor Gardner's supporters included Frank Page (first full-time chairman and principal builder of the State Highway Commission), visionary officials of the U.S. Bureau of Public Roads, and the progressive Raleigh *News and Observer*. The turning point in the debate was a fifty-minute radio broadcast by the governor on February 9, 1931, during which he urged his listeners to write or wire their representatives to support his plan. "The only clients I represent," he said, "are the three million citizens of North Carolina, and the only lobby I covet is the voice of the people made manifest to this General Assembly."[7] Governor Gardner's proposal came in the form of a bill enacted into law shortly thereafter. The counties were relieved of all road-related responsibilities except payment of existing debt incurred in connection with their previous activities in that regard. County property taxes would no longer fund building and maintenance of roads. North Carolina and Pennsylvania (which added only about twenty thousand miles of roads) were the first states whose highway departments assumed responsibility for secondary roads. As a result of passage of the 1931 road bill and subsequent additions, North Carolina boasted the nation's largest state-maintained road system from that time until the early 1990s.[8]

Another bill passed by the 1931 General Assembly created a Division of Purchase and Contract in the governor's office to oversee all acquisitions by the state. The division was able to save money by purchasing supplies, materials, and equipment for the state through required competitive bidding. Since the State Highway Commission made more purchases than the rest of state government combined, it was practical for the new Division of Purchase and Contract to set up offices in the 1921 Highway Building in Raleigh. By the end of 1932, the commission owned equipment valued at three million dollars, much of it transferred from the counties.[9] Reflecting on the importance of the bill, Edward L. Rankin Jr. (who later served as an aide to governors William B. Umstead, Luther H. Hodges, and Dan K. Moore) concluded that the awarding of state contracts on the basis of the lowest bid "worked well in North Carolina with few examples of fraud or scandal."[10]

Although Frank Page had received a salary of $15,000 per year as chairman of the State

Gov. O. Max Gardner (1929-1933) in his office. His recommendation that the Highway Commission take responsibility for 45,000 miles of county roads passed the 1931 General Assembly. As a result of this and future additions, the state boasted the largest state-maintained highway system in the nation for six decades. Photo courtesy A&H.

Highway Commission, it was decided that his successors would receive a maximum of $7,500. Rufus A. Doughton of Alleghany County served as chairman of the State Highway Commission during Governor Gardner's first two years. Doughton, a longtime member of the General Assembly and brother of Congressman Robert L. Doughton, had been one of three sponsors of the 1921 highway bill.

E. B. Jeffress, the publisher of the *Greensboro Daily News*, became the commission's chairman in 1931. As a member of the General Assembly of 1931, he had chaired the House Committee on Reorganization of State Government and had been active in drafting the highway bill. One writer concluded that Jeffress was "an outstanding chief of the far-flung department during very critical times."[11] Jeffress oversaw a reorganization of the highway department to accommodate the new legislation. The reorganization involved dividing the state into five regions, each headed by a division engineer.

Because of the deepening depression, the state was increasingly hard-pressed to balance its budget and meet its obligations. When Governor Gardner met with members of the new commission,

GARDNER ROAD MEASURE PASSED BY HOUSE AFTER DEBATE OF THREE HOURS

School Bill Advocates Adopt Resolution Abandoning All Delay at Caucus Attended By Thirty

BIG CROWD SEES ALL AMENDMENTS BEATEN; BILL PASSED, 89-18

Connor Leader In Fight For Administration Measure After Day Reads Resolution Adopted By Caucus; Crudup Pleads For Minority Bill Containing Straightout Appropriation For Counties and Argues Measure Will Preserve Local Self-Government; Connor Recalls Governor Gardner's Advocacy of Present Plan in His Inaugural Address and Denies Idea Originated With Brookings Institution; Says Counties Have Never Possessed Sovereignty and That State Must Take Over Roads in Order To Assure Tax Relief

Raleigh News and Observer *headline concerning Gov. O. Max Gardner's 1931 road bill.*

he told them: "This state is like a family of five, only one of whom [the Highway Commission] has any income. And don't spend any of it."[12] The state could ill afford to retain all former county road workers and instead sought to make the best use of the newly acquired resources of the prison department. The highway department took on the care and custody of 3,311 prisoners and fifty prison camps. The state built thirty new fireproof prison camps and closed some of the old ones inherited from the counties. The camps had to be geographically dispersed to make prisoners available throughout the state. Much of the department's focus in the early 1930s shifted from construction of new roads to maintenance of the former county roads. Very little new construction was undertaken until additional federal money became available through New Deal programs.

The new state legislation took effect on July 1, 1931. During the ensuing eighteen months, the State Highway Commission spent $6 million to maintain county roads, including improving some five thousand miles of them with topsoil, gravel, crushed stone, and other material.[13] The counties had collectively spent $9 million annually on maintenance.[14] Yet the department's strong leadership and experienced employees led to such an improved maintenance performance in the very first year that the public became highly supportive of state control of local road maintenance.[15]

In 1932 J. C. B. Ehringhaus was elected governor with the support of Max Gardner.

Beaucatcher Tunnel in Asheville, opened in 1928, carried U.S. 70/U.S. 74 traffic into downtown Asheville.
Photo courtesy Pack Memorial Library (North Carolina Collection), Asheville.

Ehringhaus, an alumnus of the University of North Carolina with undergraduate and law degrees, practiced law in Elizabeth City and, as an example of his involvement in highway matters, advocated construction of the Chowan River Bridge in the late 1920s. He had served in the legislature for two terms.[16] Despite Governor Gardner's strenuous efforts to balance the state budget in the early years of the depression, Ehringhaus inherited a deficit of fifteen million dollars. At the same time, the new governor was determined to finance a lengthening of the annual public-school term from six to eight months. To accomplish that goal, he proposed, and the General Assembly passed, a controversial 3 percent general sales tax.[17] (The General Assembly in 1931 had transferred from the counties to the state responsibility for financing public school operations.)

The 1933 legislature also combined the State Highway Commission (with its prison camps) and the State Prison Department into the State Highway and Public Works Commission; that name remained in effect until 1957. (For clarity, this study will continue to refer to the renamed agency as the State Highway Commission.) The Prison Department became the State Prison Division in an agency dominated by the Highway Commission structure and leadership.[18] The consolidation created a major governmental and political force. With the exception of Jeffress, who retained the chairmanship, Governor Ehringhaus appointed a slate of new commissioners, who took office in July 1933.[19]

The legislative action meant that the Highway Commission now had responsibility for all state prisoners, including inmates in custody at Central Prison in Raleigh, at the Caledonia prison farm (located on the Roanoke River in Halifax County), and at Camp Polk for juvenile offenders (on the western edge of Raleigh)—although none of them worked on the roads. In addition, the commission took charge of short-term prisoners anywhere in the state serving a sentence of at least thirty days (the previous minimum had been sixty days). Between 1931 and 1936 the number of prisoners in North Carolina nearly doubled to more than nine thousand. Employees of the former Prison Department, just over one thousand people, joined the State Highway Commission to create a combined work force totaling 4,463.

The combined department separated and classified prisoners, resulting in more pronounced segregation between races. Central Prison was enlarged, adding an industrial building. The prison library grew, and food served to prisoners was improved. Educational facilities were added to some units. Camp Polk, for young whites, underwent several improvements, including the addition of occupational training and a reward system for good behavior. All women prisoners were housed in one prison camp, but there were plans to build a women's prison.[20] By 1936 the state had eighty-four prison camps, forty-three of them "new, clean and reasonably comfortable," and the older units undergoing improvements.

The commission also reported in 1936 that there was "not a single chain gang in the State."[21] One scholar later offered a contradictory perspective, however, concluding that "North Carolina's practice of chain gang road building [and maintenance] persisted longer than that of other southern states, well into the middle of the twentieth century,"[22] and that charges of brutality and racism continued to plague the agency for its alleged treatment of prisoners working on the roads of the state throughout the years of the Great Depression.[23]

In reviewing the first year in which the Highway Commission and the Prison Department functioned as a consolidated agency, auditors praised the accounting department for merging the financial records and record keeping of the two agencies.[24] Chairman Jeffress and his staff worked long hours to make the consolidation a success. Jeffress suffered a stroke in 1934, leading

A "chain gang" of prisoners working on a state road in 1930. Note chains on the ground, which linked prisoners to each other.

to his early retirement. Governor Ehringhaus appointed another newspaperman, Capus Waynick, to the chairmanship. Waynick, editor of the *High Point Enterprise*, had served two terms in the legislature and helped Governor Gardner settle industrial strikes in High Point and Thomasville. He had practical experience with the New Deal, having served for a year as state director of a federal employment program.[25] (Waynick later wrote a comprehensive history of the State Highway Commission titled *North Carolina Roads and Their Builders*, published in 1952.)

The realities of the Great Depression and overall state funding shortfalls led a hard-pressed legislature to an unprecedented shift of one million dollars in highway funds to the state's General Fund in 1934. The same amount was again transferred during each of the next three years. A disappointed Chairman Waynick, while acknowledging the realities of the budget crisis, nevertheless pointed out that the loss of funds would affect essential maintenance of the state's recently expanded road network.[26] Employees of the department, like all state employees at the time, received a salary reduction of 20 percent under Governor Gardner and an additional 25 percent under Governor Ehringhaus.[27] But with jobs scarce, there was little turnover in the staff.

By that time, growing traffic was increasing the wear and tear on roads. More and more public schools were being consolidated, leading to a larger number of school buses traveling longer distances. By mid-decade, school bus routes traversed 46,000 miles of roads in the state.[28] The problem of maintenance went beyond caring for the former county roads. Faster cars and heavier trucks were wearing out the hard-surface roads built in the 1920s. All federal funds were restricted to new highway construction, so the state was obliged to fund maintenance projects through its own resources.

The State Highway Commission's operating budgets during the 1930s were considerably larger than during the 1920s. Increased income

Hackney school bus in the 1930s. The Hackney company, which assembled not only buses (with parts supplied by Ford Motor Company) but also trucks, was located in Wilson. Buses facilitated the consolidation of rural schools during the 1920s and 1930s. Photo courtesy A&H.

from gasoline taxes and federal funding, as well as consolidation with the Prison Department, led to the larger budgets. The motor vehicle license tax generated considerable funds, with a lesser amount coming from newly required driver's licenses after 1935. That year, the General Assembly passed the Uniform Driver's License Act, requiring each driver of a vehicle to have a license. The Motor Vehicle Bureau in the Department of Revenue administered the new law.[29] There were no new highway bonds. As the Great Depression began, some rural car owners stopped using their vehicles and put them on blocks. Others used an axle and two wheels to make "Hoover carts."[30] Income from the state's gasoline tax (6 cents a gallon in 1931) declined slightly in that year and again in 1933. After that period, however, gasoline-tax receipts grew steadily, nearly doubling during the decade. Increasing fuel consumption reflected both the growing number of bus and truck companies and improvements in primary and former county roads. Income from motor vehicle taxes and driver's license fees varied modestly.

Federal funding, (see table 2) especially from New Deal programs, profoundly influenced State Highway Commission budgets. Although the funding varied from year to year, the annual average was approximately $5.3 million, compared to $1.9 million the previous decade.

TABLE 2:
Federal Highway Funding in North Carolina, 1933-1948 (in millions of dollars)

FISCAL YEAR	TOTAL	REGULAR	SPECIAL	SPECIAL CATEGORIES
1933	5.471	2.550	2.888	Emergency Relief
			.032	Forestry
1934	9.522		9.522	National Recovery (NRA)
1935	4.841		4.841	National Recovery (NRA)
1936	12.483	2.939	9.544	Works Progress (WPA)
1937	3.056	2.941	.115	Forestry
1938	4.888	2.998	.600	Secondary Roads
			.045	Forestry
			1.245	Grade Crossing Eliminations
1939	4.863	2.919	.584	Secondary Roads
			1.243	Grade Crossing Eliminations
			.117	Forestry
1940	3.206	2.321	.348	Secondary Roads
			.036	Forestry
			.501	Grade Crossing Eliminations
1941	4.341	2.685	.350	Secondary Roads
			.758	Grade Crossing Eliminations
			.041	Forestry
		.507		Emergency Relief
1942	6.154	2.388	.418	Secondary Roads
			.517	Grade Crossing Eliminations
			2.234	Defense Access Roads
			.597	Strategic Highway Networks
1943	5.002	2.387	.418	Federal Aid Secondary
			.515	Grade Crossing Eliminations
			1.443	Defense Access Roads
			.239	Advanced Engineering
1944	.988		.988	Defense Access Roads
1945	.335		.335	Defense Access Roads
1946	11.460	5.433	4.454	Federal Aid Secondary
			1.492	Federal Aid Urban
			.080	Forestry
1947	11.377	5.432	4.453	Federal Aid Secondary
			1.492	Federal Aid Urban
1948	11.021	5.304	4.346	Federal Aid Secondary
			1.454	Federal Aid Urban
			.083	Defense Access Roads

SOURCE: *Biennial Reports* of State Highway Commission, 1933-1934 to 1947-1948.

A breakdown of the department's revenues for the 1934-1935 budget, not necessarily a typical year, provides another perspective: 58 percent from the state gasoline tax, 26 percent from the state motor vehicle tax, and 16 percent from federal funds.[31]

Until 1932, all federal highway funding was distributed through the use of a set formula of "federal aid" administered by the U.S. Bureau of Public Roads and requiring an equal dollar-for-dollar state match. That year Congress authorized the Emergency Relief and Construction Act, which made funds available to the states quickly, without matching requirements, in the form of loans that could be paid back years in the future. The purpose of the legislation was to provide jobs to the unemployed. North Carolina received $2.9 million in emergency funds in 1933, more than the state's allocation of regular federal aid.

Franklin D. Roosevelt became president in March 1933 and initiated New Deal spending programs to address the effects of the Great Depression more aggressively. As historian Bruce Seely has written, "highways became the largest public works program undertaken by the federal government," with 35 to 45 percent of all workers on federal relief programs building roads.[32] One of those new works programs was the National Industrial Recovery Act of 1933. Through the Public Works Administration and the Bureau of Public Roads, $9.5 million in 1934 and $4.8 million in 1935 was distributed to North Carolina without the matching requirement. The distributions represented all the federal road funds the state received during those years (see table 2). The emphasis was on creating jobs, most of which were for manual laborers. The later Works Progress Administration (WPA) was a similar program that distributed $9.5 million to the state in 1936. From 1935 to 1942, the WPA spent $173.7 million in North Carolina. Yet, in the South, from 1933 to 1935, only Virginia received less per capita from a WPA predecessor agency (the Federal Emergency Relief Administration) than did North Carolina, which likewise ranked last in the nation in per capita spending under the WPA. The main reasons for the relatively small allocations to North Carolina were probably the state's refusal to provide any local match for FERA, conflicts between state leaders and Roosevelt's WPA administrator Harry Hopkins, and reluctant provision of minimal state or local matches for other New Deal programs.[33] The federal forestry program, which sponsored road building in national parks, had provided $32,000 to North Carolina in 1933. Forestry road funding for the state increased to an average of $78,000 annually in the 1937-1940 period as officials looked toward creation of the Great Smoky Mountains National Park, which was dedicated in 1939.[34]

In the early 1930s the Skyline Drive parkway was built through the Shenandoah National Park in the Virginia mountains. Sen. Harry F. Byrd of Virginia and others proposed that a scenic parkway extend from that roadway to link the Shenandoah National Park with the Great Smoky Mountains National Park, located in the mountains of North Carolina and Tennessee. The estimated cost of such a road was $7.5 million. The proposal set off a spirited competition between North Carolina and Tennessee politicians and civic leaders for the route to traverse as much of their respective states as possible. North Carolina wanted the route to extend to Blowing Rock, Asheville, and the park. Tennessee advocated a route passing closer to the state line, with the last one hundred miles and an entrance to the Smokies in Tennessee.[35]

Though the Bureau of Public Roads, the National Park Service, and the Public Works Administration were involved in planning the road, Harold L. Ickes, U.S. secretary of the interior, had the ultimate decision as to precisely where the federally funded parkway would be built. At a hearing he arranged in Baltimore in February 1934, each state presented its recommendations. With the routing still unresolved at the conclusion of the hearing, Josephus Daniels, owner of the Raleigh *News and Observer* and U.S. ambassador to Mexico, met with his friend, Secretary Ickes, and also talked with the president, on behalf of the North Carolina position.[36]

Secretary Ickes called for a second hearing to be held in September 1934 in Washington, D.C. The North Carolina delegation, led by Governor Ehringhaus, traveled from Asheville to Washington by a special train. At the hearing, the governor introduced the state's speakers, among them Senators Robert R. Reynolds and Josiah W. Bailey, Congressman Robert L. Doughton, Robert Latham (editor of the *Asheville Citizen*), Frank Page (former chairman of the N.C. State Highway Commission), and R. Getty Browning, chief locating engineer for the North Carolina Highway Commission, who made the major presentation.[37] On November 10, 1934, Secretary Ickes sent identical letters to the governors of North Carolina and Tennessee indicating that he had decided on the North Carolina route. He reasoned that that route offered better scenery and required the acquisition of less right-of-way and the construction of fewer bridges than did the Tennessee route. The fact that Tennessee already had a huge jobs program, the Tennessee Valley Authority, was likewise a factor in the decision.[38]

Construction of the parkway commenced in September 1935. The North Carolina State Highway Commission purchased the right-of-way

As the Highway Commission's chief locating engineer, Getty Browning worked with federal officials in routing, surveying, and acquiring land for the Blue Ridge Parkway from the 1930s to the 1950s.

The Nello L. Teer Company of Durham began building the Blue Ridge Parkway in 1935, working two six-hour shifts in order to provide the maximum number of jobs to unemployed men. In this photo, employees operate a steam shovel and a tractor.

for the parkway in North Carolina (overseen by Browning) and was then reimbursed by the federal government. The Nello L. Teer Company of Durham began building the road, and members of the Civilian Conservation Corps worked on landscaping it. The following year the parkway, which had been called by various names, was officially named "Blue Ridge Parkway" because, in the words of historian Harley Jolley, "the parkway lies upon the Blue Ridge throughout most of the length of both the parkway and the ridge."[39] Routing the parkway through the Cherokee Indian reservation west of Asheville ignited a controversy that took five years to resolve. The Cherokees objected to the proposed route of the parkway because, they concluded, it would take too much land and harm the Indian tourist business. Congress in 1940 approved a compromise solution that Browning had skillfully negotiated on behalf of the State Highway Commission; it routed the parkway at a higher altitude, northwest of the reservation, with the state building a connecting road from the parkway to the town of Cherokee.[40]

Clyde R. Hoey became governor in 1937. He had grown up in Shelby, practiced law, been a newspaper publisher, and served one term in Congress. He was a brother-in-law of former governor Max Gardner, leading to speculation about the political power of the so-called "Shelby Dynasty." Frank Dunlap of Wadesboro served as chairman of the State Highway and Public Works Commission during Hoey's administration. Dunlap, an attorney and farmer, had served in the legislature. During his term as chairman, the state inaugurated an advertising campaign for tourism and a probation program for selected prisoners.[41] A number of notable highway professionals served under Dunlap and other chairmen of his era. John D. Waldrop became chief engineer in 1929. After earning his engineering degree from Virginia Polytechnic Institute, he had joined the commission in 1917. He served as district

Skilled craftsmen from Spain and Italy built stone bridges like this one for the Blue Ridge Parkway. Photo courtesy A&H.

engineer in Greensboro and as assistant state engineer. He was chief engineer for most of the period between 1929 and 1934. Leslie Ames, a native of New York, came to the commission in 1919 and became assistant to the chief engineer in 1926. Three years later he accepted an offer from Gov. Huey Long to become chief engineer in Louisiana, at double his previous salary. But, missing his old agency, he returned to North Carolina and served again as chief engineer from 1931 to 1933. He spent his last active years with a private contracting firm. W. Vance Baise, a native of Caswell County, served as chief engineer from 1934 until resigning in 1949 to become executive director of the North Carolina Asphalt Association. He had earned an engineering degree from North Carolina State College and started with the commission in 1920 as a draftsman.[42] In 1936 the commission created the Division of Statistics and Planning to strengthen the planning process. James S. Burch headed the division. He was an engineer who had worked for the department in various positions during the 1920s, then for private organizations in Washington and Chicago. He was a recognized author and lecturer on highway planning.[43]

In the mid-1930s the department purchased several small toll bridges. These included bridges linking Morehead City and Atlantic Beach, the mainland and Wrightsville Beach, and Point Harbor and Kitty Hawk, as well as spans across Currituck Sound, over Roanoke Sound east of Manteo, and across the Dan River at Milton. Despite the depression, the state responded to public opinion and eliminated tolls at all these bridges, for the Chowan River Bridge, and for the Wilmington twin bridges.[44]

A new Albemarle Sound Bridge linked Chowan's county seat, Edenton, and Washington's county seat, Plymouth, on N.C. 32. The most spectacular bridge constructed during the period, it was dedicated on August 25, 1938. At more than three miles in length (with roadway approaches totaling nearly nine miles), the bridge was the state's longest for several decades. T. A. Loving Company and Tidewater Construction Company, the primary contractors, spent seventeen months on the job. The Loving firm, with headquarters in Goldsboro, was already developing a reputation for its bridge-building specialty.[45] The span, designed under the supervision of the State Highway Commission's senior bridge engineer, William L. Craven, included a 328-foot draw span. The fir timbers for the project came from California, were treated by the Gulf States Creosoting Company of Wilmington, and were then moved by barges to the site. The bridge's cost was $1.3 million, of which $500,000 was from federal aid and the remainder from state funds.[46]

The Great Depression notwithstanding, many trucking and transportation-related companies began operations in the 1930s. These included Carolina Freight Carriers of Cherryville, Thurston Motor Lines and Central Motor Lines of Charlotte, Hennis Freight Lines of Winston-Salem, and McLean Trucking Company of Red Springs moved to Winston-Salem in 1943). North Carolina

Great Smoky Mountains brochure (1940s).
Courtesy N.C. Transportation Museum.

Equipment Company, which opened in Raleigh, furnished heavy equipment for highway and other major building projects. In the meantime, The Carolina Coach in Raleigh and Queen City Trailways in Charlotte, intercity bus companies organized in the 1920s, expanded.[47] Employing a $200,000 loan from family members, William Trent Ragland and a group of businessmen organized Superior Stone Company in Raleigh in 1939. The firm was an aggregate company that furnished basic building materials such as crushed stone, gravel, and sand. The first step was to build a plant at a stone quarry. After adding a sand pit in Dunn and a quarry at Kings Mountain, the organization furnished stone used for constructing several military bases in the state during World War II, assuring the company's continued growth.[48]

When one considers the national perspective of road building, the period of the 1920s through the mid-1930s has been called the golden age of highway building. The national highway industry was united and tied together by the leadership of Thomas MacDonald as director of the federal Bureau of Public Roads. He and his staff worked closely with Congress, the American Association of State Highway Officials, and individual state highway departments.

By the early 1940s, previously consistent federal highway policy that emphasized primary routes was unraveling as demands for other roads arose. Advocates of rural secondary roads and supporters of urban thoroughfares demanded larger shares of available dollars. They challenged the basic primary-roads approach of linking major cities and towns. Another unresolved issue was whether toll highways should be considered or discouraged. The need for new and expanded roads to prepare the nation for possible involvement in a widening war already engulfing much of the world was an important additional complication.[49] Congress, recognizing that shortfall, passed the Defense Highway Act in late 1941, just before the Japanese surprise attack on Pearl Harbor. The legislation authorized $150 million for defense access roads, such as those in the vicinity of the new Pentagon building in Washington and a war supply factory in Detroit. It authorized another $50 million for strategic network roads.

Intercity bus service expanded rapidly in the 1920s and 1930s. Carolina Coach Company (with headquarters in Raleigh) advertised its stops in 1935 by painting city names on a bus's side.

North Carolina was able to garner an annual average of $5 million a year in federal road funding during 1941, 1942, and 1943 (see table 2). A better roadway to Fort Bragg (which by the end of World War II had expanded to accommodate 100,000 troops) was deemed essential for moving newly arriving recruits by bus from the Fayetteville train station to the base.[50] In 1941 the WPA, in cooperation with military officials, financed the four-laning of N.C. 87/Bragg Boulevard from Fort Bragg to downtown Fayetteville.[51] The nine-mile road was probably the first four-lane road constructed in the state since the completion of the Charlotte-Gastonia highway in the late 1920s. Also in 1941, U.S. 17 between Wilmington and Williamston was widened from 18 to 24 feet. The road improvements, financed by WPA and defense funds, provided many relief jobs. The highway became wide enough to accommodate trucks serving rapidly growing new defense-related facilities at Cherry Point marine air base (near New Bern), Camp Lejeune marine base (at Jacksonville), Camp Davis army training base (just north of Wilmington), and the Wilmington shipyard.[52]

Defense access road funds, which financed approximately sixty projects, provided a large portion of available federal moneys in the state: $2.2 million in 1942 and $1.4 million the following year. Some of the largest high-priority projects included roads between N.C. 87 and N.C. 210 near Fort Bragg; the old Durham-Oxford road from Bragtown to Camp Butner near Durham; U.S. Highway 17 and N.C. Highway 24 near Camp Lejeune in Jacksonville; U.S. 17 from Hertford to the Harvey's Neck Seaplane Base; and N.C. 130 in Brunswick County.[53] As the war progressed, regular federal aid was cut and then eliminated. The only federal funds for North Carolina in 1944 (less than $1 million) and 1945 (only $335,000) came from defense access moneys. Income from the gas tax reached a high in 1942, then plummeted during the ensuing three years as a result of gas rationing. The loss of department employees to the military and the difficulty in obtaining needed materials slowed highway building during the 1943-1945 period.[54] In the meantime, overloaded trucks and poor weather caused roads to deteriorate while maintenance funds were limited.[55]

Visitors at 1938 opening of three-mile Albemarle Sound Bridge, the state's most extensive bridge project during the 1930s and 1940s. A newer span replaced this one in 1990. Photo courtesy A&H.

J. Melville Broughton of Raleigh was governor (1941-1945) during the war. He had graduated from Wake Forest College, become an attorney, and served two terms in the state senate. During his administration, the school term was extended from eight to nine months and the twelfth grade was added. The governor's highway commission chairmen included D. B. McCrary (an Asheboro industrialist), L. B. Prince (who reorganized the department's personnel system), and Charles Ross (the department's longtime legal counsel).[56]

R. Gregg Cherry, governor from 1945 to 1949, faced a backlog of state road needs. The governor grew up in Gastonia, earned a law degree from Trinity College (now Duke University) in Durham, practiced law, fought in World War I, and served in the legislature for several terms. He appointed Alexander H. "Sandy" Graham of Hillsborough as his commission chairman. Graham had graduated from the University of North Carolina, studied law at Harvard, and practiced law. His political career included terms in the legislature, part of them as house speaker, and as lieutenant governor under Governor Ehringhaus.[57]

Since the State Highway Commission was not capable of spending all its available

Bus station in Elizabeth City (1942). Photo courtesy A&H.

funds during the war because of shortages of labor and materials, the state accumulated $40 million for postwar construction. According to a wartime article, the department developed an ambitious (but unrealized) plan to address the people's pent-up desire to travel. This plan, designed to meet highway and employment needs, called for spending $300 million in the three years following the end of the war.[58] The 1947 legislature raised the salaries of state workers by 20 percent, offsetting some of the depression-era pay cuts.[59]

Toward the end of the conflict, Thomas MacDonald, head of the U.S. Bureau of Public Roads, said, "everybody in the United States is waiting for the close of the war to get in a car to go some place."[60] Servicemen back from the war bought cars and moved their families into new houses, often in the suburbs or countryside. Nationally, car registrations grew by almost 50 percent between 1945 and 1949.[61] The state's ability to build new highways just after the war was limited, however. Ed Rankin, who served as the department's public information officer in 1946-1947, recalls riding to meetings across the state with commission chairman Sandy Graham. "Many of his talks centered on reasons the state couldn't build highways fast enough," Rankin recalled.[62] Converting the economy from war production to domestic purposes took longer than anticipated. It was also difficult to find the necessary materials and experienced engineers. Inflation nearly doubled costs for labor and materials after the war.[63]

Federal aid to the state's highway commission reached $11 million annually in 1946, 1947, and 1948 (see Appendix A). A resurgence of new-car sales (the production of civilian automobiles had been halted during the war) led to additional income from car registrations and significant increases in gasoline-tax revenue. The 1948 budget for the State Highway Commission reached a high of $68 million.[64] Nonetheless, Congress was still unable to reach a consensus on goals and funding for a national plan of ambitious highway development.[65]

Governor Cherry's administration emphasized the need for less-traveled "farm-to-market" secondary roads and paying off old bonds. The governor declared: "I have resolved to . . . hasten the day when all-weather roads would be available to the farmer, the mail carrier, the school bus, and the church-goer, from one end of the State to the other."[66] Of the more than five thousand miles of roads paved during the Cherry administration, three thousand were rural secondary roads.[67] Using surpluses that had accumulated during the war, the governor accelerated payment on the 1920s highway bonds, although those payments were not completed until the 1950s.

In 1930, 474,000 vehicles had been registered in North Carolina, only 13 percent of which were classified as commercial (mostly buses and trucks). The number of vehicles slowly grew during the decade and leveled off at about 700,000 during World War II. Of the nearly 1,000,000 vehicles registered by 1948, the number classified as commercial had increased to 31 percent.[68] At the conclusion of Governor Cherry's term in January 1949, the state had 63,603 miles of highways in its system (14,989 of which were paved), as follows: 10,350 miles of primary highways, 51,031 miles of secondary roads, and 2,220 miles of primary and secondary road links within cities and towns.[69] Cherry's successor, W. Kerr Scott, would continue and dramatically intensify the improvement of the state's rural secondary roads.

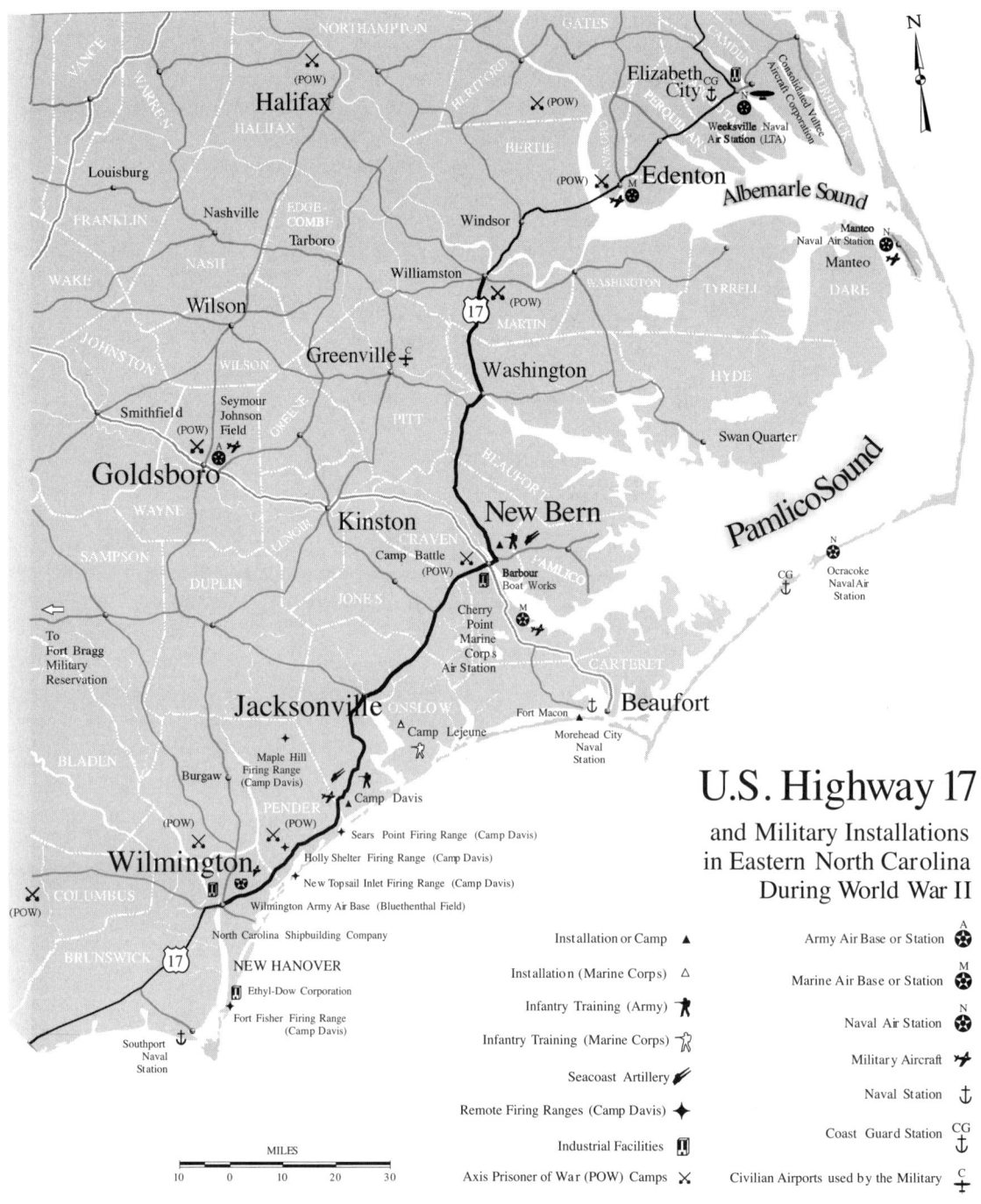

U.S. Highway 17 was widened during World War II to accommodate increased traffic from area military bases and operations. Map by Mark A. Moore, A&H.

Notes

1. O. Max Gardner (1882-1947) opened a law firm in Washington, D.C., in 1933 and was influential in state and national politics, though he never again ran for public office. He was an adviser to President Franklin D. Roosevelt and a lobbyist for corporations and other organizations. In late 1946 President Harry Truman appointed Gardner as ambassador to Great Britain, but Gardner died before he could occupy the position. *Dictionary of North Carolina Biography*, s.v. "Gardner, Oliver Maxwell (O. Max)"; Joseph L. Morrison, *Governor O. Max Gardner* (Chapel Hill: University of North Carolina Press, 1971), 28-51.

2. William S. Powell, *North Carolina through Four Centuries* (Chapel Hill: University of North Carolina Press, 1989), 481-488; John L. Bell Jr., *Hard Times: Beginnings of the Great Depression in North Carolina, 1929-1933* (Raleigh: North Carolina Department of Cultural Resources, Division of Archives and History, 1982), preface.

3. The State Highway Patrol became part of the newly established North Carolina Department of Motor Vehicles in 1941. In 1973 it was placed under the control of the Motor Vehicles Division of the North Carolina Department of Transportation (NCDOT). In 1977 it was made part of the North Carolina Department of Crime Control and Public Safety (while Motor Vehicles remained a component of the NCDOT). *Guide to Research Materials in the North Carolina State Archives: State Agency Records* (Raleigh: Department of Cultural Resources, Division of Archives and History, Archives and Records Section, 1995), 701, 702 (hereafter cited as *Guide to State Agency Records*); "From Whence We Came" (unpublished paper, N.C. State Highway Patrol, 1991), 1-9.

4. Powell, *North Carolina through Four Centuries*, 482.

5. Morrison, *Governor O. Max Gardner*, 81, 82.

6. Cecil K. Brown, *The State Highway System of North Carolina, Its Evolution and Status* (Chapel Hill: University of North Carolina Press, 1931), 52, 221.

7. "Governor Seeks Public Support," *News and Observer* (Raleigh), February 10, 1931.

8. Bruce E. Seely, *Building the American Highway System: Engineers as Policy Makers* (Philadelphia: Temple University Press, 1987), 146; John Sanders, former director, Institute of Government, University of North Carolina at Chapel Hill, telephone conversation with author, May 14, 2001; William H. Shank, *Vanderbilt's Folly* (York, Pa.: American Canal and Transportation Center, 1993), 27; "Summary of Mileage of State Highway Systems, State Highway Mileage, 1925-1975," *Highway Statistics Summary to 1975* (Washington: Federal Highway Administration, 1975); Eric DeLaughter, interim administrative manager, Transportation Planning and Programming Division, Texas Department of Transportation, telephone conversation with author, January 23, 2003; Chris J. McAdams, Research and Policy, NCDOT, telephone conversation with author, January 24, 2003. The previous seven paragraphs are based on Morrison, *Governor O. Max Gardner*, 52, 53, 75, 83-86.

9. North Carolina State Highway Commission, *Biennial Report, 1931-1932* (Raleigh: State Printer, 1933), 19, 20 (hereafter cited as *Biennial Report*, with appropriate dates); Powell, *North Carolina through Four Centuries*, 483; *Guide to State Agency Records*, 1.

10. Edward L. Rankin Jr., letter to author, October 18, 2000.

11. Capus Waynick, *North Carolina Roads and Their Builders* (Raleigh: Superior Stone Company, 1952), 76, 77. The E. B. Jeffress Park, located near the point at which the Blue Ridge Parkway intersects with U.S. 421, honors Jeffress and comprises a rest area, log cabin, and waterfalls. Dr. Houck Medford, executive director, Blue Ridge Parkway Foundation, Winston-Salem, telephone conversation with author, November 22, 2000.

12. Morrison, *Governor O. Max Gardner*, 93.

13. *Biennial Report, 1931-1932*, 16, 21.

14. *Biennial Report, 1933-1934*, 5.

15. James S. Burch, "Historical Outline of Road Administration in North Carolina" (unpublished paper written for North Carolina Historical Commission, Raleigh, April 1940), 16.

16. *Dictionary of North Carolina Biography*, s.v. "Ehringhaus, J. C. B."

17. Hugh T. Lefler and Albert R. Newsome, *North Carolina: The History of a Southern State,* 3d ed. (Chapel Hill: University of North Carolina Press, 1973), 611-613.

18. *Guide to State Agency Records,* 156.

19. *Biennial Report, 1933-1934*, 2.

20. *Biennial Report, 1935-1936*, 30-42.

21. *Biennial Report, 1935-1936*, 41.

22. Robert E. Ireland, "Prison Reform, Road Building, and Southern Progressivism: Joseph Hyde Pratt and the Campaign for 'Good Roads and Good Men,'" *North Carolina Historical Review* 68 (April 1991): 126. It is likely that Ireland and the commission had different definitions of the term "chain gang." The state employed convict labor ("chain gangs") on roads into the 1950s, but the prisoners (although accompanied by armed guards) were not always literally chained together. Jerry C. Cashion, Frank D. Gatton, and Roger C. Jones, telephone conversations with Richard F. Knapp, November 2, 9, 2000.

23. Ireland, "Prison Reform," 155.

24. *Biennial Report, 1933-1934*, 80.

25. Waynick, *North Carolina Roads and Their Builders*, 77.

26. *Biennial Report, 1933-1934*, 5.

27. Powell, *North Carolina through Four Centuries,* 485, 486.

28. *Biennial Report, 1935-1936*, 6.

29. The bureau became a separate Department of Motor Vehicles in 1941. *Guide to State Agency Records*, 701, 702.

30. Powell, *North Carolina through Four Centuries,* 477.

31. Figures are based on "Major Sources Highway Revenues, 1921-1948," a table included in the article "Financial History of N.C. Highways," *We the People of North Carolina* 10 (January 1953): 26 (hereafter cited as "Major Sources Highway Revenues" and *We the People*).

32. Seely, *Building the American Highway System*, 88-91.

33. Anthony J. Badger, *North Carolina and the New Deal* (Raleigh: North Carolina Department of Cultural Resources, Division of Archives and History, 1981), 41, 47.

34. Seely, *Building the American Highway System*, 89-91; *Biennial Reports, 1933-1934* through *1939-1940*; Powell, *North Carolina through Four Centuries,* 497.

35. Harley E. Jolley, *The Blue Ridge Parkway* (Knoxville: University of Tennessee Press, 1969), 22, 33-36, 57-64.

36. Jolley, *Blue Ridge Parkway*, 61-69, 77, 78.

37. Waynick, *North Carolina Roads and Their Builders*, 90, 91. R. Getty Browning grew up in Maryland, studied engineering at the American School of Engineers of Chicago, and worked for the Maryland Roads Commission before joining the North Carolina State Highway Commission in 1921. From 1925 to the 1950s, he was in charge of right-of-way acquisitions and the state highway maps. Waynick credited Browning for his key role in developing the Blue Ridge Parkway.

38. Jolley, *Blue Ridge Parkway,* 78-92.

39. Jolley, *Blue Ridge Parkway*, 128.

40. Jolley, *Blue Ridge Parkway*, photograph cutline opposite 92, 93-101.

41. Powell, *North Carolina through Four Centuries,* 496-498; *Dictionary of North Carolina Biography*, s.v. "Hoey, Clyde Roark"; Waynick, *North Carolina Roads and Their Builders*, 78.

42. Waynick, *North Carolina Roads and Their Builders,* 305, 87, 88.

43. John Harden, *North Carolina Roads and Their Builders*, vol. 2 (Raleigh: Superior Stone Company, Division of Martin Marietta Corporation, 1966), 88-89.

44. Burch, "Historical Outline of Road Administration," 24-25.

45. Waynick, *North Carolina Roads and Their Builders*, 225; "North Carolina Road Builders," *We the People* 14 (November 1956): 78. The Loving firm, in addition to completing enormous buildings at the state's military bases during World War II, constructed the Carteret County Bridge, which connected Morehead City and Atlantic Beach, and the Manteo-Manns Harbor Bridge over the Croatan Sound.

46. "Albemarle Prepared To Open New Bridge," *News and Observer*, August 14, 1938; *Roanoke Beacon* (Plymouth, N.C.), August 23, 1978.

47. Charles Wadelington, historian, Historic Sites Section, Division of Archives and History, Raleigh, telephone conversation with author, August 23, 2001.

48. Edward L. Rankin Jr., letter to author, March 19, 2001; Waynick, *North Carolina Roads and Their Builders*, 233-236. In 1952 William Trent Ragland arranged for Superior Stone Company to finance and publish *North Carolina Roads and Their Builders* (308 pages), by Capus Waynick. The book was a comprehensive illustrated history of the state's roads and the North Carolina State Highway Commission. In 1966 Ragland's son, William Trent Ragland Jr., authorized Superior Stone to finance and publish an updated second volume of *North Carolina Roads and Their Builders* (252 pages), to be authored by John Harden. Ragland Jr. led the company from 1953 until 1996, including its operation as a division of Martin Marietta Corporation. In 1996 Superior Stone was the founding company involved when Martin Marietta Aggregates became Martin Marietta Materials, a leading supplier of aggregates, with headquarters in Raleigh.

49. Seely, *Building the American Highway System*, 137-164.

50. Sarah McCulloh Lemmon, *North Carolina's Role in World War II* (Raleigh: Department of Archives and History, 1964), 12. Although the military decided to employ railroads for long-haul transportation of troops and supplies, highways were important to the military buildup.

51. *Fayetteville Observer*, August 12, 1941.

52. *News and Observer*, August 3, 1941.

53. Correspondence and Defense Access Files, 1935-1953, Records of Assistant Chief Engineer's Office, Federal Contact Engineer's Office, State Highway Commission Records, State Archives, Office of Archives and History, Raleigh.

54. Correspondence and Defense Access Files, 1935-1953, State Archives; "Major Sources Highway Revenues."

55. Jule B. Warren, "Thumb-Nail History of the Highway System," *We the People* 9 (March 1952): 6-8, 27.

56. Waynick, *North Carolina Roads and Their Builders*, 79-82; *Dictionary of North Carolina Biography*, s.v. "Broughton, J. Melville."

57. *Dictionary of North Carolina Biography*, s.v. "Cherry, Robert Gregg"; Waynick, *North Carolina Roads and Their Builders*, 82.

58. "$300 Million Post-War Road Building Plan," *We the People* 1 (October 1943): 8, 9.

59. John William Coon, "Kerr Scott, The 'Go Forward' Governor: His Origins, His Program, and the North Carolina General Assembly" (master's thesis, University of North Carolina at Chapel Hill, 1968), 31.

60. Seely, *Building the American Highway System*, 191.

61. Seely, *Building the American Highway System*, 193.

62. Edward L. Rankin Jr., interview with author, Concord, N.C., August 2, 2000.

63. Seely, *Building the American Highway System*, 195.

64. "Major Sources Highway Revenues."

65. This goal was finally achieved with the passage of the 1956 Federal Highway Act.

66. R. Gregg Cherry, "Some Problems Facing the State," *We the People* 4 (December 1946): 5.

67. William D. Snider, "Thirty-Five Years of Roadbuilding, 1915-1950," in *Biennial Report, 1948-1950*, 5-10; Harden, *North Carolina Roads and Their Builders*, vol. 2, 61. Harden indicates that more than five thousand miles of roads were paved. "North Carolina Road System is a Billion Dollar Investment," *We the People* 6 (January 1949): 15, gives 3,907 miles as the figure. Harden is the more reliable source.

68. "Yearly Motor Vehicle Registration," furnished by the North Carolina Division of Motor Vehicles.

69. Chester Davis, "A Progress Report," *North Carolina Roadways* 1 (September 1950): 2 (Davis is a retired reporter for the *Winston-Salem Journal*); David Leroy Corbitt, ed., *Public Addresses, Letters, and Papers of William Kerr Scott, Governor of North Carolina, 1949-1953* (Raleigh: Council of State, State of North Carolina, 1957), 453.

Chapter 4

BECOMING A MODERN AGENCY
1949-1972

After a hard-fought campaign, Kerr Scott became governor in 1949 and convinced North Carolinians to support his "Go Forward" program, which included a large bond issue to finance the paving of secondary roads. Scott grew up in Haw River, near Burlington. His father was a successful farmer who served several terms in the General Assembly. Scott graduated from North Carolina State College, where he excelled in track and debating. After serving in World War I, he began farming full-time on his family's land. With political support from the O. Max Gardner wing of the Democratic Party, Scott beat an incumbent to become the state's commissioner of agriculture in 1936.

When Scott entered the Democratic primary in 1948, he was considered an underdog to the leading candidate, state treasurer Charles Johnson. Scott appointed Capus Waynick, a former chairman (1934-1937) of the State Highway Commission, as his chief campaign aide. With no clear issues to distinguish the candidates, the better-known Johnson led Scott by 9,000 votes in a field of six hopefuls. Scott called for a runoff. Following an aggressive campaign, during which Scott advocated increased efforts by the state to pave North Carolina's numerous "farm to market" secondary roads and referred to his opponent as the "machine" candidate, Scott prevailed by a vote of 217,620 to 182,684, then easily defeated his Republican opponent in the fall.[1] As one journalist observed, "Our secondary roads were in wretched condition and the county folks demanded that this condition be corrected."[2]

As a means of financing the improvement of North Carolina's secondary roads, Governor Scott proposed a one-cent increase (from six to seven cents per gallon) in the state's gasoline tax and convinced the legislature to approve a referendum on the question of whether or not to issue $200 million in highway bonds, even though many legislators were convinced that the voters would reject the measure. The skeptical lawmakers sidestepped the question of increasing the gasoline tax and instead included it as part of the proposed referendum. The road bonds were a bold step. The most recent highway bond issue (in the amount of $30 million) approved by the General Assembly had taken place in 1927—more than two decades previously—and the gasoline tax had last been increased (from five to six cents per gallon) in 1931. The North Carolina Constitution had been amended in 1936 to require that all general-purpose bonds, including road bonds, be submitted to the voters, so a statewide vote was set for June 1949. Governor Scott traveled widely and spoke on the radio, campaigning for the bond issue. The governor and his supporters argued that: improved secondary roads would bring economic progress and help

Former governors attending Gov. W. Kerr Scott's inauguration in Raleigh on January 6, 1949. Left to right: J. Melville Broughton (1941-1945), R. Gregg Cherry (1945-1949), Governor Scott (1949-1953), Clyde R. Hoey (1937-1941), and J. C. B. Ehringhaus (1933-1937). Photo courtesy A&H.

schools; the bond revenue would finance the paving of 12,000 miles of secondary roads and stabilize an additional 35,000 miles of them with stone, gravel, and sand, whereas then-current revenues could pave only 3,000 miles; the state's credit rating was good; and the one-cent increase in the gasoline tax was necessary to pay off the debt that would be incurred.

The petroleum industry opposed the bonds, claiming that there was already enough money for the roads, that interest rates were too high, and that the gasoline tax would become burdensome. Sandy Graham, who had served as chairman of the Highway Commission for Governor Cherry, actively campaigned against the bonds, fearing that rapid new construction would hinder the proper maintenance of the expanding road network. Despite opposition within urban counties, the voters approved both the $200 million bond issue and the gasoline-tax increase by a vote of 229,493 to 174,647.[3]

Governor Scott appointed Dr. Henry Jordan chairman of the State Highway Commission. Jordan had practiced dentistry for several years, then entered the textile business in Randolph and Alamance Counties with his brother Everett (later a U.S. senator). Jordan, who had gained experience serving as a member of the commission during Governor Cherry's administration, was a tireless campaigner for the secondary road bonds.[4]

William H. Rogers Jr. became the commission's chief engineer. After earning an engineering degree at North Carolina State College, he had served in World War I. He worked in public and private organizations in the state before joining the agency in 1931 as district engineer and later served as administrative assistant to commission chairman Sandy Graham.[5]

A mild winter in 1949-1950 and the enthusiasm of the agency's workers enabled the secondary-roads program, building on beginnings achieved during the Cherry administration (1945-1949), to get off to a fast start.[6] Nor did it hurt that, according to chief engineer Rogers, the average construction cost was initially $12,000 to $14,000 per mile, which was below projections.[7] During the period, a typical secondary road selected for improvement was paved eighteen feet wide and carried between 100 to 300 vehicles daily. One of those roads reached the isolated fishing village of Merrimon, near the Neuse River below New Bern. The twelve-mile-long dirt road from Merrimon to Highway 70 had been a nightmare most of the year, especially for school buses. But paving the road opened the community to the outside world.[8]

Building such a road on isolated Ocracoke Island was a unique challenge. The Highway Commission used a special barge to bring heavy equipment from Washington, North Carolina, across Pamlico Sound. Cement came by boat from Norfolk. During the summer shrimping season, many of the men were obliged to abandon the roadwork in order to harvest the seasonal catch. "Much credit is due the older high school boys for their patience and persistence in staying on the job," a local resident recalled. In order to help preserve the island's natural beauty and rustic charm, the new road was built only ten feet wide, with wider passing areas. Completion of the road produced an unexpected result: instead of more cars, the biggest change was an increase in the number of bicycles. "A toot of the horn, the shriek of a siren, or just a big yell from the [bicycle] rider was enough to make the adult population get off the highway immediately," the same local resident noted.[9]

Governor Scott's administration achieved its ambitious goal of paving twelve thousand miles of secondary roads in four years (although fully two-thirds of the state's secondary roads remained unpaved).[10] The Raleigh *News and Observer* editorialized: "It is obvious that good business

In 1949 a reinforced-concrete bridge replaced a covered span on N.C. 53 at the Lee/Chatham County line. Only one traditional covered bridge—in Catawba County—survives in the state.

A Johnston County family watches paving of a secondary road past their home in 1950.

practices, as well as speed have been applied in this ambitious program." In writing of North Carolina's efforts to preserve its rural and pastoral areas, William D. Snider, former editor of the *Greensboro Daily News*, recently observed that the bond issue was "one of the more constructive achievements of the 20th century for a relatively poor state seeking to utilize its natural assets."[11]

Improved rural roads encouraged travel into the state's towns and cities, bringing attention to the condition of municipal and primary roads, and also began to open up rural areas for suburban development. The North Carolina League of Municipalities had argued for years that the cities and towns of the state deserved to receive a portion of the gasoline tax. The 1949 legislature appointed a study commission, which recommended that cities and towns receive one-half cent of the tax to improve municipal streets. Mayor Ben Cone of Greensboro, president of the league, took those recommendations to the 1951 legislature. Governor Scott wanted additional revenue created for that purpose, fearing that taking a portion of the existing gasoline tax would be detrimental to primary highways. But legislators, unwilling to increase the fuel tax further, enacted into law (despite Governor Scott's opposition) a bill proposed by Sen. Junius K. Powell of Whiteville that designated one-half cent of the existing gasoline tax for cities and towns. This measure, still in effect (with increases), is known as the "Powell Bill."

Half the available Powell Bill funds were distributed to municipalities according to population and half according to street mileage other than the state highway system. The funds were used for maintenance, new paving, and resurfacing of streets. In 1951, the first year the law was in effect, $4.5 million was allotted to 386 municipalities. By 1970 nearly $12 million was being distributed annually to 428 municipalities. The following year, the General Assembly doubled the amount of Powell Bill funds available to municipalities—from one-half to one cent of the state gasoline tax. Even so, the increase did not alter the state's ongoing obligation to maintain state and federal highways that passed through cities and towns. (In 2002, five hundred municipalities received Powell Bill funds.)[12]

In the meantime, the secondary-roads bond issue ($200 million) benefited the primary roads in that it freed state moneys that otherwise would have been designated for the secondary routes. Following a study of primary-road needs, Governor Scott transferred $4 million from the secondary to the primary system. North Carolina had made some progress with its primary highways since the end of World War II. U.S. 74, for example, which connected Wilmington and Asheville by way of Charlotte, had received wider roadbeds and bridges, rebuilt portions, and grade separations (such as bridges and viaducts) from railroad tracks. U.S. 1, which ran north and south through central North Carolina, connecting Maine and Florida, had been widened to 22 paved feet for its entire length through the state. But neither highway included bypasses of cities and towns during the Scott administration. U.S. 1 still passed through the heart of Raleigh, and U.S. 74 went through Lumberton, Charlotte, and Gastonia.[13] The first four-lane bypass in the state, a five-mile section of U.S. 29 (which linked Greensboro and Charlotte), bypassed Thomasville; it featured two 24-foot concrete roadways divided by a 25-foot grassy median strip and opened in 1951. A public celebration of the official opening, with Miss North Carolina as a guest, included remarks by Governor Scott, a barbecue dinner, and a cake decorated with a replica of the road.[14] A similar bypass around Lexington opened the following year.

During the last year of the Scott administration, Chairman Henry Jordan declared that about half of the state's primary roads had become obsolete. The highway department, he said, was concentrating only "on the most-used sections of our primary highways, particularly on U.S. Routes 29, 70, 64 and 301, at points where they carry the heaviest traffic."[15] Clearly, while secondary roads had received needed emphasis during the Scott years, improvement of the state's primary routes had failed to keep pace with rising demand from an increasingly mobile population.

William B. Umstead took office as governor in January 1953. Umstead was a native of Durham County who graduated from the University of North Carolina and studied law at Trinity College (now Duke University) law school. His service in Congress included three terms in the House and two years in the Senate.[16] Umstead reappointed as chairman of the State Highway Commission Sandy Graham, who brought valuable experience to the position, having served as chairman under Governor Cherry. W. H. Rogers, who had served as chief engineer since 1949, continued in that capacity. In the mid-1950s Emily Blount, daughter of C. E. Brown, head of the highway department's Third Highway Division in Wilmington, became the department's first female engineer. She had worked at the department in the summers while earning two engineering degrees from North Carolina State College.[17]

In the spring of 1954 Chairman Graham and the Highway Commission hired the New York City engineering firm of Parsons, Brinkerhoff, Hall & Macdonald to conduct a comprehensive study of the state's highway needs for the ensuing ten years, with particular attention to the primary-road system. The Parsons study, published in November 1954, concluded that $1.4 billion would be needed during that time for constructing and maintaining highways. The Parsons report included the following conclusions:

The secondary-roads program initiated in 1949 was practically complete and would suffice for many years.

Despite improvements over the years, the current primary system was essentially the one developed in the 1920s.

Limiting access to major highways through use of service roads (eliminating driveways, including entry to restaurant and motel parking lots directly connecting with the highways) was important to ensure the flow of traffic.

Increased vehicular speeds, sizes, and weights had damaged highways.[18]

While the study was being carried out, Governor Umstead's health was failing. He died in office in November 1954. His successor, Luther H. Hodges, had grown up near Leaksville (now Eden), graduated from the University of North Carolina, and lived in Leaksville and then New York City while pursuing a career in textiles with Marshall Field and Company. For a year in the early 1930s, he served on the State Highway and Public Works Commission. Despite a lack of political experience, he was elected lieutenant governor in 1952 and became governor when Umstead died. Two years later he easily won a full four-year term.[19]

One of Hodges's first encounters with the State Highway Commission as governor came in the form of a visit from Chairman Sandy Graham in early 1955. According to the governor's published memoirs, Graham bluntly told the governor, "We want your support for a $150 million bond issue for building some primary roads. I won't even sit down. This has all been worked out and I just want your permission." Graham and the commissioners were responding to the Parsons report, which documented the shortcomings of existing primary highways. The commissioners' apparent strategy was to improve aging highways by spending a total of $610 million over the next six years, using the proposed bond revenues while also raising truck and automobile taxes and

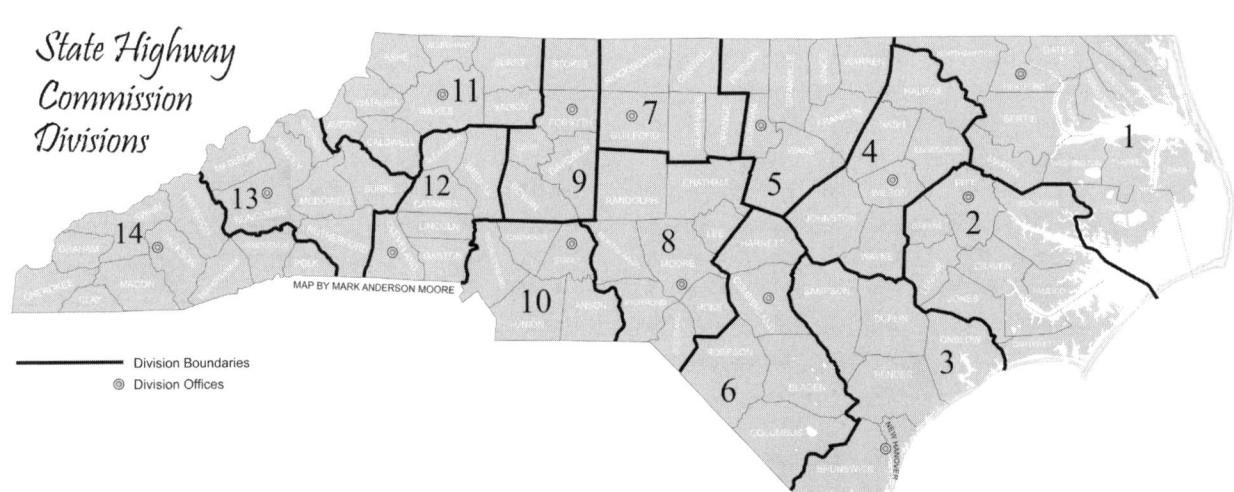

The State Highway Commission often reorganized the number and location of administrative divisions before implementing this 1953 plan, which has remained unchanged except for the headquarters location of Division 1 (presently Edenton rather than Ahoskie). Map by Mark A. Moore, A&H.

Repaving a highway in the 1950s.

fees. Governor Hodges told Graham he needed to study the department's request for the bond issue while preparing for his upcoming budget message to the General Assembly.[20]

While reviewing the proposed bond issue, Hodges discovered that the commissioner-led department was already spending approximately $200 million each biennium—fully one-third of the state budget—and that unlike those of other state agencies, the department's budget received only cursory review from the Budget Bureau and the legislature. In addition, any surplus highway funds went into a "governor's surplus fund," enabling the governor to order roads built as political favors. At Hodges's urging, the 1955 General Assembly authorized a study committee, chaired by Sen. Claude Currie of Durham, to make recommendations regarding the State Highway and Public Works Commission.[21] The Currie committee recommended:

That a full-time "executive-administrator" with experience in engineering, planning, and administration be employed to run the department and report to the commissioners. This administrator would become responsible for overall policy, and the position of commission chairman would change from full time to half time.

That construction and maintenance of secondary roads be organized on a priority basis as determined by a formula instead of being controlled by the commissioners.

That the department's commissioners become a smaller group representing the entire state rather than districts, and that commissioners be granted less authority, confined mainly to activities of advice and public relations.[22]

Governor Hodges also provided leadership on another issue involving the highway department: a proposal to separate the state penal system from the highway program. The State Highway and Public Works Commission had had total responsibility for all prison-related functions since 1931. That arrangement had worked reasonably well, inasmuch as many prisoners worked on the roads. By the mid-1950s, however, machines could do much work that previously had been done by manual labor, and the department needed fewer prisoners for road work. Nevertheless, the agency was still accepting one thousand excess prisoners each year for highway service because alternative employment was unavailable for them.

At the governor's urging, the 1955 General Assembly authorized creation of another highway study committee, this one to consider the feasibility of separating the state prison system from the highway commission. The resulting body, though concerned about how to find suitable employment for the prisoners and how to finance the prison system from the state's General Fund, recommended a separation of the agencies. Funds for the State Highway Commission came from the separate Highway Fund (as they had for the department since 1919), while all other state agencies relied upon the General Fund. The 1957 General Assembly passed both sets of recommended reforms: establishing the State Highway Commission and the Prison Department as separate agencies and changing the leadership structure of the State Highway Commission. The Prison Department, which initiated work-release programs, was funded by the Highway Fund until 1961, after which its funding came from the state's General Fund. The Highway Commission continued to utilize prisoners by contracting with the Prison Department.[23]

Governor Hodges convinced W. F. Babcock to leave a professorship in engineering at North Carolina State College to take the new position of state highway administrator. Hodges remarked that "This is one of those rare occasions when the job actually did seek the man."[24] What started as a five-year appointment turned into a twelve-year career at the State Highway Commission. "The result," John Harden wrote in *North Carolina Roads and Their Builders*, "was a well-tuned, efficient agency utilizing the most modern engineering techniques."[25]

Following a reorganization of the State Highway Commission, Gov. Luther Hodges (left) in 1957 appointed W. F. Babcock as the agency's chief executive officer. Babcock, who served in that capacity for twelve years, emphasized comprehensive planning, training programs, and updated technology. Copy of cover photo from July-August 1957 issue of *North Carolina Roadways*.

Babcock had grown up in Boston, where his father was an engineering professor at the Massachusetts Institute of Technology (MIT). He earned degrees in civil engineering with an emphasis on transportation at MIT and in 1940 began a teaching career at North Carolina State College, becoming a full professor in 1952. He was also a private consultant on traffic engineering studies and thoroughfare plans to fifty towns and cities in the state. Two noteworthy members of Babcock's initial team were Harold Makepeace, formerly mayor of Sanford and a member of the Currie study commission, who filled the new position of secondary roads officer, and chief engineer Bill Rogers, who retired two years later and was replaced by Cameron W. Lee. J. Melville Broughton Jr., son of the former governor, served as the first part-time commission chairman, heading the seven-member body for the remainder of Hodges's time in office (1957-1961).[26]

One of W. F. Babcock's first actions was to create the Advanced Planning Department, nicknamed "the department of first assumptions."[27] The department was charged with conducting thorough reviews of every proposed new highway involving state or federal funds, which then required endorsement by a planning board before entering the engineering stage. The reviews covered land-development potential, traffic characteristics, and population trends. The duties of the advanced planning team also included cooperating with the federal government in implementing special highways funded by Congress's 1965 Appalachian Regional Development Act, which paid for improving 196 miles of highways in the state's mountain region.[28]

Under highway administrator Babcock's leadership, the State Highway Commission developed budgetary controls, acquired mainframe computers for engineering work, added aerial photography to assist it in mapping, and strengthened in-service training programs. Billy Rose, who worked as an assistant to Babcock, remembers him as a quick thinker. "He could upset people by giving quick, direct answers to their questions," Rose recalled—especially if the answer was not what they wanted to hear.[29] Edward L. Rankin Jr., private secretary to Governor Hodges, recalls that Babcock, not attuned to the political world, "did not suffer fools gladly" and could be tactless. "The governor once had to insist he go to Charlotte and sit down with folks there to talk about a road complaint," Rankin remembered.[30]

Administrative assistant Cameron Lee (left) and maintenance supervisor Frank W. McCracken visit Avery County to inspect the aftermath of a 1958 snowstorm.

On the national level, discussions continued about the need for expressways and a modern interstate highway system. In many states, there was progress in building four-lane expressways. The Pennsylvania Turnpike, for example, financed by New Deal agencies at President Roosevelt's insistence, had opened in 1940 as a 160-mile, controlled-access (allowing motorists to enter or exit the turnpike only at designated ramps) toll highway connecting Harrisburg and the outskirts of Pittsburgh. The turnpike, which initially required lower speeds at points at which it decreased in width from four to two lanes in order to pass through mountain tunnels, nevertheless dramatized the potential of expressways for increasing traffic speed and efficiency; it also generated a national debate about the merits of toll roads.

The Federal-Aid Highway Act of 1944 had projected a coordinated interstate highway system totaling 40,000 miles. Though no special funding was designated for implementation, states were encouraged to begin building the system using traditional federal aid, which included funds for urban as well as primary and secondary roads. The act authorized use of federal-aid funds for land acquisition but provided no separate funding for that purpose.[31] Under the leadership of Thomas MacDonald, the U.S. Bureau of Public Roads involved the entire highway community in planning what essentially became the present interstate system.

Beginning in February 1945 each state highway department was invited to offer recommendations for interstate routes through their respective states. Meeting behind closed doors in June 1945, the North Carolina State Highway Commission, chaired by Sandy Graham, made modest and unimaginative recommendations for statewide routes that did not even include Raleigh. Despite a public hearing at which the Raleigh Chamber of Commerce and citizens of the capital city expressed their displeasure, the commission did not change its recommendations, which were included in the 37,681-mile "National System of Interstate Highways" approved by MacDonald and the federal public works administrator on August 2, 1947. That final decision left Raleigh one of only six state capitals not included in the interstate system. The commission's recommendations and the map that accompanied the report were significant, in that the same general routes were unaltered by later (1956) legislation that provided financing for the proposed interstate system.

In the 1947 plan North Carolina was allocated only 708 miles of interstate highways. In contrast, Virginia received 911 miles; Tennessee, 1,052; Georgia, 1,141; and much smaller South Carolina, 706. North Carolina was concentrating on building secondary roads during that period. Indeed, state leaders were so focused on such roads that they failed to grasp the future significance of interstate thoroughfares. In a 1947 article in *Better Roads* magazine, North Carolina's state highway engineer, Vance Baise, commented on the lack of special federal funding for interstate highways and added, "we certainly do not feel justified in improving any part of the

Alexander H. "Sandy" Graham, a former lieutenant governor, served two terms as chairman of the Highway Commission, 1945-1949 and 1953-1957. During those years the state missed opportunities to obtain adequate interstate mileage.

system [with state funds] except as traffic needs require."³²

As recommended by the State Highway Commission, the 1947 scheme designated interstate routes much unchanged half a century later. The north-south, Maine-Florida route, which became known as Interstate 95 (the interstates were first numbered in 1957), would skirt the Rocky Mount and Fayetteville areas—a more direct path for long-distance travelers than routing the highway westward toward Raleigh.³³ In order to pass through most of the state's industrialized Piedmont crescent, the specific route of another projected interstate highway (future Interstate 85, linking Richmond and Atlanta) entered the state near Henderson and Durham. It then continued west, roughly along the route of the old North Carolina Railroad built a century earlier, to Greensboro and then southwestward to Charlotte and beyond. The future Interstate 40 began at Greensboro and continued westward through Winston-Salem to Asheville and ultimately on to the West Coast. Finally, the future Interstate 26 was routed to connect Asheville and Charleston, South Carolina, via Columbia. The route that later became Interstate 77 was not included in the 1947 plan. The interstate system did not include either of North Carolina's principal ports—Wilmington and Morehead City—but did include both Norfolk and Charleston. The larger volume of tonnage at those port cities in neighboring states, in contrast to that of North Carolina's much smaller ports, may have influenced the decision.

Once North Carolina and the nation had approved a routing for an interstate system, the question became one of implementation. When President Dwight Eisenhower (1953-1961) took office, the highway program was administered by the Bureau of Public Roads, an agency of the U.S. Department of Commerce. In addition to its headquarters in Washington, the bureau maintained an office in every state, nine regional divisions, and offices in several foreign countries. Eisenhower, determined to see an interstate program started, decided it was time to replace Thomas MacDonald, who was then seventy-two years old and had headed the federal highway program since 1919. (From Eisenhower's decision forward, leadership of the bureau customarily changed with each new administration.)³⁴ For several years, Congress debated how to finance the interstate system. President Eisenhower, who believed that the interstates offered military as well as economic advantages, was determined to find a solution. During World War II he had admired the autobahns, the superhighways constructed in Germany during the 1930s.

Debates on the pros and cons of building toll roads continued after World War II. The Pennsylvania Turnpike was proving financially successful, though the newer West Virginia Turnpike was having troubles. Several new toll turnpikes opened, especially in the Northeast and Midwest, among them the New Jersey Turnpike in 1953. Turnpikes represented a way for states to construct needed expressways in the absence of sufficient federal funding. By the mid-1950s, toll highways were being constructed to connect Miami and Fort Pierce in Florida and Richmond and Petersburg in Virginia.³⁵ The U.S. Department of the Interior even advocated charging tolls on the Blue Ridge Parkway. Governor Hodges led the state's opposition, stating that such tolls "would be unwise, unsound and extremely difficult to administer," and the parkway toll proposal was shelved.³⁶

In the 1950s, states were encouraged to apply for urban additions to the proposed interstate system. In September 1955 the Bureau of Public Roads published maps of the approved designations in its "Yellow Book"—so named because its cover was yellow. Virginia and Tennessee each gained bypasses around several cities, as well as routes through downtowns. South Carolina had received such additions for Columbia, Greenville, and Spartanburg, cities with an average population of 61,000 in 1950. North Carolina, in which the average population of the five largest cities was 87,000, made no requests at all and thus was one of only five states not included.³⁷

Congress finally passed a historic, expanded Federal-Aid Highway Act in June 1956. The legislation authorized the building of a 41,000-mile network of modern, interstate highways by 1972. Financing would be on a "pay-as-you-ride" basis, with the federal government paying 90 percent and the states 10 percent. Funding would come from increasing federal taxes on gasoline (from 2 cents to 3 cents per gallon), tires, and highway vehicles of exceptional weight, as well as excise taxes on trucks, buses, and trailers. The state highway departments would construct and maintain the interstates in their respective states. Although some toll highways became part of the interstate system, the legislation had the effect of slowing the building of new toll roads. Rep. George Fallon of Maryland and Sen. Albert Gore Sr. of Tennessee, the bill's chief authors, declared that the bill would lead to "the greatest government construction program in the history of the world."[38]

Construction specifications included traffic lanes 12 feet wide. Most interstates had four lanes, according to volume of traffic, though that particular specification was not made mandatory until 1966. The width of medians (usually 36 feet) and rights-of-way (typically 300 feet, providing enough room to add two more lanes later) varied. The specifications also included wide overpass bridges; limited-access entrances and exits; 10-foot-wide shoulders; and exclusion of restaurants, motels, and other businesses from direct connection to the road's right-of-way.[39]

North Carolina was allotted 714 miles for what became Interstates 95, 85, 40, and 26, according to the basic map and plan approved in 1947. Fortunately for North Carolina, a route connecting Charlotte and Canton, Ohio (near Cleveland), was added to the interstate system in October 1957; the route, designated as Interstate 77, was designed to link the growing Piedmont to the industrial Midwest.[40] It gave North Carolina a revised total of 776 miles of allotted interstate highways.

Meanwhile, the State Highway Commission had been attempting to build expressways compatible with the 1947 interstate plan, using the traditional 50-50 federal aid match. By autumn 1955 the highway department's magazine, *North Carolina Roadways*, referred to an "80-mile continuous toll-free expressway," part of U.S. Highways 29 and 70 from the Yadkin River northeast of Salisbury to Hillsborough, as the "Longest Expressway in [the] South." The article included the following points about the road: that it was "Comparable in design and construction to many of the big turnpikes in the North and East"; that it "does not enter a single town, has no delay points and has no restricted speed zones" (the speed limit was 55 m.p.h.); that "No railroads or other highways intersect or cross the expressway at grade"; and that it is "well marked with large reflectorized signs." The portion from the Yadkin River to Greensboro (most of which is currently I-85 Business) was four lanes. The Greensboro-Hillsborough portion (which became I-40/85) was new construction of two lanes, but right-of-way was acquired for adding two additional lanes when needed.[41]

By the mid-1950s, a new four-lane portion of U.S. 70 was built in the mountains between Old Fort and Ridgecrest, replacing an unsafe, narrow, winding road. The department claimed that this six-mile, three-million-dollar project required the movement of more dirt per mile than any other road built in the nation.[42] W. E. Graham & Sons (of Cleveland, North Carolina) successfully carried out the impressive feat of engineering and grading. Although the company worked throughout the eastern United States, its North Carolina resources included rock-crushing operations in Mount Airy, as well as in Winston-Salem, where it also operated a granite quarry.[43] Other portions of four-lane highways completed about that time included routes between Canton and Lake Junaluska, Charlotte and China Grove, Charlotte and Monroe, Gastonia and Kings Mountain, New Bern and Cherry Point, and Durham and Raleigh.[44]

In the mid-1950s the highway department constructed numerous two-lane bypasses around central business districts and towns, including those at Asheboro, Charlotte, Clinton, Elizabeth City, Goldsboro, Henderson, Laurinburg, Lumberton, Morganton, Oxford, Reidsville, Rocky Mount, Sanford, Southern Pines, and Wilson. The department planned for selected bypasses to eventually become portions of interstate highways. Such plans involved opening two lanes and acquiring the necessary right-of-way for adding two additional lanes later. Examples included U.S. 29/70 in Greensboro (which became Interstates 40 and 85), U.S. 64 in Statesville (Interstate 40), and U.S. 70 in Durham (Interstate 85).[45]

Likewise built during this period were the first city expressways in the state. The 1944 Federal-Aid Highway Act had designated funds for urban road planning and included an urban road category as part of annual federal aid.⁴⁶ In the early 1950s Greensboro built Cone Boulevard, a four-lane road with a grassy median, along the northern edge of the city and began four-laning Lee Street/N.C. 6 to allow east-west traffic to avoid downtown. In 1955 one-and-one-half miles of Downtown Boulevard (now known as Capital Boulevard) opened in Raleigh as an expressway to ease traffic on U.S. Highway 1 to and through the city's downtown. The thoroughfare included grade separations at Peace Street, Wade Avenue, and old Wake Forest Road.⁴⁷

According to Billy Rose, an agency planner in the 1960s and later highway administrator, the most important urban expressways in North Carolina were Independence Boulevard in Charlotte, Winston-Salem's East-West Expressway, and the Asheville Expressway. All were initiated by their respective cities but involved cooperation with the State Highway Commission.⁴⁸

Former Charlotte mayor Ben Douglas, known as an airport booster, served as a member of the State Highway Commission in the late 1940s and led the effort to create Independence Boulevard in his city. Charlotte voters approved the issuance of $200,000 in street bonds in 1946, which likely provided enough local share to match federal funding of more than $2 million. Independence Boulevard opened in two segments in 1949 and 1950 with four lanes (though it was not a controlled-access expressway); it extended eight miles—from the southwest edge of downtown eastward as U.S. Highway 74.⁴⁹ In the mid-1950s, the Charlotte Coliseum was built on East Independence, and the boulevard's new grade-separation intersection with Morehead Street and South Boulevard was completed, providing a quicker connection with four-lane Wilkinson Boulevard/U.S. 29/74.⁵⁰

Winston-Salem and the state built the East-West Expressway, which cost $16 million, from downtown westward six miles. The first segment opened in 1958, requiring the removal of a low-income downtown neighborhood, and the remainder of the road opened two years later. "At the time, it was very progressive, and John Gold (the city manager) deserves credit," Billy Rose declared.⁵¹ It featured four lanes, controlled access, and was even lighted at night. As traffic escalated, however, the expressway's "Hawthorne Curve" gained publicity. Drivers heading eastward encountered a steep downhill grade, followed

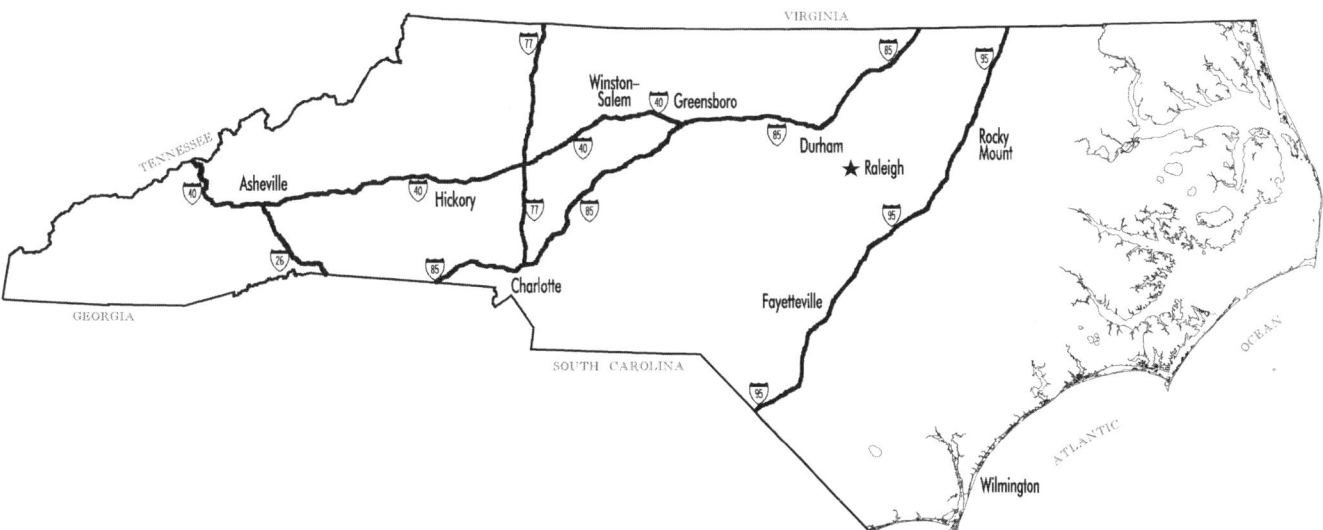

Interstate Highway System Authorized in 1956 and 1957

The Federal-Aid Highway Act of 1956 authorized funding for the interstate highway system. North Carolina was allotted only 714 miles—in contrast to South Carolina's 769, Virginia's 1,008, Tennessee's 1,093, and Georgia's 1,171. In 1957 a new interstate (now I-77) was added to connect Charlotte and Ohio, adding 62 miles within North Carolina. Map by Brian Padfield, NCDOT.

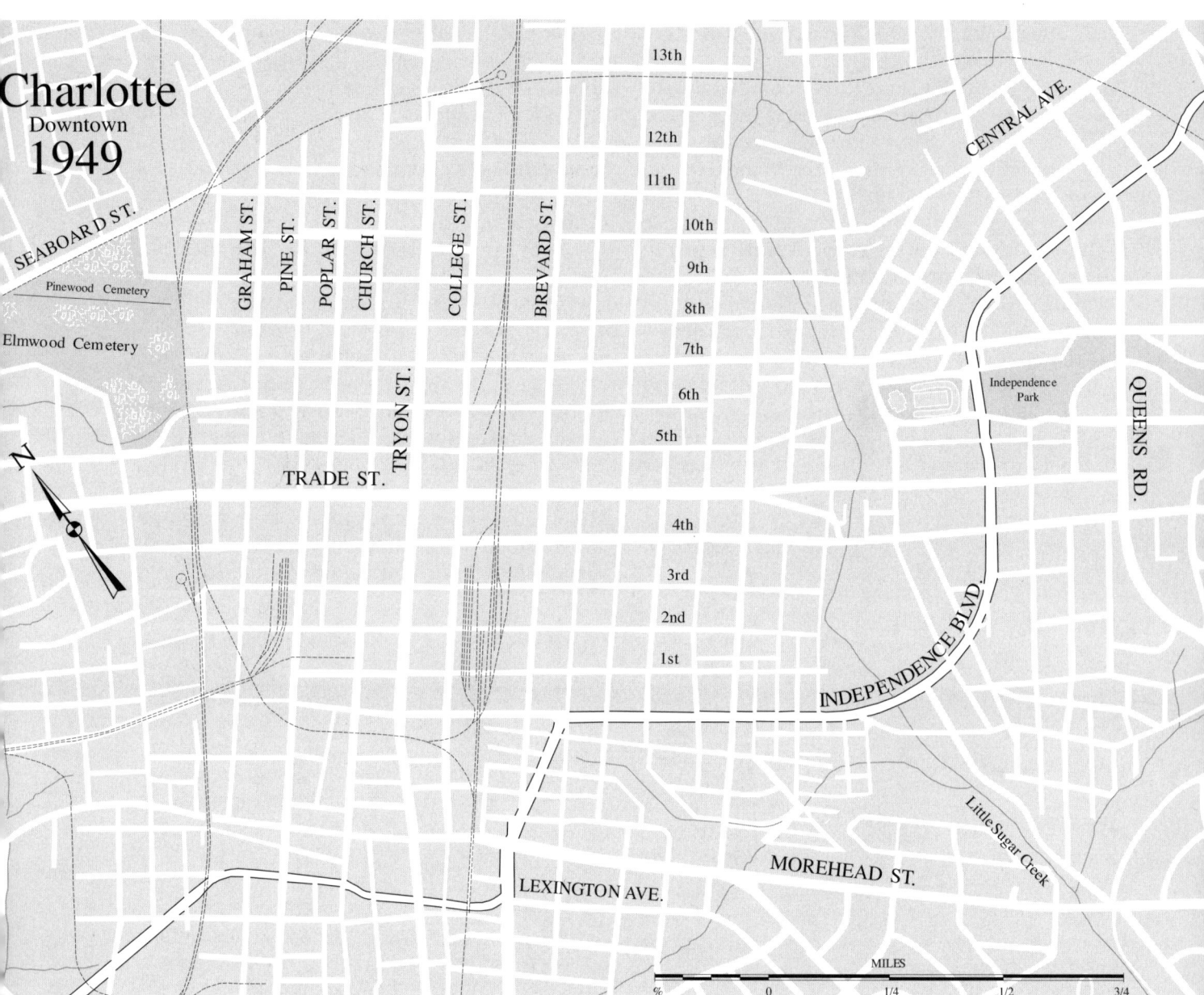

Independence Boulevard, the state's first urban expressway, opened in Charlotte in 1949. This map from that year shows the route through the city's center. Map courtesy Special Collections Unit, UNC-Charlotte Library; adapted by Mark A. Moore, A&H.

The East-West Expressway, which opened in 1958 in Winston-Salem and became part of Interstate 40, included the dangerous Hawthorne Curve. The curve was finally straightened in the 1990s and is presently part of I-40 Business.

immediately by a sharp, dangerous curve over Hawthorne Road, near North Carolina Baptist Hospital. When the road was being built, the city discovered that acquiring the property necessary to eliminate the curve would have cost $500,000, a prohibitive amount at that time. Before the highway opened, federal highway officials had planned to build I-40 south of town, but they yielded to the city's desire to include the East-West Expressway as part of the interstate. One journalist called that decision "a terrible blunder." An I-40 bypass finally opened on the south side of the city in 1992, and a few years later the Hawthorne Curve (now part of I-40 Business) was straightened.[52]

The Asheville Expressway was a four-lane, controlled-access highway that opened in 1960 between Beaucatcher Tunnel and the French Broad River. It was intended to move east-west and north-south traffic around downtown on U.S. 70, U.S. 25, and U.S. 19/23. Wilbur Smith and Associates (with headquarters in Columbia, South Carolina) designed the road, and George R. Prescott, resident engineer for the State Highway Commission, directed construction. Although just short of two miles in length, the expressway required the removal of 282 structures and the construction of nine bridges. It was a key factor in Asheville's success years later in gaining approval for construction of the I-240 loop through the center of town, which opened in 1981.[53]

Another significant expressway was the Raleigh Beltline. By 1964, ten miles of the highway were open around the west and north sides of Raleigh from Apex to U.S. 64 East. It offered a means by which U.S. 1 could bypass the downtown business district and facilitated growth in the northern portions of the city. The road had four lanes with controlled access. The portion from New Bern Avenue/U.S. 64 to Poole Road opened in 1976.[54]

The gubernatorial administrations of both Terry Sanford (1961-1965) and Dan K. Moore (1965-1969) advocated additional interstate designations for North Carolina. An unfulfilled 1963 request recommended adding Durham-Raleigh-Morehead City and Charlotte-Wilmington routes. In 1968 the U.S. Department of Transportation announced the addition of 1,492 interstate miles in twenty-eight states. North Carolina was granted a forty-nine-mile extension of I-40 from near Durham via Raleigh eastward to Smithfield at I-95 and a nine-mile extension of I-77 from Independence Boulevard in Charlotte southward to the South Carolina state line (as part of an overall extension of that highway to Columbia, South Carolina). The two segments were the state's first extensions of interstate highways since 1957.[55]

While education was clearly the priority of Terry Sanford, who became governor in 1961, he also supported a strong highway program.[56] Governor Sanford made the chairmanship of the highway commission a full-time position again (it had been part-time for the previous four years) and appointed businessman Merrill Evans of Ahoskie to head an eighteen-member commission. Evans had worked for the department as a young man and served as a member of Gov. Gregg Cherry's highway commission.[57] Despite the fact that W. F. Babcock (state highway administrator) and Cameron Lee (chief engineer) continued in their positions through both the Sanford and Moore administrations, the position of director of secondary roads changed with each new governor. Ben Roney of Rocky Mount held the position during the Sanford years; George S. Willoughby Jr. did so in the Moore years.

The State Highway Commission (and later the Department of Transportation) consistently expressed concerns about continuing funding of "non-highway" undertakings from the Highway Fund. The 1961 General Assembly addressed that matter by transferring administration of the Paroles Commission, the Probation Commission, and the State Prison Department from the Highway Fund to the General Fund. The Highway Commission had spent approximately $15 million to fund those areas during fiscal year 1961 alone.[58]

Two years later, the Herbert C. Bonner Bridge, 2.4 miles in length and costing nearly four million dollars, opened on the Outer Banks, enabling N.C. Highway 12 to span Oregon Inlet. The bridge was built to withstand winds of 120 miles per hour.[59] By 1964 interstate construction was on schedule, and nearly half of the state's 59,000 miles of secondary roads had been paved. Meanwhile, construction of primary roads, which took more time and money to build than did secondary roads, languished, even as traffic increased. One editorial writer declared that the state needed a "good primary roads governor."[60]

Dan K. Moore became governor in 1965. He earned undergraduate and law degrees from the University of North Carolina and then practiced law in Sylva, forty miles west of Asheville. He served in the legislature and in World War II, was a superior court judge, and then was a legal counsel for Champion Paper Company in Canton.[61] Governor Moore appointed Joseph M. Hunt of

The Asheville Expressway, which stretched two miles on U.S. 70/U.S. 74 between the Beaucatcher Tunnel and the French Broad River, opened in 1960 and is now part of Interstate 240.

Greensboro, a former Speaker of the state house of representatives, commission chairman.⁶² The governor convinced the 1965 General Assembly to endorse a $300 million bond issue, which included $150 million for primary roads and $75 million each for secondary and urban roads, and to continue the one-cent gasoline tax levied in 1949 for the improvement of secondary roads. Voters approved the bonds. The bond revenue accelerated planning of new or improved roads, including the four-laning of U.S. 70 between Raleigh and Morehead City and the continued upgrading of U.S. 74 between Wilmington and Asheville.

The State Highway Commission built the first segments of North Carolina's interstates to relieve congestion on busy primary highways. By the mid-1960s, the Tar Heel State was ahead of many other states, having completed about half of its modest original system. At that time, there were only two remaining portions of unfinished interstate highways in the state that required traffic to be diverted temporarily to non-interstate two-lane (rather than four-lane) roads: I-85 between Durham and Henderson and I-40 between the Mocksville area and Statesville.⁶³ The spectacular twenty-two-mile Pigeon River Gorge section of Interstate 40 through rugged mountains cost $33 million. When that section's two tunnels opened, they were the first to be incorporated into the Interstate Highway System east of the Mississippi River.⁶⁴ The Green River Bridge opened in 1969, enabling I-26 to span a deep gorge in Polk County.

The pace at which interstate highways were being constructed nationwide was unimpeded until the mid-1960s. One highway historian has pointed out that after 1965 environmentalists and those opposed to the routing of interstate highways through cities were able to secure legislation that effectively slowed the earlier rates of growth.⁶⁵ Historic preservationists, for instance, increasingly questioned the destruction of landmarks resulting from highway construction. The National Historic Preservation Act of 1966 provided

This view, looking northeast, shows early construction of the Raleigh Beltline. Note U.S. 1/U.S. 64 (Hillsborough Street) at bottom of photograph paralleling railroad tracks. This portion of the Beltline, close to the state fairgrounds, opened in 1964; the Beltline was completed around Raleigh in 1985. Copy of cover photo from May-June 1961 issue of *North Carolina Roadways*.

funding to establish a National Register of Historic Places, as well as state staffs to identify and attempt to preserve eligible buildings and districts. That same year the Department of Transportation Act directed the new U.S. secretary of transportation not to approve "any program or project which requires the use of any land from an historic site of national, state or local significance" unless there was no "feasible and prudent alternative" that could minimize harm to such a site. The National Environmental Policy Act of 1969 required federal agencies (and others using federal funds) to "prepare an environmental impact statement for every major federal action affecting the natural and man-made environment. . . ."⁶⁶

The new federal regulations affected urban states more than North Carolina, at that time a basically rural state with its interstate and expressway routes primarily located on the outskirts of cities. On the other hand, two major North Carolina roads resulted in the destruction of minority inner-city neighborhoods: I-77 resulted in the demise of Charlotte's McCrorey Heights, and the Durham Freeway destroyed the inner core of Durham's historic Hayti.[67] By 1972, originally the target year for completing the interstate system, a new federal timetable reset completion for 1980—a delay the North Carolina Department of Transportation blamed largely on "increased costs and cutbacks and freezes of federal funds."[68] Of the state's 838 authorized interstate miles, 562 were open to traffic in 1972.

Meanwhile, Congress passed the Highway Beautification Act in 1965. The legislation encouraged landowners to make land adjacent to federal aid highways more attractive by, among other measures, regulating outdoor advertising, junkyards, and littering. The act also advocated creation of rest areas and scenic overlooks along major highways. The rest areas could not be located close to municipalities or be parts of community parks. Garden clubs and other civic groups were asked to participate in beautification. Governor Moore appointed a special commission to work on related issues. The state's first welcome center, located on I-85 near the Virginia state line, opened in 1968.[69]

There was progress on safety issues as well during the period. The Carolina Motor Club (an affiliate of the American Automobile Association) and the State Highway Patrol had always advocated safety measures. In 1957 the legislature for the first time appropriated funding for driver education in high schools. Congress passed the Highway Safety Act in 1966. The Traffic Engineering Section of the State Highway Commission, organized in 1945, studied the causes of accidents and hazardous locations and took action to rectify such situations.

Thirty-nine-year-old Robert W. Scott, son of former governor Kerr Scott, became the state's governor in 1969. After attending Duke University for two years and then graduating from North Carolina State University, he operated the family dairy farm in Haw River and served as lieutenant governor from 1965 to 1969.[70] As governor, he brought in a new leadership team at the State Highway Commission. He appointed as chairman Duncan M. "Lauch" Faircloth, a farmer and businessman from Clinton who had served on Governor Sanford's highway commission. As part of the new administration's shake-up, Scott replaced respected professional highway administrator W. F. Babcock, though his reasons for doing so were not widely publicized. Babcock quietly rejoined the engineering faculty at North Carolina State University. The dismissal of Babcock was part of a political effort to restore more power to the highway commission and its chairman.[71] In a report issued at the end of 1969, Chairman Faircloth publicly declared that "rather than have decisions of construction and highway improvements made from the central offices in Raleigh, he [Governor Scott] felt priorities should be determined where they existed."[72] George Willoughby was promoted from secondary roads officer to highway administrator, Billy Rose became assistant highway administrator, and Jack Murdock began a tenure as secondary roads officer.[73] The commission was enlarged to twenty-three members, but all did not go well. Two members of the commission resigned in 1972 following newspaper reports that the men had "violated conflict-of-interest statutes prohibiting members of the Highway Commission from doing business with the Highway Department."[74]

During the first biennium of the Scott years, the available funds from the 1965 bond issue were depleted. In response, Governor Scott led efforts to convince the 1969 General Assembly to increase the gasoline tax by two cents to a total of nine cents per gallon, the highest of any state in the nation.[75] Some lawmakers wanted to take back one cent of the increase in the ensuing session, but the decision stood. As a result, "the state was able to break all records for dollars spent for construction."[76] Urban projects completed during that time included Church Street in Burlington, a U.S. 64 bypass in Asheboro, Garrison Boulevard in Gastonia, Ward Boulevard in Wilson, and a central business-district loop in Fayetteville. Greensboro's Wendover Avenue, a major east-west expressway that passes two miles north of downtown, was completed in 1972 following a fifteen-year effort. The entire road, which cost a total of $12.5 million, extended eleven miles (mostly in six lanes) between U.S. 29 North on the city's east side and I-40 on the west side. The Cape Fear River Bridge at Wilmington, fed by traffic on U.S. Highways 17, 74, and 76, opened at a cost of $16 million. The handsome, vertical-lift span features two huge pillars. Bridges also opened over the French Broad River in Asheville and across Bogue Sound, connecting the mainland with Emerald Isle.[77]

Growth of the Tar Heel highway system between 1949 and 1972 can be documented in a number of ways. An analysis of the overall funding and number of State Highway Commission full-time staff, as well as state population and vehicle numbers, is revealing. The department had 9,395 employees (including those in prison work) in 1948. With the issuance of the secondary road bonds in 1949, the staff grew to 12,369 by 1953. To accommodate the increased staff, the department moved into a new, five-story (plus full basement) building, facing the State Capitol, early in 1953. The new 61,000-square-foot headquarters building included a 400-seat auditorium and a cafeteria. Though a typical government building of the period, containing fluorescent lighting and

The Oregon Inlet Bridge (now the Herbert C. Bonner Bridge), more than two miles long and built at a cost of four million dollars, opened on the Outer Banks in 1963, replacing a ferry. Note ferry slip at lower right.

Green River Bridge, spanning a deep gorge and rising 220 feet above the river, opened on Interstate 26 in Polk County in 1969.

sound-absorbent ceilings, the attractive main entrance on Wilmington Street featured Italian marble, as well as aluminum doors and grillwork.[78] The new headquarters provided almost twice the space of the overcrowded 1921 building (approximately 36,247 square feet) it replaced; the older structure was remodeled to accommodate the North Carolina Museum of Art.[79]

In 1957 all prison functions were transferred from the State Highway Commission to a Department of Prisons. This is the primary reason why the total staff of the State Highway Commission had shrunk to 9,600 employees by 1960. Staff growth during the 1960s (to 10,642 by 1970) was in part a response to new fed-eral programs (such as interstate highways) and mandates. (During the 1960s the department also hired 1,500 to 2,000 people each year as part-time or seasonal staff.) To accommodate the growth, a six-story, 100,000-square-foot annex building was added to the agency complex in 1968. When the new North Carolina Department of Transportation (NCDOT) was organized in 1971, it encompassed not only the State Highway Commission but also the Division of Motor Vehicles and the State Ports Authority (both agencies retained their respective office space in the transfer), which accounts in large part for still another expansion in the size of the NCDOT staff—to a total of 11,500 workers by 1972.[80]

By 1960 the total annual revenues for the State Highway Commission were $150 million, which represented steady though unspectacular growth during the previous decade. During the 1960s the agency's revenues more than doubled to $399 million for fiscal 1970. It is noteworthy that federal funds accounted for 25 percent of the commission's total revenues by 1972 (see Appendix A).[81] The cost of building highways has increased steadily for many reasons, including inflation, the use of expensive technology, and the necessity of meeting increasing federal regulations. In 1953, for example, when many roads required only 100 feet of right-of-way, the department's annual budget for right-of-way was only $4 million. By 1970 the department employed three hundred people and spent $25 million annually for right-of-way, which amounted to as much as 400 feet for some interstates.[82]

Traffic increased dramatically across the state and nation after World War II. Between 1945

The state's first welcome center opened in 1968 on Interstate 95 in Northampton County. N.C. now has nine such centers; a new one opened in 2003 on I-26 in Madison County. Welcome centers are constructed and owned by the NCDOT and operated by the N.C. Department of Commerce.

High-school students enjoying the first McDonald's in North Carolina, which opened in 1959 on Summit Avenue near downtown Greensboro. By 2002 there were 371 McDonald's restaurants along roads in the state. Photo courtesy Carol W. Martin/Greensboro Historical Museum Collection.

and 1950 the number of vehicles in the state swelled by an astonishing 59 percent, from 686,000 to 1,171,000, and the state's population grew to four million. By 1960 the state's 4,556,000 people possessed 1,907,000 vehicles. The statewide ratio of cars to people increased from 1-to-3.5 in 1950 to 1-to-2.4 in 1960. North Carolina's population topped five million in 1970. The number of vehicles continued to increase faster than the population, and the statewide ratio of vehicles (3,200,000) to people ballooned to 1-to-1.6.[83] From 1949 to 1971 the State Highway Commission added more than 10,000 miles of roads to the highway system. Most of that growth was in secondary roads. By 1971 the commission was responsible for a total of 73,990 miles of roadways, as follows: 11,710 miles of primary roads (including interstate highways); 58,600 miles of secondary roads; and 3,680 miles of primary and secondary links within cities and towns.[84]

In 1948 the North Carolina State Highway Commission, like the state's highway system, operated much the way it had in the 1920s and 1930s. During the period from 1949 to 1972, the department transformed itself into a modern state agency, with relatively efficient management

Jack Murdock, all-American guard for the Wake Forest College basketball team in 1956-1957, drives for a lay-up in a game against UNC. After several years of helping coach the team, he directed the NCDOT's secondary roads program for nearly three decades.

utilizing new technology. By 1972 the organization was building and administering an extensive network of roadways and interacting with a large number of outside entities, ranging from environmental organizations to an expanded federal bureaucracy with new funds and new mandates. Except for gaps at Hickory and near Asheville, motorists were able to drive on an interstate highway from the Tennessee border to Durham without encountering a stoplight. The state's residents and visitors were introduced to a growing interstate and primary highway system, as well as to the initial development of bypasses, urban expressways, and paved secondary roads.

In 1966 Congress created the U.S. Department of Transportation (which began operations in April 1967) to encourage cooperation among the nation's existing transportation modes—principally highways, aviation, and rail. The venerable Bureau of Public Roads became a part of that department's Federal Highway Administration. Mass transit was incorporated into the new federal department in 1968. Even more changes were on the horizon, as the federal government began to explore ways to broaden acceptable transportation options beyond highways. In 1970, for instance, Congress authorized the creation of Amtrak, a national passenger train network, in hopes of reinvigorating rapidly declining rail travel.[85]

The 1971 North Carolina General Assembly passed the Executive Organization Act, mandating that 350 separate agencies, boards, and commissions be consolidated into fewer than twenty executive departments of state government. Each department was to be headed by a secretary

Highway officials in early 1969. First row, left to right: W. F. Babcock, highway administrator; and Duncan M. "Lauch" Faircloth, commission chairman. Standing, left to right: Billy Rose, assistant highway administrator; Cameron W. Lee, chief engineer; and George S. Willoughby Jr., secondary roads officer. Willoughby replaced Babcock as highway administrator later that year.

appointed by the governor. As mentioned earlier, the enormous State Highway Commission, as well as the Department of Motor Vehicles and the Ports Authority, became divisions in the newly created Department of Transportation and Highway Safety.[86] Fred Mills, an attorney from Wadesboro, served as the first secretary of the new agency, although the State Highway Commission continued to operate independently during two ensuing years of transition. North Carolina was among the first thirteen states to organize departments of transportation.[87] The following two chapters will consider how, in subsequent years, the reorganized department initiated efforts to grow from a highway-focused entity to an agency broader in concept and deed.

The Cape Fear River Bridge opened at Wilmington in 1969 at a cost of sixteen million dollars. Note the unique vertical-lift span in raised position.

Notes

1. John William Coon, "Kerr Scott, the 'Go Forward' Governor: His Origins, His Program, and the North Carolina General Assembly" (master's thesis, University of North Carolina at Chapel Hill, 1968), 15-30; *Dictionary of North Carolina Biography*, s.v. "Scott, William Kerr"; John Harden, *North Carolina Roads and Their Builders*, vol. 2 (Raleigh: Superior Stone Company, Division of Martin Marietta Corporation, 1966), 55, 56.

2. Chester Davis, "A Progress Report," *North Carolina Roadways* 3 (September 1950): 4.

3. John Sanders, former director, Institute of Government, University of North Carolina at Chapel Hill, interview with author, Raleigh, July 13, 2001; Coon, "Kerr Scott, the 'Go Forward' Governor," 31-35, 39-65. In June 1949 voters also approved a $25 million bond issue proposed by Governor Scott to benefit public education.

4. Harden, *North Carolina Roads and Their Builders*, vol. 2, 57.

5. Capus Waynick, *North Carolina Roads and Their Builders* (Raleigh: Superior Stone Company, 1952), 89-90.

6. "Roads Are Bustin' Out All Over!" *North Carolina Roadways* 1 (July 1950): 10.

7. Davis, "A Progress Report," 3.

8. "A Paved Road Opens a 'Lost Province,'" *North Carolina Roadways* 1 (August 1950): 12.

9. Mrs. Theodore Rondthaler, "Paved Roads Come to Ocracoke," *North Carolina Roadways* 1 (January-February 1951): 2, 3.

10. Davis, "A Progress Report," 2.

11. "Solid Accomplishment," *News and Observer* (Raleigh), October 27, 1952; William D. Snider, "The Precious Nature of North Carolina," *News and Record* (Greensboro), January 14, 2001.

12. Harden, *North Carolina Roads and Their Builders*, vol. 2, 36; "Now It's a Full Powell Penny Going to Those City Streets," *North Carolina* 29 (July 1971): 46, 105.

13. "Are Our Primary Highways Neglected?" *North Carolina Roadways* 1 (August 1950): 21. By that time, larger cities in the Northeast and upper Midwest were building urban expressways.

14. "Two N.C. Cities Open Up Million Dollar By-passes," *North Carolina Roadways* 2 (November-December 1951): 20.

15. "Primary Road Needs in North Carolina," *We the People of North Carolina* 9 (March 1952): 4, 5, 28 (hereafter cited as *We the People*). Kerr Scott (1896-1958) was elected to the U.S. Senate in 1954 and served until his death in 1958. *Dictionary of North Carolina Biography*, s.v. "Scott, William Kerr."

16. *Dictionary of North Carolina Biography*, s.v. "Umstead, William Bradley."

17. "Traffic Engineer is First N.C. Woman to Become Licensed," *North Carolina Roadways* 10 (November-December 1960): 9.

18. North Carolina State Highway Commission, *Biennial Report, 1955-1956* (Raleigh: State Printer, 1956), 34-44 (hereafter cited as *Biennial Report*, with appropriate dates).

19. *Dictionary of North Carolina Biography*, s.v. "Hodges" (all entries).

20. Luther H. Hodges, *Businessman in the Statehouse* (Chapel Hill: University of North Carolina Press, 1962), 126-129.

21. Other members of the committee were Sen. T. Clarence Stone of Stoneville, Rep. James Stikeleather of Asheville, Rep. Carroll Holmes of Hertford, Rep. B. T. Falls Jr. of Shelby, Harold Makepeace of Sanford, and John G. Clark of Greenville. Hodges, *Businessman in the Statehouse*, 132.

22. Hodges, *Businessman in the Statehouse*, 132-135.

23. Hodges, *Businessman in the Statehouse*, 140-149; *Guide to Research Materials in the North Carolina State Archives: State Agency Records* (Raleigh: Department of Cultural Resources, Division of Archives and History, Archives and Records Section, 1995), 691 (hereafter cited as *Guide to State Agency Records*); *Biennial Report, 1961-1962*, 12.

24. "W. F. Babcock Named Director of Highways," *North Carolina Roadways* 8 (July-August 1957): 1. This position was sometimes referred to as "director of highways." The first title was chief executive officer, then chief administrative officer (1961), and, later, state highway administrator (1965). *Guide to State Agency Records*, 691.

25. Harden, *North Carolina Roads and Their Builders*, vol. 2, 80.

26. Broughton graduated from Wake Forest College, earned a law degree at the University of North Carolina, and served in World War II before establishing a law practice in Raleigh. Lee, a native of Asheville, earned an engineering degree at the University of South Carolina in 1935 and joined the State Highway Commission. In 1961 President John F. Kennedy appointed Luther Hodges (1898-1974) U.S. secretary of commerce, a post he held until 1965. Afterward, Hodges resided in Chapel Hill, working for the North Carolina Research Triangle Foundation and lecturing at the UNC School of Business. *Dictionary of North Carolina Biography*, s.v. "Hodges, Luther Hartwell."

27. Billy Rose, telephone conversation with author, October 5, 2000. Rose grew up on a farm near Kenly in Johnston County. He earned bachelor's and master's degrees in civil engineering at North Carolina State College and studied two more years at Massachusetts Institute of Technology in Boston. He joined the Highway Commission in 1959 as an urban planner, became Bill Babcock's assistant in 1963, and assistant highway administrator in 1969. He served as highway administrator for the Department of Transportation from 1973 to 1985 and thereafter as deputy secretary for one year.

28. "Advanced Planning," *North Carolina Roadways* 13 (September-October 1966): 1.

29. Billy Rose, telephone conversation with author, November 22, 2000.

30. Edward L. Rankin Jr., telephone conversation with author, October 5, 2000.

31. Bruce E. Seely, *Building the American Highway System: Engineers as Policy Makers* (Philadelphia: Temple University Press, 1987), 175-177, 187-191; Richard F. Weingroff, information liaison specialist, Federal Highway Administration, e-mail to author, June 5, 2001; U.S. House, *Interregional Highways, A Report of the National Interregional Highway Committee, Outlining and Recommending a National System of Interregional Highways*, 78th Cong., 2d sess., January 12, 1944, H. Doc. 379, 7.

32. "National Interstate System Long-range Goal," *Better Roads* 17 (September 1947): 20, 48.

33. "Group Continues Highway Efforts," *News and Observer*, August 5, 1947; David Cooper, "N.C. Interstate Limits Set in 1945," *News and Observer*, March 18, 1962; U.S. Department of Transportation, Federal Highway Administration, *America's Highways, 1776-1976* (Washington, D.C.: U.S. Department of Transportation, Federal Highway Administration, 1976), 157, 158; Billy Rose, interview with author, Raleigh, January 9, 2001; "The National System of Interstate and Defense Highways," *We the People* 14 (November

1956): 12-83; John D. Morris, "Roads Bill Sent to White House; 'Gas' Tax to Go Up," *New York Times*, June 27, 1956.

34. Tom Lewis, *Divided Highways: Building the Interstate Highways, Transforming American Life* (New York: Penguin Group, 1997), 91, 92.

35. Seely, *Building the American Highway System*, 204-208; "Toll-Road Era Coming to an End," *U.S. News & World Report* 41 (July 13, 1956): 54, 55.

36. "Protest Parkway Toll," *North Carolina Roadways* 5 (March-April 1955): inside front cover; "No Parkway Tolls This Year," *North Carolina Roadways* 5 (May-June 1955): inside front cover. A fifty-mile toll road from Virginia Beach to North Carolina's Outer Banks was proposed in 1964 but never built. "Highway Approves N.C. Toll Road," *North Carolina Roadways* 13 (September-November 1964): 3.

37. "List of Maps," *General Location of National System of Interstate Highways, Including All Additional Routes at Urban Areas Designated in September 1955* (Washington, D.C.: U.S. Department of Commerce, Bureau of Public Roads, September 15, 1955). At that time, the commission was again chaired by the influential Sandy Graham, who had been chairman in 1945 when the state refused to include access to the state capital in its interstate recommendations. Tennessee's four cities receiving urban loops averaged a population of 207,000 in 1950. Virginia's average, not counting the loop portions in the Washington, D.C. area or in Bristol (a town divided between Tennessee and Virginia), was 205,000. *Census of Population:1950,* Volume II, *Characteristics of the Population* (Washington, D.C.: United States Government Printing Office, 1952), Parts 33, 40, 42, 46.

38. John D. Morris, "Roads Bill Sent to White House," *New York Times*, June 27, 1956; John D. Morris, "Eisenhower Signs Road Bill; Weeks Allocates 1.1. Billion," *New York Times*, June 30, 1956.

39. "Chairman Graham Announces the First Links in the New Road Program," *We the People* 14 (November 1956): 40, 42. After completing his four-year term as chairman in 1957, Sandy Graham ((1890-1977) retired from public service. He was an active member of the board of Rocky Mount Mills and became its chairman. *Dictionary of North Carolina Biography*, s.v. "Graham, Alexander Hawkins ('Sandy')."

40. *Biennial Report, 1957-1958*, 16.

41. "State Boasts Longest Expressway in South," *North Carolina Roadways* 6 (January-February 1956): 1.

42. *Biennial Report, 1955-1956*, 9; *We the People* 9 (March 1952): 23.

43. "North Carolina Road Builders," 78.

44. *Biennial Report, 1955-1956*, 18, 19.

45. *Biennial Report, 1955-1956*, 18, 19; "Bypasses Give Major Traffic Relief to Cities and Towns," *North Carolina Roadways* 5 (May-June 1955): 1, 2, 4.

46. Seely, *Building the American Highway System*, 187-191.

47. "Transportation Highways," *We the People* 12 (November 1955): 40; "Downtown Boulevard Opened to Traffic," *North Carolina Roadways* 6 (November-December 1955): 3.

48. Rose interview.

49. Jack Claiborne, "Airport Memorializes Former Mayor Ben Douglas," *Charlotte Observer*, April 25, 1982; Dan Morrill, "The Road that Split Charlotte," *Parade*, May 2, 1982, 12, 15, 19; Thomas H. Hanchett, *Sorting Out the New South City* (Chapel Hill: University of North Carolina Press, 1998), 239, 240.

50. "Transportation Highways," 38.

51. Rose interview.

52. Frank V. Tursi, *Winston-Salem, A History* (Winston-Salem: John F. Blair, 1994), 231-233. According to Billy Rose, the Federal Highway Administration wanted to widen I-40 instead of constructing the new southern route but agreed to build the route after an NCDOT financial study showed it to be the less-expensive alternative.

53. "$6-Million Expressway Will Be Opened Today," *Asheville Citizen*, December 15, 1960.

54. Daniel C. Hoover, "Light at the End of the Beltline," *News and Observer*, July 5, 1978; "Raleigh Beltline Nears Completion," *North Carolina Roadways* 13 (May-June 1964): 1; "New Connection," *North Carolina Roadways* 13 (December 1964): 21.

55. *Biennial Report, 1969-1970*, 14; United States Department of Transportation press release, December 13, 1968, 1, 2, 3, 4; David Cooper, "N.C. Gearing Up Campaign for More Interstate Roads," *News and Observer*, December 8, 1963; "State Short-Changed on Interstate Roads," *Wilmington Morning Star*, June 17, 1967. The portion of I-40 originally projected to connect Raleigh and Smithfield was later routed in a more southeasterly direction, ultimately connecting Raleigh and Wilmington via Benson.

56. Sanford grew up in Laurinburg, graduated from the University of North Carolina, served as a paratrooper in World War II, returned to the university for a law degree, then practiced law in Fayetteville. He served a term in the state senate and managed Kerr Scott's successful campaign for U.S. Senate in 1954. Harden, *North Carolina Roads and Their Builders*, vol. 2, 68, 69.

57. Evans graduated from the College of William and Mary. In Ahoskie he worked in the supply and fertilizer business and operated a life insurance and public relations firm. Harden, *North Carolina Roads and Their Builders*, vol. 2, 70.

58. *Biennial Report, 1961-1962*, 12.

59. *Biennial Report, 1961-1962*, 63-65; *Biennial Report, 1963-1964*, 23; Harden, *North Carolina Roads and Their Builders*, vol. 2, 26, 27.

60. "Thinking about Primary Roads," *We the People* 21 (July 1963): 24; Roger R. Jackson Jr., "Our Highway System Today," *We the People* 22 (July 1964): 73.

61. Harden, *North Carolina Roads and Their Builders*, vol. 2, 72, 73.

62. Hunt grew up in Greensboro and graduated from Duke University. He worked for an insurance firm and served several terms in the legislature; he was Speaker of the house of representatives in the 1961 legislative session. Harden, *North Carolina Roads and Their Builders*, vol. 2, 77, 78, 84.

63. *Biennial Report, 1965-1966*, 13.

64. *Biennial Report, 1969-1970*, 7, 8.

65. Mark H. Rose, *Interstate Express Highway Politics, 1939-1989*, rev. ed. (Knoxville: University of Tennessee Press, 1990), 102.

66. Barbara Church, N.C. Department of Transportation, telephone conversation with author, October 3, 2000; Steve Claggett, "Federal and State Statutes Affecting Archaeological Resources in North Carolina" (unpublished report, Office of State Archaeology, Division [now Office] of Archives and History, Raleigh).

67. One resident of Durham estimates that 80 percent of the Hayti neighborhood—including approximately 600 residents and some 140 businesses—was displaced by the Durham Freeway. Andre D. Vann, telephone conversation with author, October 22, 2002.

68. *Biennial Report, 1971-1972*, 10. When the Durham Freeway was later extended westward to I-85—a very lengthy, embattled process—another largely minority neighborhood was destroyed.

69. F. H. Brant, "New Emphasis on Highway Beauty," *North Carolina Roadways* 13 (March-April 1966): 1, 2, 3; "Conference on Beautification," *North Carolina Roadways* 13 (March-April 1966): 11; Paul Stankiewicz, telephone conversation with author, January 29, 2003. By 2003 the state had nine welcome centers, located where Interstate 40 enters the state; at the Tennessee and South Carolina borders on Interstate 26; and at the Virginia and South Carolina borders on Interstates 85, 77, and 95. "Organization and Functional Overview, North Carolina Department of Transportation," informational notebook for NCDOT board members (Raleigh: North Carolina Department of Transportation, January 2001), 6-3.

70. Beth G. Crabtree, *North Carolina Governors, 1585-1974* (Raleigh: Division of Archives and History, Department of Cultural Resources, 1974), 140-142.

71. "State Government Roundup," *North Carolina* 27 (October 1969): 6, 7. "I was offered the position, but turned it down because I did not think Bill Babcock should have been fired," Billy Rose recalled. Rose interview. Willard Farrington Babcock (1917-1991) retired from teaching in 1984 and worked for North Carolina State University's (NCSU) Institute for Transportation Research and Education from 1984 to 1988. In a 1988 interview, he talked about the challenges of building interstate highways and the difficulties of recruiting engineers for the State Highway Commission. Transcription of oral history interview, NCSU Libraries, Special Collections and University Archives, North Carolina State University, Raleigh; W. F. Babcock, interview with Darwin Stolzenbach, American Association of State Highway and Transportation Officials Interstate Highway Research Project, [Raleigh], January 12, 1988, transcript at NCSU Libraries; Jack Murdock, interview with author, Raleigh, January 5, 2001.

72. "Highway Summary 1969," *North Carolina Roadways* 16 (January-February 1970): 2, 3.

73. Jack Murdock grew up in Raleigh, was an All-American basketball player at Wake Forest College, taught high school, returned to Wake Forest as an assistant basketball coach, and was head coach for one year. He joined the State Highway Commission in 1966 as assistant secondary roads officer. He served as secondary roads officer from 1969 to 1993 and as assistant secretary of secondary roads and economic development from 1993 to 1996. He retired in 1996. Murdock interview.

74. "Interview: D. M. Faircloth," *North Carolina* 30 (July 1972): 27.

75. "North Carolina's Gasoline Taxes No Longer Highest in the Nation," *North Carolina* 30 (July 1972): 39. By 1972 seven other states had a nine-cent tax, and Connecticut's was ten cents.

76. *Biennial Report, 1971-1972*, 6.

77. *Biennial Report, 1969-1970*, 17, 19; *Biennial Report, 1971-1972*, 13, 15; "Across Town in 15 Minutes," *Greensboro Daily News*, August 15, 1972; John Watkins, division engineer, Division 7, North Carolina Department of Transportation (NCDOT), 1973-1999, telephone conversations with author, February 9, 12, 2001.

78. "Here's the First View of Our New Highway Building," *North Carolina Roadways* 1 (July 1950): 23.

79. Peggy Jo D. Kirby, *North Carolina Museum of Art: The First Fifty Years, 1947-1997* (Richmond, Va.: Carter Press, 1997), 32; "Fact Sheet: The North Carolina Museum of Art" (undated report, North Carolina Museum of Art); Myra Fulmer, management analyst, NCDOT, telephone conversation with author, January 12, 2001. The Museum of Art's renovation of the 1921 building, which cost $400,000, gutted most of the interior to

create larger rooms. When the museum moved to a new location in 1983, the Department of Transportation reclaimed the building and integrated it with the remainder of the DOT complex. The exterior of the building, including the signage "State Highway Commission" (which appears below the roofline), retains its original design.

80. "Number of Full-Time Employees," unpublished listing supplied by Division of Human Resources, NCDOT; Kathi Johnson, Division of Human Resources, N.C. Department of Transportation, telephone conversations with author, January 3, February 14, 2001.

81. *Biennial Report, 1971-1972*, 22; *Biennial Report, 1965-1966*, 47; *1990 Census of Population and Housing Unit Counts, North Carolina* (Washington, D.C.: U.S. Department of Commerce, 1992), 1; "Yearly Motor Vehicle Registration" (unpublished document, Division of Motor Vehicles, NCDOT). All of the State Highway Commission's revenues were in the Highway Fund. Funds from bond issues are not considered revenues.

82. "Getting the Land Where Highways Go," *North Carolina* 28 (July 1970): 50.

83. *1990 Census of Population and Housing Unit Counts*, 1; "Yearly Motor Vehicle Registration."

84. *Biennial Report, 1971-1972*, 8, 12; Billy Rose, "The System and Its Future Needs," *North Carolina* 29 (July 1971): 35. For 1949 statistics, see conclusion of chapter three.

85. Lewis, *Divided Highways*, 201, 218; *America's Highways*, 298.

86. The following programs retained their statutory powers and duties, although managerial responsibility for their operations was transferred to the secretary: the State Highway Commission, the Department (now Division) of Motor Vehicles, the State Ports Authority, the Board of Commissioners of Navigation and Pilotage for the Cape Fear River and Bar, and the boards of the North Carolina Railroad and the Atlantic and North Carolina Railroad Companies. Four additional state entities, including the Governor's Highway Safety Program, the North Carolina Traffic Safety Authority, the Governor's Aviation Committee, and the Vehicle Equipment Safety Compact, were brought directly under the authority of the department and secretary. *Guide to State Agency Records*, 682.

87. William S. Powell, *North Carolina through Four Centuries* (Chapel Hill: University of North Carolina Press, 1989), 544-547; Alan L. Porter and Thomas D. Larson, "State Departments of Transportation: A Perspective," in *Management of Transportation and Environmental Review Functions* (Washington, D.C.: National Academy of Sciences, 1976), 12.

Chapter 5

BROADENING THE FOCUS FROM HIGHWAYS TO TRANSPORTATION
1973–2003

In a political upset in 1972, James E. Holshouser Jr. was elected North Carolina's first Republican governor of the twentieth century. He had graduated from Davidson College, earned a law degree from the University of North Carolina at Chapel Hill, practiced law in Boone, and served three terms in the General Assembly. When he took office in January 1973, he talked about paving roads where they were needed, without regard to politics. He suggested that highway officials meet more often with local governmental bodies and chambers of commerce. Holshouser envisioned the creation of a modern transportation system consisting of a network of highway corridors that would serve to unite communities and lay the groundwork for a mass-transit system.[1]

James B. Hunt Jr., a young Democratic leader and lawyer from Wilson, was elected lieutenant governor in 1972 and, by holding the highest state office of his party, gained influence with the legislature. Governor Holshouser appointed Bruce A. Lentz of Charlotte as secretary of the North Carolina Department of Transportation (NCDOT) in January, although full implementation of the new "North Carolina Department of Transportation and Highway Safety" would not take place until July 1, 1973. The North Carolina State Highway Commission (including operation of six ferries), the North Carolina Department of Motor Vehicles (including the State Highway Patrol), and the State Ports Authority became divisions of the NCDOT.[2] Billy Rose became highway administrator, and Jack Murdock continued as secondary roads officer.[3] The position of assistant secretary for planning was created to organize "multi-modal transportation planning efforts in the Department to better serve the transportation needs of the State," including aviation and mass transportation.[4]

A new twelve-member Board of Transportation and a fourteen-member Secondary Roads Council replaced the board of the State Highway Commission. All twelve members of the Board of Transportation—nine chosen by the governor, one by the lieutenant governor, one by the Speaker of the state House of Representatives, and one by the joint caucus leader of the minority party—were appointed on a statewide basis rather than to represent specific areas. The secretary of the NCDOT served as chairman of the board. The mission of the board was "to construct, maintain, and operate an efficient, economical, and safe transportation network."[5] Each member of the Secondary Roads Council, appointed by the governor, represented one of fourteen highway divisions. Working with Jack Murdock, they developed plans for the improvement, construction, and maintenance of the state's secondary roads.[6]

There was substantial turnover in NCDOT leadership during the Holshouser years: four secretaries of transportation, three commissioners of the motor vehicles division, and two executive directors of the State Ports Authority division. Bruce Lentz served as secretary of the Department of Transportation for one and one-half years and then left to become secretary of administration. Troy Doby, a Raleigh civil engineer, followed and served as secretary for a year before returning to his private engineering business. Jake F. Alexander of Salisbury then served as secretary for a year before resigning to run for governor. G. Perry Greene of Boone was the administration's fourth and final secretary at the NCDOT.

When new governors (all Democrats) had taken office in the past, they traditionally had chosen a new chairman and almost a full set of new board members for the State Highway Commission but otherwise made few personnel changes beyond the department's top staff.[7] The Republican Holshouser administration eventually dismissed one hundred employees of the Highway Division (the former State Highway Commission), an agency whose leadership had always been tied to the traditionally dominant Democratic Party. The General Assembly held hearings about the issue but took no action.[8]

The biggest challenge at the NCDOT during that period resulted from a national energy crisis, coupled with inflation. Arab states in the Middle East withheld shipments of crude oil to America. North Carolinians faced long lines at service stations in 1974. Speed limits on interstate highways were lowered to 55 miles per hour, and sales of compact cars increased. By 1975 the costs of both

Former North Carolina governors. Left to right: James G. Martin (1985-1993), James B. Hunt Jr. (1977-1985 and 1993-2001), James E. Holshouser Jr. (1973-1977), Robert W. Scott (1969-1973), and Terry Sanford (1961-1965).

gasoline and highway construction were climbing. Even though the Federal-Aid Highway Act of 1973 revised the formula for matching federal aid from 50-50 to 70 percent federal and 30 percent local funds, the pace of new highway construction slowed.[9]

The organization of the NCDOT provided new opportunities for long-range planning. Previous State Highway Commission boards had focused on highways to be built in particular highway divisions. It was hoped that the Secondary Roads Council, with a representative from each division, would concentrate on specific issues relevant to secondary roads and that the Board of Transportation would provide a broader statewide policy perspective. The first significant planning document to emerge from the NCDOT was *North Carolina Highways, a Seven Year Highway Improvement Program, July 1973 thru June 1980*, published in October 1973. Public hearings were held throughout the state to solicit citizen response to the plan. The name of the planning document was changed to *Highway Improvement Program* the following year, although it continued to project highway improvements seven years into the future.

In 1975 the agency's name was shortened from North Carolina Department of Transportation and Highway Safety to simply North Carolina Department of Transportation, though many referred to the agency as the "DOT" or the "NCDOT." Some non-highway programs, including Public Transportation (1974), Ferry (1974), and Aeronautics (1975; later renamed Aviation), gained division status within the NCDOT.

In 1976 Democratic lieutenant governor James B. Hunt Jr. was elected governor. He took office in January 1977. He had grown up on a farm near Wilson and had earned bachelor's and master's degrees in agricultural economics from North Carolina State University and a law degree from the University of North Carolina at Chapel Hill. Governor Hunt appointed Thomas W. Bradshaw Jr. as NCDOT secretary. Bradshaw, who grew up in Raleigh, graduated from Broughton High School and later attended an executive development program at the University of North Carolina at Chapel Hill. After serving a term on the Raleigh City Council, he was elected mayor at age thirty-two. A personable leader who worked long hours, he was president of the North Hills Realty Company.[10] Billy Rose as highway administrator and Jack Murdock as secondary roads officer continued their roles during the first two Hunt administrations (1977-1985), adding stability during the NCDOT leadership transition. D. W. Patrick was appointed chief engineer. Subsequent chief engineers included Don Overman (1979-1981) and R. Frank Coleman (1981-1986).

The 1977 General Assembly enacted legislation to refine the NCDOT's organizational structure. The Ports Authority Division, with its focus on the oceangoing movement of goods, proved not to be a suitable fit for the NCDOT and was transferred to the state Department of Commerce (where it remains at the present time).[11] The Highway Patrol segment of the Motor Vehicles Division became a part of the newly established Department of Crime Control and Public Safety (but was still funded at $30 million annually from the Highway Fund). The Motor Vehicles Division remained with the NCDOT and retained responsibility for vehicle registration, issuance of driver licenses, driver education programs, highway safety, vehicle inspections, police information services, and school bus driver training.[12]

The legislature, in a bow to past practices, also enlarged the Board of Transportation from twelve to twenty-four members, including the NCDOT secretary, and abolished the Secondary Roads Council. Lawmakers transferred the basic functions of the council to the board; each of the fourteen highway divisions would henceforth be represented by a board member, but that person would represent *all* state highways (and not just secondary roads) within a given highway division. The governor's twenty-one appointees to the new board would include one from each of the fourteen highway divisions and seven from the state at large. (Legislative leaders continued to appoint three board members.) The traditional makeup of the board, including both highway-division and statewide representation, has continued to the present.[13]

North Carolina voters, in 1977, approved a constitutional amendment allowing governors to run for a second consecutive term. Governor Hunt, a prime advocate of the change, won re-election in 1980. The

Thomas W. Bradshaw Jr. (third from right), with Gov. James B. Hunt Jr. looking on, takes oath as NCDOT secretary with other cabinet appointees in 1977. Left to right: Joseph W. Grimsley, Administration; Sarah T. Morrow, Human Resources; Howard N. Lee, Natural Resources and Community Development; Sara W. Hodgkins, Cultural Resources; Bradshaw; D. M. Faircloth, Commerce; and Mark Lynch, Revenue. Photo courtesy A&H.

resulting stability, coupled with a more balanced and focused structure, enhanced the NCDOT's effectiveness. Secretary Bradshaw strengthened the annual planning document, changing its name from *Highway Improvement Program* to *Transportation Improvement Program* (*TIP*), and increased the number of hearings to solicit public opinion. The *Transportation Improvement Program, 1979-1985*, dated October 1978, also inaugurated a tradition of finalizing the document the year before it was to take effect rather than in the first year it was actually in effect. (That edition included aeronautics and public transportation, and the next year's *TIP* added bicycles.) With a few exceptions, the NCDOT published the *TIP*s annually until 1999, when the agency issued its first biennial issue, *Transportation Improvement Program, 2000-*

2006. That change allowed more time for the agency to obtain public comment.

Another Bradshaw goal was to improve the east-west highways connecting the Piedmont to the coast. To promote that cause, he oversaw the completion of the Raleigh Beltline, the first segments of which had opened nearly two decades previously. The roadway, originally intended to connect with Western Boulevard south of downtown, was reconfigured; it opened in 1985 with a wider southwestern arc that carries I-40 traffic around the west and south sides of the city.[14]

To the west, the biggest challenge in building I-240 through the downtown area of Asheville, encompassing the Asheville Expressway, was surmounting Beaucatcher Mountain. Controversy over whether to build a second tunnel paralleling the existing one on U.S. 70 or to remove enough of the mountain for the new road persisted for more than a decade. Despite sentiment about the expense of tunnels and concern that the open-cut option would subject nearby areas to increased air pollution, the cut was built. According to the road's project engineer, that option was chosen because it allowed for a wider roadway and possible expansion in response to increased traffic. One noteworthy feature of I-240, which opened in 1980, was that it included three tri-level interchanges, unusual for that time and place.[15]

All sections of the Interstate Highway System originally scheduled for North Carolina in 1956 and 1957 were completed by the mid-1980s. These included I-26 (Asheville to the South Carolina line) in 1976, I-77 in 1977, and I-95 in 1980. The "temporary I-85" between Greensboro and Lexington never qualified for full interstate status, primarily because it had too many access roads. But when the newly aligned, six-lane section opened in 1984, I-85 was completed in North Carolina. A more formidable challenge was to gain federal approval for additional interstate mileage in the state. The Hunt administration insisted that I-40 be extended to Wilmington and sought federal discretionary funds to begin acquiring right-of-way.[16]

The most immediate highway crisis during the late 1970s was money. According to the NCDOT's *Biennial Report* for 1977-1978, "construction and maintenance costs have more than doubled in the past decade while gasoline tax revenues, reacting appropriately to growing environmental and energy conservation concerns, have risen at a much slower pace."[17] As the price of gasoline escalated, the tax percentage of the total fuel bill decreased. Seeking a remedy, the 1977 General Assembly proposed a $300 million bond issue (and retained a one-cent gasoline tax from the previous bond issue), which the voters approved that November by a two-to-one margin. The bonds were projected to generate more than $2 billion in improvements during the ensuing seven years, against total needs estimated to be $7 billion. Inasmuch as the improvements included roads that would later need to be maintained, the legislature also increased annual vehicle registration fees from two to three dollars. Another way the Hunt administration found to deal with the recession of the late 1970s, with its resulting financial problems, was to eliminate twenty-five hundred NCDOT jobs over two years in order to increase efficiency.[18]

For many years, North Carolina was a "donor" state in relation to federal highway spending. By the 1970s it ranked dead last among the fifty states in the proportionate amount of federal aid for highways that it received.[19] There is disagreement about the degree of donor status. One research study calculated that in 1972 the state received an equivalent of only 52 cents for every dollar of federal highway taxes paid by North Carolinians. The *Highway Improvement Program, 1978-1984*, concluded that 64 cents was returned. The problem had begun soon after World War II with the state's lack of foresight in seeking interstate highways. The Federal-Aid Highway Act of 1956 confirmed the fact that, compared with other states, North Carolina had requested and received relatively small amounts of interstate mileage. Annual allocations of interstate federal aid in subsequent years were primarily based on the number of uncompleted interstate miles. Since North Carolina had proportionately fewer uncompleted miles than other states, it was always at a disadvantage. Its donor status did improve in later years, especially during the 1990s.[20]

A dramatic problem emerged when national newspapers reported that the U.S Justice Department in 1979 had begun investigating bid-rigging in fourteen (primarily southern) states. During the spring of 1980 two officials of a paving contractor firm in North Carolina entered guilty pleas to charges of rigging contract bids. It was revealed that bid-rigging had been widespread among some of the state's highway contractors for many years; in time, many were convicted and served prison terms. A number of contracting firms were suspended from the NCDOT list of qualified bidders. The bid-rigging revelations represented the first significant scandal to emerge from the state's many years of highway building.[21] The 1981 General Assembly endorsed strong new laws to add safeguards to the bidding process. No revelations of bid-rigging have surfaced since that time.[22]

In 1980 Governor Hunt easily defeated former governor Robert W. Scott in the Democratic primary and I. Beverly Lake Jr. in the general election to become the first North Carolina governor to serve more than one four-year term. Hunt had previously appointed another former governor, Dan K. Moore, to head a "Governor's Blue Ribbon

Mainframe computer used by the NCDOT's Division of Motor Vehicles in the early 1980s.

Commission on Transportation Needs and Financing." That commission hired the respected firm of Wilbur Smith and Associates as consultants. In December 1980 the Moore commission offered its findings, pointing out that:

The rising costs of highway-construction materials exceeded the overall 20 percent inflation rate of the previous several years.

More energy-efficient vehicles were consuming less gasoline.

When the state's gasoline tax was last increased (to 9 cents in 1969), a gallon had cost an average of 32 cents but that average cost had risen to $1.20 per gallon by 1980.

Funds from the 1977 bonds would be depleted by 1982, and thereafter the state would be unable to match available federal-aid allocations.[23]

The Moore commission recommended alternative plans for significantly raising highway taxes. One plan would add 5 cents per gallon to the gasoline tax. Another would create a 4 percent sales tax on the wholesale price of gasoline. The latter approach had been discussed for years as a way to capture more revenues as the price of gasoline climbed. In an editorial, the influential business-oriented magazine *North Carolina* advocated additional funding for highways. But Governor Hunt, who had promised not to increase taxes, suggested a 3-cents-per-gallon tax increase.[24] A national recession and fallout from the bid-rigging controversy made it a difficult time to raise any taxes. Nevertheless, the 1981 General Assembly agreed with the governor and increased the gasoline tax by 3 cents—from 9 to 12 cents per gallon—and directed that the new funds be used primarily for maintenance and resurfacing. Hunt later characterized the question of raising highway taxes as "the toughest legislative fight I was ever in."[25]

The same session of the General Assembly resolved to increase the Powell Bill gasoline-tax allocation to municipalities from 1 cent to 1.375 cents per gallon.[26] Following legislative guidelines for utilizing the increased taxes, the emphasis soon shifted away from construction to "demands of maintaining the 76,000-mile state highway system—patching potholes and resurfacing worn pavements."[27] A former NCDOT division engineer recalls that the prevailing lack of money made it possible only to fill potholes, not to carry out needed resurfacing.[28]

William R. Roberson Jr., a businessman and former legislator from eastern North Carolina, became NCDOT secretary in July 1981. Despite the gasoline-tax increase of that year, there was a mood of retrenchment. In his cover letter introducing the new *TIP* that December, Secretary Roberson attributed a decision by the Board of Transportation to adopt a less ambitious version of the *Transportation Improvement Program* to an ongoing decline in gasoline-tax revenues and the effects of inflation. To allow additional time to complete projects with available funding, the time frame of the *TIP*, which had been projected for seven years, was temporarily extended to ten. The secretary also called attention to "the contributions that other forms of transportation can make in helping relieve the demands being placed on our highway system." One magazine expressed disappointment at the secretary's remarks, glumly forecasting dim prospects for the state's "ever again enjoying a thriving road program at the level we knew for so many years."[29] New construction no longer dominated the department's budget. The NCDOT spent approximately equal amounts on construction and on maintenance in 1981. During the following fiscal year, the department spent $247 million on maintenance, compared with only $56 million for construction.[30]

In 1982 Congress passed the Surface Transportation Act, which more than doubled the federal gasoline tax from 4 to 9 cents per gallon. The legislation also increased the amount of federal aid available to North Carolina. In fiscal year 1982 the state's federal allocation was only $176 million. It jumped to $275 million in 1983, $362 million in 1984, and $313 million in 1985. There was initial concern about finding matching state funds (30 percent) sufficient to qualify for the federal aid (70 percent), especially with the then-prevailing state emphasis on maintenance; however, the matching funds were eventually secured (see Appendix A).[31]

By 1983 there was a more positive mood. Secretary Roberson reported that as a result of field-management reorganization and other efforts to trim costs, as directed by the General Assembly, the NCDOT had reduced expenses by $40 million in fiscal year 1982—double his initial goal. Annual projects for resurfacing, which all roads need periodically, increased from 380 miles in fiscal 1981 to 3,330 in 1982. Continuing the emphasis on maintenance, the Board of Transportation in 1983 approved a three-year, $165 million plan to replace obsolete bridges. The effort was made possible by

Rev. and Mrs. Billy Graham and Governor Hunt, with NCDOT Equipment Unit superintendent Lloyd Young, attend dedication of Billy Graham Parkway in Charlotte in 1983. The north-south thoroughfare connects I-85 with N.C. 49 at a point near I-77.

the increased federal gasoline tax.³² In addition, nearly all the right-of-way for I-40 to Wilmington was acquired.³³

James G. Martin, a Republican, was elected governor in 1984 and took office in January 1985. Martin grew up in Winnsboro, South Carolina, and earned degrees in chemistry from Davidson College (B.S.) and Princeton University (Ph.D). He was an associate professor of chemistry at Davidson College before serving six terms as congressman from North Carolina's Ninth District.³⁴ Governor Martin appointed James E. Harrington as secretary of the NCDOT. Harrington, a native of New Hampshire, grew up in Southern Pines, graduated from Virginia Military Institute, and worked as a resort developer. He had served as secretary of the Department of Natural and Economic Resources in the Holshouser administration from 1973 to 1977.³⁵ Billy Rose served one year as deputy secretary at the NCDOT before taking early retirement. To replace Rose as highway administrator, Secretary Harrington appointed George W. Wells, who served five years in the position. Earl H. McEntire became chief engineer in 1986 and served four years, while Jack Murdock continued as secondary roads officer.

The one highway-related promise Governor Martin made during his gubernatorial campaign was to complete I-40 from Raleigh to Wilmington. The Wilmington-Wallace segment, the first portion to open, was subsequently dedicated to basketball superstar Michael Jordan. Special interstate funding was used to construct the Raleigh-Wallace segment. The completed I-40 opened with fanfare and jubilation on June 28, 1990. The mileage sign at the Wilmington terminus of I-40 reads: "Barstow, Calif. 2,554."³⁶

By 1990, I-85 between Greensboro and Hillsborough also carried the designation I-40; I-40 was open from Hillsborough past Chapel Hill to the Research Triangle Park; and the busy Research Triangle Park segment had been widened to six lanes.³⁷ Meanwhile traffic on I-40 through downtown Winston-Salem was reaching crisis proportions. All other interstate highways in the state had been constructed to bypass major urban areas (except for I-77 through Charlotte and interstates built specifically to serve downtowns, such as Asheville's I-240 and Charlotte's I-277). State and federal officials were able to secure $114 million in federal discretionary funding for an I-40 southern

Jim Harrington, NCDOT secretary from 1985 to 1989, found more permanent funding for non-highway programs and advocated creation of the Highway Trust Fund, passed in 1989, to provide increased resources for highways.

Gov. Jim Martin; Bill Pope, mayor of Barstow, Calif.; Wilmington mayor Don Betz; and Raleigh mayor Avery Upchurch (pictured left to right) celebrate completion of Interstate 40 from Raleigh to Wilmington in 1990.

bypass of Winston-Salem. Hannah Byron, the NCDOT's lobbyist in Washington, was a key advocate. Added to a federal appropriations bill passed by Congress was a provision restricting the resulting funds to the exclusive use of Winston-Salem and Spartanburg, South Carolina. At a Washington ceremony, President Ronald Reagan presented to Governor Martin a check for the Winston-Salem project, with U.S. Department of Transportation (USDOT) secretary Jim Burnley (from High Point) and NCDOT secretary Harrington in attendance. The twenty-three-mile bypass opened in 1992.[38]

I-277 in Charlotte was completed in 1988. Coupled with I-77 on the west side, I-277 provides a circle around downtown Charlotte. The four-laning of U.S. 64 eastward from Raleigh was extended to Tarboro in 1989. By 1990 new bridges had been erected over the Albemarle Sound (replacing the 1938 bridge serving N.C. 32/N.C. 37) and between Morehead City and Atlantic Beach.

Some rural legislators were concerned that large cities could sell city bonds to buy rights-of-way and build roads that would more quickly utilize federal-aid funds, leaving less money for small towns and rural areas. But that concern was offset by another increase in Powell Bill tax share, from 1.375 to 1.75 cents per gallon, which benefited more than four hundred communities. The legislature also mandated that secondary roads be funded at the same level as the Powell Bill program.[39]

Construction of the Blue Ridge Parkway, begun in 1935, was completed by 1967 except for a seven-mile segment around Grandfather Mountain. For many years the federal government advocated a "high route" that would have destroyed much of this scenic mountain. Another contentious issue was an effort by the federal government to impose tolls on parkway users. Hugh Morton, the owner of Grandfather Mountain and one of the state's best-known photographers, insisted on no tolls and a routing that would preserve the pristine landscape. Several North Carolina governors endorsed Morton's position. The final "middle route," costing ten million dollars and opened in 1987, included a daring S-curved bridge known as the Linn Cove Viaduct. The

In 1987 construction of the Linn Cove Viaduct, a ten-million-dollar bridge at Grandfather Mountain, completed the Blue Ridge Parkway. The bridge includes 153 fifty-ton segments, each one a different shape. Photo courtesy Hugh Morton.

completed Blue Ridge Parkway, which attracts more than twenty million visitors yearly, extends 470 miles between Virginia's Shenandoah Valley and the Great Smoky Mountains National Park.[40] In a related development, the state established a Scenic Byways program in 1990. Scenic roads throughout the state were identified through the use of appropriate signage and maps. The system now includes forty-five routes covering a total of 1,700 miles.

The NCDOT, in collaboration with Keep North Carolina Clean and Beautiful, inaugurated the Adopt-a-Highway program in 1988. In its first year, nearly one thousand businesses and other organizations volunteered to keep their own designated two miles of highway clean by picking up trash at least four times a year. First Citizens Bank led the way by adopting three hundred miles of roadway. Jean H. Dodd, director of the state program, characterized it as one of the nation's most successful statewide volunteer clean-up efforts.[41] By 2002 more than 5,000 volunteer groups had adopted 12,000 miles, saving the state five million dollars a year in road clean-up costs.[42]

The format of the *Transportation Improvement Program, 1986-1995* changed to list specific information about the highway program for each of the fourteen highway divisions and individual counties. Planning a "strategic highway corridor network" (a series of four-lane highways coupled with the interstates) and addressing urban congestion were the goals Governor Martin listed for the 1988-1996 *TIP*. Other *TIP*s in the period added the ferry program to the document and discussed the possibility of dedicated funding for non-highway programs.[43]

The issue of inadequate funding, which had plagued the State Highway Commission/NCDOT since the 1930s, would not go away. Although North Carolina had always followed the principle that those who use the highways should pay for them, it was clear that highway funding was not keeping pace with needs. By 1985 the cost of construction was rising by 15 percent annually, while highway revenues were growing at only 3 percent.[44] The 1986 General Assembly supported the NCDOT by transferring the cost of administering driver education to the General Fund, thus saving the agency thirty million dollars per year. Furthermore, the legislature increased the state gasoline tax by an additional 2 cents and also levied a percentage-of-price gasoline tax (as opposed to a fixed tax expressed in cents per gallon) of 3 percent at the wholesale level. Those actions increased the total gasoline tax to 15.5 cents per gallon. But the following year the legislature refused the governor's request for a bond issue in the amount of $450 million.[45]

During 1987 and 1988 a Highway Study Commission appointed by Governor Martin and the legislature reviewed highway needs. Secretary Harrington, considering a number of potential new taxes, reminded citizens that the twenty-first century was rapidly approaching and that any system devised to meet the future needs of the state's roadways "should have the resources and staying power to get us there."[46] Both the Highway Study Commission and Secretary Harrington recommended creation of a North Carolina Highway Trust Fund, an ambitious program subsequently passed by the 1989 General Assembly. The bill called for a $9.2 billion highway construction program, which included the following four objectives to be realized over a 13 1/2-year period:

Completion of an "Intrastate Highway System," which would bring 90 percent of North Carolinians within ten miles of a four-lane highway (61.95 percent of trust funds);

Construction of urban loops and connectors around seven cities: Asheville, Charlotte, Durham, Greensboro, Raleigh, Wilmington, and Winston-Salem (25.05 percent);

Paving all state-maintained secondary roads carrying fifty (instead of one hundred) or more vehicles a day (6.5 percent);

Doubling Powell Bill funds for municipal streets (6.5 percent).

The newly created state "Highway Trust Fund" was designed to finance the aforementioned specified projects, while the traditional "Highway Fund" continued to match federal aid, build new roads, and address maintenance (see Appendixes A and B). Twenty-five percent of total state gasoline-tax revenues, increased by 5.2 cents per gallon as part of the Highway Trust Fund bill, was designated for the Trust Fund. A key new

U.S. 13 through North Carolina was named in honor of R.B. Nelson, a resident of Robersonville (Martin County). Nelson, a lifelong promoter of highways, was buried with a N.C. highway map in his lap.

funding source for the NCDOT was the state's tax on new and used vehicles, which had been 2 percent and had been added to the state's General Fund. Under new legislation, that levy (now called a "use tax") was increased to 3 percent. The use tax, from which $170 million would be transferred each year to the General Fund, was the largest source of revenue for the Trust Fund. Because of an economic downturn and a decline in automobile sales during 1990 and 1991, revenues from the use tax were less than expected during that start-up period.[47] Creation of the Highway Trust Fund was a major step forward, facilitating a faster pace of construction in the 1990s. Many observers, however, were concerned that funds for maintenance were not included in the program.

After three years as NCDOT deputy secretary, businessman Thomas J. Harrelson of Southport was promoted to secretary in 1989.[48] The following year William G. Marley was appointed highway administrator, and Wayne D. Bailey became chief engineer; each man served three years. Secretary Harrelson's greatest challenge was dealing with the recession of the early 1990s. The crunch came in the 1991 General Assembly, which had to close a gap of $1.2 billion to balance the 1992 fiscal-year budget. In fiscal year 1991 state funding for education ($4.9 billion) was more than four times that for the NCDOT ($1.2 billion). The Highway Fund and the Highway Trust Fund were less vulnerable to budget cuts than were state programs funded from the General Fund. The legislature still controlled the NCDOT budget, however. In defending his agency, Secretary Harrelson commented: "Money must be found for education, but not at the expense of the majority of North Carolinians, who were willing to pay taxes and user fees for what they were promised would be a better system of highways."[49] The 1991 General Assembly balanced the 1991-1992 budget by cutting programs and raising taxes in approximately equal degree. The legislature diverted nearly forty million dollars from the Highway Fund to the General Fund to pay for driver education and medium-custody inmate labor. (Though driver education had been funded from the General Fund for four years, the previous General Assembly had begun shifting the expense back to the Highway Fund.) Consequently, the NCDOT had to delay projects set forth in the *TIP* and postpone maintenance work. Secretary Harrelson also addressed safety issues. Initiatives included work zones and workplace safety for construction employees, improved visibility for night driving, and enhanced speed-limit enforcement.[50]

In 1991 Congress passed the Intermodal Surface Transportation Efficiency Act (ISTEA), the first major change in federal transportation funding policy since the beginning of the Interstate Highway System in 1956. The historic legislation funded both highway and non-highway programs for six years. It required that state departments of transportation and planners take an integrated approach to all forms of transportation, increase participation in decision-making on the part of citizens and local governments, and be more flexible in the ways transportation dollars were spent. Congress debated the percentage of federal funds each state would receive in return for the federal user gasoline taxes paid by its citizens. Should reimbursements continue to favor urban states of the Northeast, as in the past, or the faster-growing states of the Southeast? The act raised North Carolina's reimbursement formula from 79 percent to 87.5 percent of the federal gasoline taxes actually paid by Tar Heels. The act also authorized funds to be administered by state DOTs for enhancement activities, including historic preservation, bicycle and walking facilities, and beautification. Although enhancement funding of $3 billion over six years represented only 2 percent of the total ISTEA allocation, it brought new opportunities to the states. Preservationists and other community leaders both in urban and rural settings warmly endorsed the revised national transportation policies mandated by ISTEA. The Transportation Equity Act for the 21st Century ("TEA-21"), a six-year highway/transportation bill enacted into law by Congress in 1998, increased funding for nearly all programs and further mitigated North Carolina's donor status.[51]

Jim Hunt surprised many citizens by running for governor again. Defeating Republican lieutenant governor Jim Gardner, he won an unprecedented third term in 1992 and easily won a fourth term in 1996.[52] The governor appointed Sam Hunt (no relation) NCDOT secretary in January 1993. Secretary Hunt, who had served in the General Assembly, stayed two and one-half years before leaving to raise funds for Governor Hunt's reelection campaign. Other appointments included Larry R. Goode as state highway administrator and J. Don Goins (still serving in 2003) as chief engineer. When Jack Murdock retired in 1996 as head of secondary roads, the position was filled by Larry Peters, then Chris McGee in 1998 and Jim Rand in 2000. The new Hunt administration escalated road building, taking advantage of increased funding from the Highway Trust Fund, and likewise made significant strides in non-highway programs. The most obvious growth occurred in the realms of interstate extensions, intrastate four-lane roads, and urban loops.[53]

The 1991 ISTEA legislation changed the composition of basic federal highway aid, which had been a 70 percent (federal)/30 percent (state) split for nearly two decades, to 80 percent (federal) and 20 percent (state). Since the interstate system was substantially completed, the special 90 percent (federal)/10 percent (state) interstate funding formula was discontinued. States could still build new interstate highways that had been authorized, but only with the basic 80/20 match. At the same time, ISTEA authorized a new Interstate 73 from Detroit to Charleston, S.C., to pass through North Carolina's Piedmont region.[54] North Carolina's strategy in creating I-73 through the state was to upgrade existing four-lane highways to interstate standards, requiring limited new corridors. The plan was for I-73 to enter the state from Virginia on I-77, follow U.S. 52 to Winston-Salem, U.S. 311 to High Point, and U.S. 220 to Asheboro and Rockingham before entering South Carolina. Everything changed in 1995 when Virginia congressmen proposed routing the Virginia portion of the interstate through Roanoke, which pointed the highway toward Greensboro instead of Winston-Salem. With competition between the Triad's two major cities and uncertainty about the state's plan, North Carolina took advantage of the situation to acquire more

Engineering intern using transit.

interstate mileage. Garland Garrett, who became NCDOT secretary that fall, and U.S. senator Lauch Faircloth (who had served as highway commission chairman under Gov. Robert W. Scott), led the state's efforts.[55]

The National Highway System Designation Act, passed in late November 1995, finalized the interstate routing. The future Interstate 73 followed a Roanoke-Martinsville-Greensboro-Rockingham route, basically along U.S. 220 through the state. But North Carolina also gained new I-74, which followed the original I-73 route to Winston-Salem and High Point, U.S. 220 to Rockingham, but then turned southeast on U.S. 74 to the Shallotte area, then south to Myrtle Beach and Charleston. "Future I-73/I-74 Corridor" signs began to appear on U.S. 220 in 1996. Secretary Garrett persuaded Rodney Slater, secretary of the U.S. Department of Transportation, to designate thirteen miles of the newly constructed interstate

Gov. Jim Hunt (left) meets with Sam Hunt, NCDOT secretary from 1993 to 1995. Sam Hunt is now president of the North Carolina Railroad.

highway in Randolph and Montgomery Counties as "I-73/I-74," despite the fact that the new segment would not connect to an existing interstate highway, as generally required by policy. In 1999 and 2000 the NCDOT completed two thirteen-mile projects that will form part of the future I-74: a segment in Surry County linking I-77 southward from Virginia to four-lane U.S. 52, and the U.S. 74 bypass around Rockingham and Hamlet. Without designated interstate funding, completing the projected new interstates will take years. Nicholas L. Graf, federal highway administrator for projects in North Carolina, has observed that the state appears more committed than either of its neighbors on the north and south to completing the new highways.[56]

About 1990 North Carolina and Tennessee received authorization from the Federal Highway Administration of the USDOT to extend another interstate, I-26, from Asheville north to Johnson City, Tennessee. The Volunteer State completed future I-26 to the North Carolina line by 1995. That same year the NCDOT was authorized to upgrade four-lane U.S. 19/23 to interstate standards between Asheville and Mars Hill (with the project scheduled to commence in 2008) and to build a new alignment between Mars Hill and the Tennessee line. The nine-mile, new-construction segment of I-26, successfully completed on time in late 2003, was one of the most challenging construction projects undertaken by the NCDOT, both from engineering and environmental perspectives. The road was built through the undeveloped Walnut Mountain range in Madison County, which required heavy blasting, huge equipment to move the earth, and a work schedule of twenty-four hours a day, six days a week. That roadway, along with a connecting fifteen-mile segment in Tennessee, has been designated a "scenic highway" and is the first such interstate highway in the nation. In 1995 the NCDOT board awarded a $105.6 million contract—its largest single contract ever issued—to Gilbert Southern Corporation of Atlanta for heavy grading and placing base stone for six miles of the projected nine-mile road.

After construction started, the NCDOT concluded that the nine-mile segment should consist of six rather than four lanes in order to facilitate truck traffic. (If I-40 west of Asheville needed to be closed for any reason, I-26 could be used as an alternate route for truck traffic over the mountains.) Although I-26 includes a 6 percent grade (similar to ones on I-40 at Old Fort and on I-26 at Saluda), trucks do not slow overall traffic. The nine-mile segment cost $230 million, or $25.5 million per mile. Stan Hyatt, resident NCDOT engineer on the job, has remarked that although the construction job was "extremely dangerous," there had been few injuries, and the environment has remained largely undisturbed.[57]

Other interstate ventures include a possible plan, initiated by Virginia, to designate U.S. 29 between Greensboro and Danville as I-785. Such a designation, which has lukewarm support in North Carolina, could help Virginia eventually acquire interstate designation for U.S. 29 to connect to I-66 in northern Virginia. Widening (from four to eight lanes) and upgrading, although behind schedule, is proceeding along eleven miles of I-40 between Greensboro and Winston-Salem (to be open in 2003). A thirteen-mile segment of upgrade on I-85 in Rowan County, to include a modern diamond

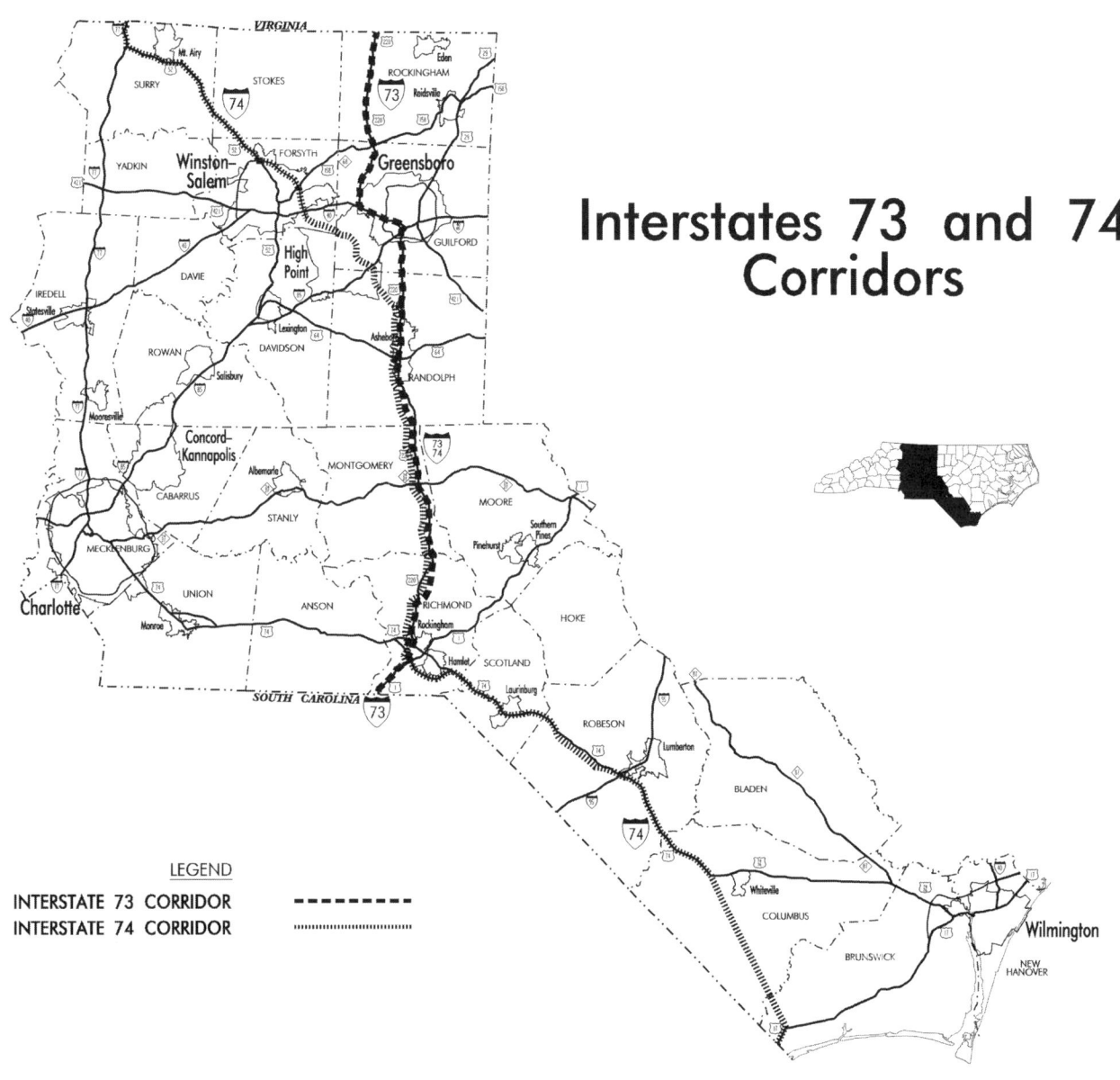

In 1995 North Carolina was allotted portions of planned new Interstates 73 and 74. Construction will take many years, partly because the federal share of costs is now 80 rather than 90 percent. Map by Brian Padfield, NCDOT.

interchange and the rearrangement of adjacent city streets in Salisbury, is scheduled for completion in 2005.[58]

In the east, the most spectacular bridge built in the state in recent years opened in New Bern in 1999 at a cost of $120 million: a one-and-a-half-mile span connected to U.S. 70 and carrying U.S. 17 across the Neuse River. Ralph Whitehead Associates of Charlotte was the lead design engineering firm, and Traylor Brothers of Evansville, Indiana, was the contractor.[59] Another U.S. 17 project under construction is the Jacksonville bypass. A segment of U.S. 64 in Edgecombe and Martin Counties and a U.S. 264 bypass of Wilson recently opened. The five-mile Virginia Dare Memorial Bridge across Croatan Sound, the state's longest such span, opened in 2002 as part of the Manteo bypass on U.S. 64/264. At the peak of construction, more than fifty barges brought supplies to the site.[60]

Urban expressways were completed in Greensboro and Fayetteville in the mid-1990s. Greensboro built Bryan Boulevard (named for the late Joseph Bryan, a businessman and philanthropist), a controlled-access road connecting Benjamin Parkway with the Piedmont Triad International Airport, giving the Gate City an attractive way for airport passengers to access the city's northwest and downtown areas. Fayetteville completed the missing link of the controlled-access expressway that connects I-95 with the central business district loop and U.S. 401 North. The portion inside the city limits is called Martin Luther King Jr. Parkway. In the late 1990s Wilmington opened two-thirds of Smith Creek Parkway, likewise now known as Martin Luther King Jr. Parkway, a limited-access road connecting the area in which I-40 begins to 23rd Street near the Wilmington airport. The remaining portion, now under construction, will connect the expressway to downtown Wilmington, offering an alternative to overcrowded Market Street.

In the midst of criticism of such road-building enthusiasm, Gov. Jim Hunt appointed a blue-ribbon study committee in 1995. The impressive result, *Transit 2001*, appeared in January 1997. The report, which includes a number of recommendations, warned that North Carolina had "dramatically under-invested in transit facilities and services and . . . reinforced auto-dependent development patterns."[61]

A more immediate and dramatic challenge to the NCDOT status quo arose in September 1997 when the agency received negative publicity for building roads and bridges for political insiders. Three NCDOT board members resigned, citing conflict of interest.[62] State Auditor Ralph Campbell ordered a review of the department's policy making. At a January 1998 news conference, Governor Hunt admitted, "Over many decades and through many administrations—Democratic and Republican, mine and others—a system has evolved that no longer gives citizens and taxpayers confidence in how priorities are set and decisions are made."[63] The governor announced changes: NCDOT secretary Garland Garrett would become an adviser to the governor, and Norris Tolson would become the new NCDOT secretary. Tolson, a graduate of North Carolina State College, concluded a career with DuPont as a salesman and manager that had included an assignment in Europe. He retired and returned to his home at Pinetops in Edgecombe County in 1993, served in the legislature, and then spent a year as secretary of the North Carolina Department of Commerce.

In March 1998 Secretary Tolson announced his reorganization plans, which were fully supported by Governor Hunt. Larry Goode, who had been highway administrator for five years, was placed on permanent loan to North Carolina State University's Institute for Transportation Research and Education. Len Sanderson, who had headed the department's construction office, became highway administrator. David King, deputy secretary for transit (supervising ferry, aviation, bicycle, public transportation, and rail operations), became deputy secretary for transportation, with supervision of the highway administrator. Tolson also created a Planning and Environment Division responsible for statewide planning for all transportation needs. Later that year Janet D'Ignazio, a Michigan transportation official noted for her environmental planning expertise, became chief planning and environmental officer for the new division. She had previously worked for the NCDOT's Public Transportation Division and as assistant general manager of the Chapel Hill Transit Authority.[64]

Stan Hyatt is the resident NCDOT engineer in charge of building a new nine-mile segment of Interstate 26 through rugged mountains in Madison County. This fifty-ton Caterpillar dump truck, too large to travel on highways, must be moved to building sites in segments and reassembled.

Secretary Tolson's reorganization plan had several purposes. One was to curb the powers of the highway administrator, who for years had controlled planning and financing of the *Transportation Improvement Program* process and thus scheduling for all NCDOT projects. A new NCDOT controller, Wayne Stallings, began providing revenue projections and budgeting information for the *TIPs*, and the Planning and Environment Division was given increased responsibilities in both areas. Another goal was to provide better coordination of all NCDOT programs. The Planning and Environment Division would work with public and private environmental officials and groups concerning environmental issues. David King, who had creatively built the department's multimodal programs, could now work to integrate those programs with highways.[65] To address the controversies surrounding the Board of Transportation, Governor Hunt and the legislature implemented Secretary Tolson's recommendations. All members of the board were required to disclose financial and political matters and receive annual training in ethics policies. Many board members felt that the negative publicity the board had received was unfair, since only three of the body's twenty-four members had been involved in unethical practices.

The legislature also resolved that, effective in 2001, the board would have nineteen instead of twenty-four members (all to be appointed by the governor and none by legislative leaders) and that the board would elect a chairman each year from among its members rather than having the secretary serve as chairman. A board member would represent each of the fourteen highway divisions, and five members at-large would represent the interests of mass transit, state ports and aviation, rural transportation, environmental issues, and finance and accounting issues.[66] The reorganization received favorable reaction, though some observers concluded that Tolson did not go far enough. During his one-and-one-half years as NCDOT secretary, Tolson returned credibility to the department. In May 1999 Secretary Tolson resigned in order to run for governor and was replaced by David McCoy, Governor Hunt's deputy chief of staff. Secretary McCoy continued to implement the reorganization strategy.[67]

Michael F. Easley was elected governor in 2000 and took office in January 2001. Easley, a native of Rocky Mount, graduated from the University of North Carolina at Chapel Hill and earned a law degree from North Carolina Central University in Durham. He was a district attorney for Brunswick, Bladen, and Columbus Counties for ten years, then served as the state's attorney general from 1993 to 2001. Governor Easley named Lyndo Tippett, who had served eight years as an NCDOT board member, to be secretary of the department and Eugene A. Conti Jr. as the agency's chief deputy, a new position. (Secretary Tippett thereupon assigned oversight of the Highway Division to Conti.) Tippett grew up in Johnston County, graduated from Barton College (formerly Atlantic Christian College) in Wilson, and worked as a certified public accountant in Fayetteville. Conti, who has worked for state and federal governments, served as assistant secretary for transportation policy for the USDOT. Governor Easley appointed all nineteen members of the NCDOT Board of Transportation, which included seven incumbents who had served under Governor Hunt. J. Douglas Galyon of Greensboro, a board member since 1993, has served as chairman of that body since 2001.[68]

Secretary Tippett worked with the 2001 General Assembly on a bill to authorize the NCDOT to use a portion of a cash balance in the Highway Trust Fund for other transportation purposes; the transfer would avoid delaying ongoing construction projects scheduled in the *TIP*.

Inasmuch as the Trust Fund had a balance of $858 million and the Highway Fund $270 million at the end of fiscal year 1999-2000, a consultant, as well as a special legislative committee, recommended such a move. Senate Bill 1005, which the legislature approved in 2001, authorized the NCDOT to use highway trust funds totaling $680 million over three years for purposes other than those originally specified; of that total $470 million would be for maintenance of primary highways and $120 million for public transportation (primarily for mass-transit systems in the Raleigh-Durham and Charlotte areas). The Raleigh *News and Observer* endorsed the legislation, pointing out that spending on mass transit had not kept up with growth and that road maintenance was an important safety issue.[69]

In an unprecedented move, additional Highway Trust Fund moneys were transferred to the state's General Fund to bolster an ailing state budget. Governor Easley diverted $80 million for fiscal 2001-2002, the 2002 legislature moved $205 million for the 2002-2003 budget, and the 2003 legislature transferred $80 million for fiscal 2003-2004. Unlike previous, special-purpose transfers authorized for transportation programs since the establishment of the Trust Fund in 1989, these diversions supported the general state budget. The 2002 legislature also passed a bill permitting toll roads (the first since the plank-road era of the 1850s) to be built in the state. The governor and legislative leaders appointed a North Carolina Turnpike Authority, which will have the authority to build at least three toll roads to interstate standards in urban areas. A Charlotte-Gastonia route will possibly be one of the thoroughfares built.[70]

The annual revenues of the NCDOT tripled between 1971 ($400 million) and 1989 ($1.223 billion). During that period, the state gasoline tax increased by 12 cents per gallon and the federal gas tax by 5 cents, and vehicle registration fees sustained one modest increase. The Highway Trust Fund had been created in 1989 by raising the gasoline tax by 5.25 cents, increasing vehicle-registration and several

This $120 million bridge at New Bern, opened in 1999, is the most expensive one ever built in N.C. This view looks northeast across the Neuse River and shows the intersection of U.S. 17 and U.S. 70.

The five-mile Virginia Dare Memorial Bridge, the state's longest, opened in 2002 to carry U.S. 64/U.S. 264 traffic across Croatan Sound as part of a planned Manteo bypass. This photo shows a few of the fifty barges used during construction.

other fees, and establishing a separate fund for highway construction. By 2002 the state's motorists were paying 22.3 cents of state tax and 18.4 cents of federal tax on each gallon of gasoline.[71] Largely because of the additional resources provided by the trust fund, NCDOT revenues doubled in the 1990s to $2.655 billion. For the 2001 fiscal year, for example, the Trust Fund provided 33 percent of the NCDOT's revenues, with the traditional Highway Fund providing 41 percent. Federal aid furnished 26 percent, about the same percentage as during the previous thirty years (see Appendixes A and B).

Two state bond issues—$300 million in 1977 and $950 million in 1996 ($500 million for urban loops/connectors, $300 million for intrastate highways, and $150 million for secondary roads)—provided additional resources for highway construction, although they are not considered revenues. By 2003 only $250 million in proceeds from the 1996 bonds had been spent. The delay in spending occurred because projects took longer than anticipated and the NCDOT was able to fund planned construction from the Highway Trust Fund. On Governor Easley's recommendation, the 2003 legislature authorized the agency to spend the remaining $700 million in bond funds over two years to provide jobs and enhance safety.

Of that amount, $630 million will be used for major maintenance and improvement of existing highways—projects such as widening shoulders, adding turn lanes, improving intersections, and replacing unsafe bridges. The remaining $70 million will be used for public transportation projects such as mass-transit systems and rail, ferry, and bicycle programs. Inflation continued to be a factor in assessing the actual increase in available resources. The costs of acquiring right-of-way, especially for urban areas, escalated. The NCDOT's annual expenditures for right-of-way increased from $25 million in 1970 to $186 million in 2000, using approximately the same-size staff.[72]

Legislators who had created the Trust Fund in 1989 specified that 25 percent of the revenues would fund construction of seven urban loops and connectors—complete loops around Charlotte, Raleigh, and Greensboro; partial loops around Winston-Salem and Durham; an interstate connector in Asheville; and a bypass in Wilmington. The 1996 bonds furnished additional funds for those expensive projects.

Construction on Charlotte's sixty-three-mile loop, known as I-485 and projected to cost $1.1 billion, began in 1988. Although nearly all of the completed twenty-six miles are only four lanes, they include extra-wide medians in some sections that will allow additional lanes to be added easily. The completed portion starts west of I-77 South and extends around the southern edge of Charlotte, past U.S. 74 East to Lawyers Road. A short six-lane portion northeast of the city between I-85 and N.C. 49 is also open. The remaining sections of I-485 will be six lanes. The connecting portions between Lawyers Road and N.C. 49 and between I-85 South and N.C. 160 are under contract. The remaining link (I-85 South to I-85 North) could be completed as early as 2010 or as late as 2013.[73] I-485 will serve several purposes. It will provide bypasses (especially for I-77, to relieve heavy traffic through the city) and provide access to U.S. 74 East. Charlotte citizens are impatient for its completion. Bob Morgan, group vice-president at the Charlotte Chamber of Commerce, points out that "Charlotte is the largest metropolitan area in the U.S. without an outer loop."[74]

Raleigh's outer loop, I-540, is similar to Charlotte's in price ($1.2 billion) and at a total of seventy-one miles is about the same length. (Raleigh already has the state's first loop, I-440, completed in the mid-1980s.) Construction of the six-lane outer loop commenced in 1992. Eleven miles are open northwest of the city, extending from I-40 past the Raleigh-Durham International Airport to U.S. 1 North. By 2008 twenty-nine miles of the loop are scheduled to be completed, extending the route to U.S. 64 East and to U.S. 1

Gov. Michael F. Easley (first row, far right) and NCDOT Secretary Lyndo Tippett (first row, far left) meet with the NCDOT Board of Transportation in 2001. First row, left to right: Secretary Tippett, Nancy W. Dunn, Nina S. Szlosberg, J. Douglas Galyon (board chair), Governor Easley. Second row: Frank L. Johnson, Tyrone Y. Cox, Margaret Kluttz. Third Row: Lanny T. Wilson, Larry S. Helms, Louis W. Sewell Jr., Samuel L. Erby Jr. Fourth Row: G. R. Kindley, Alan Z. Thornburg, Paul Waff. Fifth Row: Collice C. Moore, D. M. Campbell Jr., Conrad Burrell, Cameron W. McRae. (Not shown are Clark Jenkins and Edward Dolby.)

southwest of the city. The remainder of the project could take until 2025 to complete. Though I-540 will not serve as a bypass to the degree that Charlotte's I-485 does, it will be a true loop, will relieve congestion on major roads to I-440 and I-40, and will give north Raleigh residents quicker access to the airport. Large residential and retail developments are already under way or planned for the vicinity of the loop and its future path; examples include Wakefield Plantation, a burgeoning 2,200-acre development within a mile of the town of Wake Forest. Some environmentalists claim that the loop, as well as its counterparts in Charlotte and Greensboro, will hasten undesirable urban sprawl.[75]

In 1954 the city of Greensboro hired W. F. Babcock, an engineering professor at North Carolina State College and later state highway administrator, to create an urban road plan for the city. That plan included a loop. Thirty-five years later, moneys from the Highway Trust Fund made possible the long-envisioned roadway, to be known as Painter Boulevard and designated as I-840.[76] Greensboro resolved the final remaining routing controversy in the early 1990s, extending the western loop farther west to avoid land and other historic properties belonging to Guilford College. Except for that change, the loop essentially follows the alignment Babcock recommended.[77] Construction of Painter Boulevard finally began in 1997. The first major segment, fifteen miles in length, will open by early 2004 and will serve as the I-85 bypass, so that drivers on that interstate can avoid the congested "Death Valley," the section in which I-85 and I-40 now meet. The loop will consist of at least six lanes on the I-85 bypass and western sections and probably four lanes on the less-busy northern and northeastern segments.

The NCDOT's cost estimates for 2000 show that present construction on the state's three urban loops has a consistent cost per mile. Greensboro's I-85 bypass loop is costing $20.3 million per mile; Charlotte's northern and western portions of I-485, $21 million per mile; and the initial twenty-nine miles of Raleigh's I-540, $20.5 million per mile. Yet the cost of the Greensboro project could change as the NCDOT buys right-of-way and actually begins building through the crowded western part of the city, which will require numbers of houses and businesses to be relocated. Significantly, in contrast to the price of constructing urban loops such as the aforementioned, rural interstate construction in 1996 carried an average cost of only $3.3 million per mile.[78]

Winston-Salem's partial loop is designed to extend from I-40 West around the western and northern portions of the city to I-40 East. Although some right-of-way was acquired and a contract was let to build four miles of the loop, a group of citizens successfully delayed the project by obtaining a federal court order to prohibit the state from claiming their residences or dividing their farms. The matter remains unresolved, and construction has been postponed indefinitely. Durham's plans for a partial loop through the northern and eastern areas of the city, extending from I-85 South across I-85 North to U.S. 70 East,

Since 1991 the NCDOT's Incident Management Assistance Patrol has provided emergency services to stranded motorists and removal of debris along urban expressways.

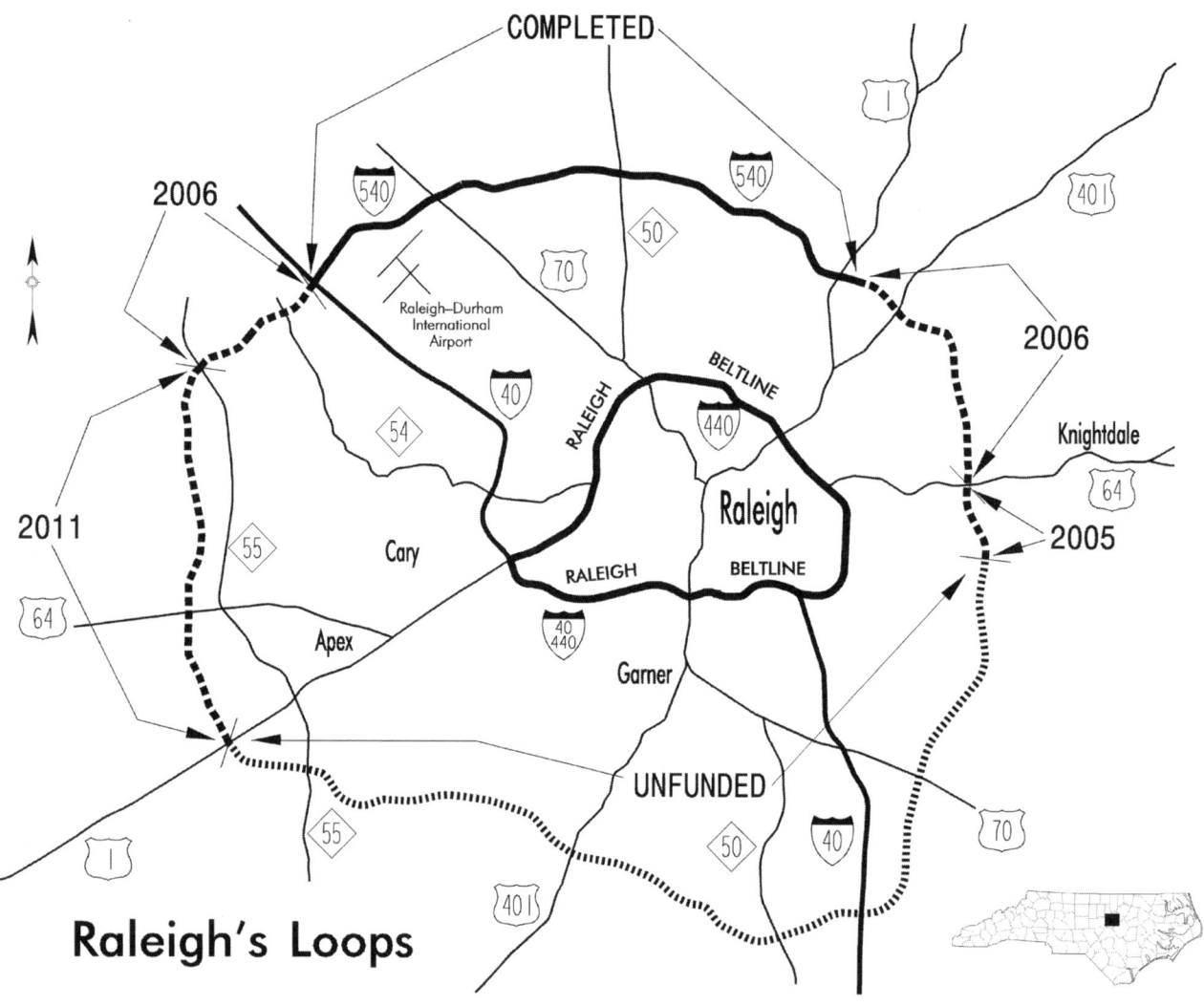

About half of the Raleigh Beltline (now Interstate 440) was built during the 1960s, but the loop was not completed until 1985. Eleven miles of a planned seventy-one-mile outer loop (Interstate 540) are now open. Map by Brian Padfield, NCDOT.

are likewise on hold. A portion of the loop's route, projected to pass near the Eno River, is unresolved because of opposition from environmentalists and local residents. Asheville's plan, still to be designed, is a connector for I-26 (where it meets I-40 West) to extend three miles northward to connect with present U.S. 19/23 (and future I-26). Wilmington's road will be the U.S. 17 bypass around the western perimeter of Wilmington, linking I-40 travelers to the beaches of Brunswick County and points further south. The portion between I-40 and U.S. 421 is currently under construction.[79]

Once these urban highways are opened, the NCDOT must maintain them. Maintenance has always been a challenging and complex issue for the agency. For example, the American Automobile Association (AAA), which annually rates the condition of the nation's bridges, revealed in March 2001 that North Carolina ranked in the bottom fourth among the fifty states for its substandard spans. David E. Parsons, chief executive officer and president of AAA Carolinas, recently warned that the need to upgrade the state's bridges, as well as its roads, is "greater than ever" and that "additional funding must be found before the situation worsens."[80]

Interstate 540 bridge construction, showing curved steel girders.

During the period from 1973 to 2000, vehicle owners expected and sometimes demanded through the political process an emphasis on building all categories of new highways as quickly as possible, leaving maintenance a low priority. Maintenance became a serious problem in the 1970s. The legislature responded by raising the gasoline tax by three cents in 1981 and targeted the new funds for maintenance. That action led to a noticeable, but not permanent, improvement in maintenance. Highway Trust Fund legislation in 1989 created significant new funding sources for the major categories of highways but authorized no additional funds for maintenance. The fast-growing highways have included intrastates (62 percent of trust funds), urban loops and connectors (25 percent), and secondary roads (6.5 percent). While new-highway construction escalated in the 1990s, problems with maintenance became more pronounced.

Policies pertaining to secondary roads illustrate the maintenance dilemma. "A Report on Transportation Needs in North Carolina," a research report issued by the state Department of Administration in 1973, concluded that "the 'pave everything' policy [regarding secondary roads] is undermining the entire highway program in North Carolina by [incurring] spiraling maintenance costs at a disproportionate rate" and suggested that the state selectively upgrade the roads found to be the most deficient.[81] During the 1970s, the NCDOT began paving secondary roads on a priority basis, based on the number of unpaved miles and with the requirement that eligible roads must carry at least one hundred vehicles daily. By 1983 the department was authorized to pave subdivision roads that were located on the edges of cities and towns and which carried more than one hundred vehicles each day. The Trust Fund legislation of 1989 established the goal of paving all secondary roads that carried at least fifty vehicles daily. As a result, 8,600 miles of secondary roads—more than triple the amount of the previous decade—were paved during the 1990s. While newly paved secondary roads in 1990 had served more than 24,000 homes, those paved in 2000 served fewer than 10,000. The average annual cost in 2001 of maintaining an unpaved secondary road (typically gravel) was $2,500 per mile; a paved road required $5,000.[82]

Maintaining interstate highways posed a different challenge. Since only about two-thirds of North Carolina's allotted interstate mileage was completed by 1973, completing the system was an NCDOT priority. Although the interstate program included limited funds for maintenance (increased in the 1990s), the states always had the lion's share of responsibility for maintaining the highways. The widened portion of I-40/I-85 near Burlington, for example, includes lighting that must be maintained.[83] The NCDOT also had to maintain many miles of roads within the state's cities, including all N.C. and U.S. highways. In Greensboro, for example, such routes included not only Lee Street (N.C. 6), Battleground Avenue (U.S. 220), and Wendover Avenue (U.S. 70), but

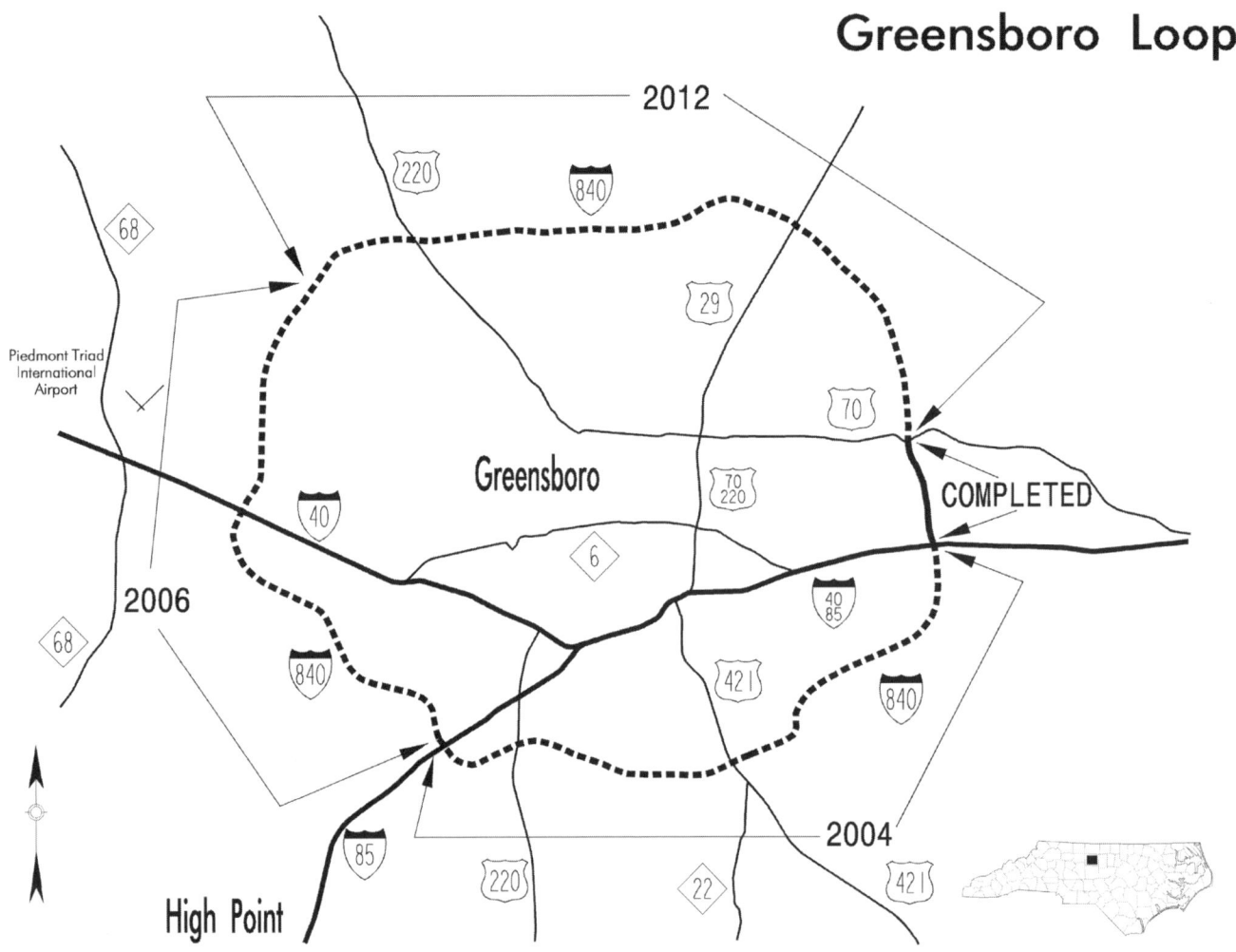

The Greensboro loop (Interstate 840, also known as Painter Boulevard) will provide a faster and safer route for interstate motorists. Map by Brian Padfield, NCDOT.

also Market Street and Friendly Avenue (formerly U.S. 421), Freeman Mill Road, and several downtown streets that constituted an inner loop. The mandate requires traffic servicing (traffic signals, signs, painting); landscaping (seeding, erosion control, beautification); and construction (engineering and inspections for widening or upgrading).

Governor Hunt's third and fourth administrations made efforts to address maintenance problems. As required by Trust Fund legislation, available revenue freed by the retirement of bonds had been transferred from the Highway Fund to the Trust Fund. Beginning in 1999, however, that revenue ($38 million annually) remained in the Highway Fund, earmarked for maintenance.[84] Nevertheless the maintenance dilemma continues to be problematic.

Safety is another important issue for the NCDOT. According to a study by the Insurance Institute for Highway Safety, North Carolina presently ranks among the top five states in terms of stringent safety laws. Nevertheless, the study recommended that North Carolina take action to require seat-belt use for passengers in rear seats, to use additional cameras to record violations at traffic signals, and to revoke licenses for first offenders on the charge of Driving under the Influence (of illegal drugs or the inappropriate use of prescription drugs—"DUI") or Driving While Intoxicated (with alcohol—"DWI") laws.[85]

The NCDOT's process of awarding construction projects is another issue. For several years, minority contractors have alleged that the department does not treat them fairly. An association representing minority contractors in the two Carolinas sued the NCDOT in federal court in 1999; the two parties reached a settlement in 2001. The department agreed to a series of steps, including monitoring the progress of minority firms and encouraging their participation. In February 2002, however, Ty Cox of Durham, at that time the NCDOT's only African American board member, voted against awarding contracts as a means of protesting what he perceived as the agency's lack of progress.[86]

The public is relatively familiar with the NCDOT's Division of Motor Vehicles (DMV) through its activities in issuing driver's licenses, license plates, and vehicle registrations. But when that division was established (as the *Department of Motor Vehicles*) in 1941, it also included the State Highway Patrol, as well as a Division of Highway Safety and was likewise charged with licensing, inspecting, and certifying motor vehicles. The department helped to implement legislation passed by the General Assembly during the late 1940s and 1950s that required annual automobile inspections, insurance and liability coverage for motorists, and high school driver training. Parts of the DMV—including the State Highway Patrol in 1977 and the Enforcement Section in 2002—have been transferred from the NCDOT to the North Carolina Department of Crime Control and Public Safety. The Enforcement Section ensures compliance with state safety regulations applicable to private and commercial vehicles. It administers a statewide program of vehicle inspections that includes the testing of exhaust emissions. It also maintains nine weigh stations along major highways to assess usage fees based on the weight of trucks' cargo and to prevent overweight trucks from damaging pavement.[87]

Citizens can obtain or renew driver's licenses at one of about 130 driver's license offices (at least one office in each county). For many decades, licenses had to be renewed every four years. In 1995 North Carolina implemented a new timetable for license renewal. Driver's licenses are renewed for a period of four to eight years, depending on one's birth date. The cost varies according to the yearly charge for the type of license obtained. Eventually, all drivers over the age of twenty will renew their license every five years. The division also operates about 130 additional offices that issue license plates, collect vehicle taxes and fees, and maintain electronic records for all vehicles. Motorists have the option of ordering license plates or annual stickers by mail, telephone, or via the Internet. In addition, the division offers assistance to non-English-speaking customers.[88]

Surprisingly, the size of the NCDOT staff has had modest growth since its organization. In late

Workers repair bridge in southeastern N.C.

1977, after the State Ports Authority and State Highway Patrol were moved to other departments, the NCDOT had 13,499 employees. The largest staff increases occurred in preparation for the active road building of the 1990s with the addition of engineers (numbering eight hundred in 2001) and planners. At the same time, about one-third of the department's planning, design, and environmental functions, including some highway inspection and oversight, had been contracted to private companies. Although the NCDOT spent only $13 million for consultants in 1988, the figure increased to $133 million by 2000.[89] The agency had a total of 14,462 employees in January 2001. In 1990 the NCDOT leased and later purchased two new buildings on Birch Ridge Drive in Raleigh known as Century Center. That complex accommodates one thousand employees. A staff of nine hundred works at the Transportation Building (with its 1921, 1953, and 1968 segments interconnected) across from the State Capitol in downtown Raleigh.[90]

At the dawn of the twenty-first century, North Carolina had an impressive 78,267-mile highway system—exceeded only by Texas, with 78,820 miles.[91] The state could boast a variety of roads, from scenic pastoral settings to modern urban loops. Yet between 1970 and 2000 the population of North Carolina grew by 64 percent—from about 5 million to 8 million. During the same period, the number of vehicles in the state more than doubled—from 3,218,292 to 6,978,046 (1999). The state ratio of cars to persons increased from 1 vehicle for each 1.6 persons in 1970 to 1-to-1.15 in 2000—an average of almost one vehicle for each person.[92]

But could new road construction keep pace with an exploding population that made North Carolina the ninth-fastest-growing state in the nation? Would more loops continue to attract new traffic and congestion? Could the state continue to meet strict air-quality and environmental regulations as the numbers of vehicles outpace population? This volume's final chapter will explore the North Carolina Department of Transportation's efforts to create alternatives to highways and build a comprehensive, more environmentally responsible transportation system for the future.[93]

Notes

1. Beth G. Crabtree, *North Carolina Governors, 1585-1974* (Raleigh: Division of Archives and History, Department of Cultural Resources, 1974), 143-145.

2. The General Assembly established the North Carolina State Ports Authority (SPA) in 1945 to oversee the developing ports at Wilmington and Morehead City in order to increase water-borne commerce. *Guide to Research Materials in the North Carolina State Archives: State Agency Records* (Raleigh: Department of Cultural Resources, Division of Archives and History, Archives and Records Section, 1995), 125 (hereafter cited as *Guide to State Agency Records*).

3. Billy Rose, interview with author, Raleigh, January 9, 2001; Harden, *North Carolina Roads and Their Builders*, vol. 2, 99.

4. North Carolina State Highway Commission, *Biennial Report, 1973-1974* (Raleigh: State Printer, 1975), 8, 9 (hereafter cited as *Biennial Report*, with appropriate date).

5. *Guide to State Agency Records*, 682; *Biennial Report, 1972-1973*, 1.

6. Jack Murdock indicates that the act establishing the NCDOT "put into law our existing policies" of paving on a priority basis secondary roads carrying one hundred or more vehicles per day. Jack Murdock, interview with author, Raleigh, January 5, 2001.

7. Between 1921 and 1969 the governor chose all the members of the State Highway Commission. "Public Transportation," *www.ncdot.org* (NCDOT website).

8. "Department of Transportation—Four Stormy, Controversial Years," *North Carolina* 34 (July 1976): 29-32.

9. J. F. Alexander, "To the Citizens of North Carolina," *Highway Improvement Program, 1975-1982* (Raleigh: North Carolina Department of Transportation and Highway Safety, 1975), unpaged (hereafter cited as *Highway Improvement Program*, with appropriate dates); *Highway Improvement Program, 1974-1981*, 35. By 2000 the United States imported a significantly larger percentage of its annual oil usage than during the energy crisis of the early 1970s.

10. "New Transportation Secretary is Young but Experienced Leader," *North Carolina* 35 (July 1977): 34.

11. Also transferred from NCDOT to Commerce was the Board of Commissioners of Navigation and Pilotage for the Cape Fear River and Bar. *Guide to State Agency Records*, 683.

12. "Transportation Secretary Thomas W. Bradshaw, Jr.," *North Carolina* 36 (August 1978): 22; *Guide to State Agency Records*, 702. The Ports Authority had about 350 employees at this time, while the State Highway Patrol had 1,138 uniformed personnel and between 300 and 400 support staff. "An Overview of North Carolina Transportation Policy and Recommendations for Policy Planning" (research report, State Planning Division, North Carolina Department of Administration, April 1973), 12; "North Carolina State Highway Patrol Authorized Strength Uniformed Members, 1929-2000" (unpublished report, Research and Planning Section, North Carolina Department of Crime Control and Public Safety, 2000).

13. *Guide to State Agency Records*, 683; Jack Murdock, telephone conversation with author, October 3, 2002. One member must be a member of a political party other than that of the governor. The lieutenant governor appoints a state senate member, and the Speaker of the state House of Representatives appoints a House member. *Guide to State Agency Records*, 683.

14. "Contract Let for 4.3 mile Beltline Link," *Raleigh Times*, August 12, 1977.

15. William G. Marley, NCDOT highway administrator, 1990-1993, telephone conversations with author, January 30, February 12, 2001. The tri-level interchanges on present-day I-240 include one built at the intersection

of I-40 and I-26 (the first such interchange in the state), which now includes the beginning of I-240 on the city's west side; another originally built in the late 1960s to serve the junction of U.S. 70 and U.S. 19/23; and still another built at the intersection of I-240 and U.S. 70 East as part of the overall construction of I-240.

16. Robert W. McDowell, "Getting Educated about Highways," *North Carolina* 49 (July 1991): 24, 25; John Watkins, division engineer, Division 7, NCDOT, 1973-1999, telephone conversations with author, February 9, 12, 2001. Major delays included the expense of building I-77 through a large urban area in Charlotte and a lawsuit filed by the city of Fayetteville in opposition to the I-95 bypass.

17. *Biennial Report, 1977-1978*, 2.

18. Thomas W. Bradshaw Jr., telephone conversation with author, April 11, 2001.

19. *Highway Improvement Program, 1978-1984*, 4.

20. "A Report on Transportation Needs in North Carolina," (research report, Office of State Planning, North Carolina Department of Administration, 1973), 24, 25; *Highway Improvement Program, 1977*, 4.

21. "Bid Collusion," *North Carolina* 38 (July 1980): 10; "Money Problems Are Nothing New in State's Roadbuilding History," *North Carolina* 39 (July 1981): 22, 24, 26, 91; Wendell Rawls Jr., "Scandal Builds in Southeast," *New York Times*, July 6, 1980.

22. Thomas O'Toole, "Everyone Got a Piece of the Paving Job; Justice Department Unearths Bid-Rigging in 14 States," *Washington Post*, October 15, 1981; Mary Thornton, "Bid-Rigging Probe Has Grown to Largest U.S. Antitrust Case," *Washington Post*, August 10, 1982.

23. "Statement by Former Gov. Dan K. Moore, Chairman of the Governor's Blue Ribbon Study Commission on Transportation Needs and Financing," November 24, 1980, *Biennial Report 1979-1980*, 1-3; Wilbur Smith and Associates, *Report of Governor's Blue Ribbon Commission on Transportation Needs and Financing*, December 16, 1980.

24. Wilbur Smith and Associates, *Report of Governor's Blue Ribbon Commission*, 381-384; A. L. May, "Hunt to Try to Show Woes of Highways," *News and Observer* (Raleigh), December 17, 1980; "The Hard Choices," *North Carolina* 39 (February 1981): 10.

25. Stan Swofford, "Building a Power Base," *News and Record* (Greensboro), January 1, 2001.

26. "Money Problems Are Nothing New in State's Roadbuilding History," *North Carolina* 39 (July 1981): 23; "The 1981 Good Roads Package Just Bought Some Extra Time," *North Carolina* 40 (July 1982): 22.

27. "The 1981 Good Roads Package," 22.

28. Watkins telephone conversations.

29. W. R. "Bill" Roberson Jr., "To the Citizens of North Carolina," in *Transportation Improvement Program, 1982-1991* (hereafter cited as *TIP*, with appropriate years); "About Highways," *North Carolina* 39 (July 1981): 20. There was no *TIP* published for the 1983-1992 period.

30. "The 1981 Good Roads Package," 22; W. R. Roberson Jr., letter to Gov. James B. Hunt Jr., January 13, 1983, in *Biennial Report, 1981-1982*.

31. Roberson letter to Governor Hunt; "Highway Program Perking Up with New Federal Tax Funds," *North Carolina* 41 (July 1983): 20, 21, 22, 56; "Highway Fund Revenue, Fiscal Years 1952 through 2001" (unpublished report, NCDOT, 2002).

32. Roberson letter to Governor Hunt.

33. James E. Harrington, letter to Gov. James Martin, February 5, 1985, in *Biennial Report, 1983-1984*; Bradshaw telephone conversation.

34. Julie W. Snee, ed., "James Grubbs Martin, Governor," in *North Carolina Manual, 1991-1992* (Raleigh: Department of the Secretary of State, 1992), 15.

35. James E. Harrington, "North Carolina Highways in the Near and Far Terms," *North Carolina* 46 (July 1988): 14.

36. Mark Schreiner, "I-40, Road Changed How Southeastern N.C. Gets Around," *Wilmington Morning Star*, June 28, 2000; Nicholas L. Graf, telephone conversations with author, January 30, March 7, 2001. One disadvantage to concentrating resources on I-40 was that projects such as guardrail maintenance and similar improvements to other interstate highways fell behind schedule. Two notable examples were the widening of I-40/I-85 between Greensboro and east of Burlington and construction of an I-40 bypass of Winston-Salem.

37. In the 1960s the State Highway Commission had constructed with secondary federal-aid funds a new two-lane roadway that linked Wade Avenue in Raleigh with the Research Triangle Park by way of the Raleigh-Durham Airport. The route also connected with N.C. 54. It was later expanded to become I-40. Rose interview.

38. Rose interview; Graf telephone conversations; James E. Harrington, telephone conversation with author, February 5, 2001.

39. "State's Roadbuilding Efforts Beefed Up by New Tax Revenues," *North Carolina* 45 (July 1987): 24-52; Bradshaw telephone conversation, April 11, 2001.

40. Hugh M. Morton and Edward L. Rankin Jr., *Making a Difference in North Carolina* (Raleigh: Lightworks, 1988), 134-143. The Nello L. Teer Company of Durham built most of North Carolina's portion of the parkway.

41. Lisa Trent, "One Thousand N.C. Businesses 'Adopt-a-Highway' to Clean Roads," *North Carolina* 47 (July 1989): 50.

42. "Scenic Byways" and "Adopt-a-Highway," 2002 NCDOT State Transportation Map.

43. *TIP, 1986-1995*, HP-3, HP-4; *TIP, 1987-1995*, 4; *TIP, 1988-1996* (edition of November 1987), 1; *TIP, 1988-1996* (edition of December 1988), 4.

44. *TIP, 1986-1995*, HP-2, HP-3. The General Assembly established the Highway Fund in 1919 to receive state revenues earmarked for highways, so the funds could be safely separated from the state's General Fund. The U.S. Highway Trust Fund, created by the 1956 Federal-Aid Highway Act of 1956, operates in a similar manner.

45. *TIP, 1986-1995*, HP-2, HP-3; "1988 Transportation Improvement Program Funding Update," *Executive Summary, Transportation Improvement Program, 1988-1996* (November 1987), unpaged; "State's Roadbuilding Efforts Beefed Up by New Tax Revenues," 24, 26, 27, 52.

46. James E. Harrington, *Planks, Pavement and Progress* (Raleigh: North Carolina Department of Transportation, 1989), 42.

47. Harrington, *Planks, Pavement and Progress*, 47, 48; House Bill 399, "An Act to Establish the North Carolina Highway Trust Fund, to Provide Revenue for the Fund, to Designate How Revenue in the Fund is to be Used, and to Raise Revenue for the General Fund," 1989 session, North Carolina General Assembly; Crissty Martin, Program Development, NCDOT, telephone conversations with author, January 12, February 20, 2001.

48. Secretary Harrelson graduated from the University of North Carolina at Chapel Hill, earned a master's degree in business from the University of Pennsylvania, spent two years with Chevron Corporation, and worked in a family business (grocery and appliance stores) in Southport.

49. McDowell, "Getting Educated about Highways," 22-27.

50. McDowell, "Getting Educated about Highways" 22-27; "Highway Fund Crisis," *TIP, 1993-1999*, unpaged.

51. Graf telephone conversations; *"ISTEA, a Road Map for the Future"* (Washington, D.C.: National Trust for Historic Preservation, 1996), 4, 5.

52. In 1984 Hunt ran against Sen. Jesse Helms for a U.S. Senate seat, but Helms won by a margin of 52 percent to 48 percent. Hunt joined the Raleigh law firm of Poyner and Spruill, specializing in corporate law, and was active in national educational efforts. Stan Swofford, "A History-Making Comeback," *News and Record*, January 2, 2001.

53. Sam Hunt, a native of Burlington who earned an A.B. degree from East Carolina University, served as a first lieutenant in the U.S. Army, a member of the N.C. House of Representatives (1985-1993), and as owner and president of Hunt Electric Supply Company in Burlington. The title of the position relating to secondary roads was changed in 1996 from assistant secretary of secondary roads and economic development to assistant to the chief engineer for secondary roads.

54. Graf telephone conversations; "ISTEA," *TIP, 1993-1999*, unpaged.

55. Garland Garrett graduated from Virginia Polytechnic Institute and served as vice-president of Cape Fear Music Company, a business owned by his family in Wilmington. He was a member of the NCDOT board from 1977 to 1982 and deputy secretary from 1993 to 1995. He was a fund raiser for Governor Hunt during his campaigns. "Transportation Secretary; Wilmington's Garrett Leads Roads Office; Hunt Rewards Longtime Ally," *Wilmington Morning Star*, September 1, 1995.

56. Graf telephone conversations; Justin Catanoso, "New Proposal for I-73 Stirs Triad Rivalry," *News and Record*, April 14, 1995; Andrew Barron, "Congress OKs Interstate 73/74 through N.C.," *News and Record*, November 21, 1995; Jane Reynolds, "Plans for Highway Picking Up Speed," *News and Record*, August 19, 1996.

57. Stan Hyatt, resident engineer, Division 13, NCDOT, telephone conversation with author, November 14, 2001.

58. Graf telephone conversations; Richard Rogoski, "Still the Good Roads State?" *North Carolina* 58 (July 2000): 21, 23.

59. "NCDOT Wins National Highway Award," press release, NCDOT, December 5, 2001.

60. Rogoski, "Still the Good Roads State?" 21, 23; Vicki Hyman, "DOT Presses for Toll Roads," *News and Observer*, March 3, 2001; memorandum from Sherri Johnson, NCDOT Public Information Office, to author, October 24, 2001; Anna Griffin, "New N.C. Bridge Is Poetry for Motion," *Charlotte Observer*, August 11, 2002.

61. "The Transit 2001 Executive Summary," *Transit 2001* (Raleigh: North Carolina Department of Transportation, 1997).

62. Norman Gomlak and Ames Alexander, "Official's Role Questioned in Road Projects," *Charlotte Observer*, September 8, 1997. The *Charlotte Observer* and the Raleigh *News and Observer* won public service awards from the North Carolina Press Association for their coverage of conflict-of-interest allegations of NCDOT board members.

63. Kevin Sack, "A Road-Building Scandal Forces a Governor's Hand," *New York Times*, January 14, 1998.

64. Press releases, "Transportation Secretary Tolson Announces Overhaul at DOT" and "NC Department of Transportation Reorganization Plan," North Carolina Department of Transportation, March 4, 1998.

65. King, a native of Lumberton, graduated from Davidson College and earned an M.B.A. from UNC at Chapel Hill. After serving two years in the army, he joined the NCDOT in 1973, working in administration; as director of the public transportation division; and as deputy secretary for transit, rail, and aviation. Wade Rawlings, "'Transit Guy' Gets Broad Power at DOT," *News and Observer*, March 8, 1998.

66. "Problems at DOT," *Charlotte Observer*, March 3, 1998; Jack Betts, "In the DOT Driver's Seat," *Charlotte Observer*, February 6, 2001; David King, interview with author, Raleigh, March 21, 2001.

67. Chris FitzSimon, "Real Problem Remains at State DOT," *Triangle Business Journal*, March 6, 1998, 47; "Has Been Acting Chief since Tolson's Resignation; Hunt Names David McCoy DOT Secretary," *Wilmington Morning Star*, June 23, 1999; Tim Gray, "Now He Wants to Make Agriculture His Business," *Business North Carolina* 20 (April 2000): 17. After a few months as a candidate, Tolson withdrew from the 2000 governor's race, then entered and lost the race for agriculture commissioner. In 2001 Gov. Mike Easley appointed him secretary of the North Carolina Department of Revenue. McCoy, a Chippewa Indian, earned degrees at the University of Georgia (A.B. and M.S. in educational psychology) and UNC at Chapel Hill (M.S. in public health and a law degree). He served as deputy secretary of the North Carolina Department of Administration (1995-1997) and deputy chief of staff for operations and personnel for Governor Hunt's office (1997-1999).

68. "Easley Names Tippett/Conti Team to Head D.O.T.," press release, NCDOT, January 25, 2001. Secretary Tippett appointed Roger Sheats, who had worked with local governments and environmental issues as executive director of the Mid-Carolina Council of Governments, to a newly created position, deputy secretary for environment, planning, and local government affairs.

69. "Eyes on Highway Surplus," *News and Observer*, May 22, 2001; "Transportation Secretary Lyndo Tippett, Summary of Accomplishments, July 10, 2001" (unpublished fact sheet, Public Information Office, NCDOT, 2001).

70. Chris J. McAdams, Research and Policy, NCDOT, telephone conversation with author, October 10, 2002.

71. Nicole Burns, Public Information Office, NCDOT, e-mail to author, July 15, 2002.

72. Mike Stanley, program development staff engineer, NCDOT, telephone conversation with author, July 24, 2003; Kirby Warrick, Right-of-Way Section, NCDOT, telephone conversation with author, March 2, 2001.

73. Charlie Jones, transportation planner, city of Charlotte, telephone conversations with author, March 23, 2001, October 22, 2002; project breakdown maps of Charlotte outer loop from *TIP, 2002-2008*; Heidi Russell Raferty, "Open Road," *North Carolina* 60 (July 2002): 46, 48-53; Carroll Leggett, manager, Program Development Branch, NCDOT, telephone conversation with author, August 5, 2002.

74. Rogoski, "Still the Good Roads State?" 21.

75. Rogoski, "Still the Good Roads State?" 21; Rob Christensen, "New Jersey Sprawl Is Here, Y'all," *News and Observer*, May 6, 2001.

76. Painter Boulevard is named for Pennell C. Painter, Greensboro's progressive city manager during the 1920s. Jim Schlosser, "Leader Plagued by Work, Injury," *News and Record*, May 26, 2002; Watkins telephone conversations.

77. Watkins telephone conversations.

78. Doug Lane, preliminary estimate engineer, NCDOT, telephone interview with author, March 27, 2001; Warrick interview. Thirteen miles of new construction of I-73/I-74 in Randolph and Montgomery Counties

(not merely the upgrading of U.S. 220) opened August 27, 1996, at a cost of $43 million.

79. Al Avant, assistant branch manager, Program Development Branch, NCDOT, telephone conversation with author, March 21, 2001; intrastate corridor maps from *TIP, 2000-2006*.

80. "The State of Bridges in the Carolinas," *Go* (newsletter of AAA Carolinas), March-April 2001, 6.

81. *A Report on Transportation Needs*, 31.

82. House Bill 399, Chapter 692, Sec. 1.8, G.S. 136-44.5, 1989 Session, North Carolina General Assembly; "Secondary Road Paving Program," in *TIP, 1998-2004*; Watkins telephone conversations.

83. Graf telephone conversations; "Interstate Maintenance (IM)" (unpublished fact sheet, Federal Highway Administration, ca. 1998).

84. Former NCDOT secretary James E. Harrington considered this action a diversion from the Highway Trust Fund, which was intended for construction rather than maintenance. James E. Harrington, telephone interview with author, July 27, 2001.

85. "How the Carolinas' Traffic Safety Laws Measure Up," *Go*, March-April 2001, 7; Jacquie Hughett, public relations manager, AAA Carolinas, Charlotte, telephone conversation with author, September 6, 2001.

86. Lynn Bonner, "DOT Contracts Protested," *News and Observer*, February 8, 2002.

87. *Guide to State Agency Records*, 701, 702; McAdams telephone conversation. In June 2002 a federal grand jury began investigating charges that Division of Motor Vehicles enforcement officers and supervisors, primarily in the state's Mountain region, fixed tickets, accepted gifts and bribes to avoid enforcing truck-safety regulations, and engaged in political activities while on the job. In October of that year an administrative judge ordered the DMV to revamp its hiring and promotion procedures in order to prevent racial discrimination. Quintin Ellison and Tonya Maxwell, "DMV Officers Appear before Grand Jury," *Asheville Citizen-Times*, June 5, 2002; Andrea Weigl, "Judge Finds Bias at DMV," *News and Observer*, October 2, 2002.

88. "Organization and Functional Overview, North Carolina Department of Transportation," informational notebook for NCDOT board members (Raleigh: North Carolina Department of Transportation, January 2001), 5-1, 5-2, 5-3; "Division of Motor Vehicles," *www.ncdot.org* (NCDOT website).

89. Len Hill, deputy administrator for preconstruction, Division of Highways, NCDOT, telephone conversation with author, May 14, 2001.

90. "Organization and Functional Overview," 2-1; Myra Fulmer, management analyst, NCDOT, telephone conversation with author, January 12, 2001.

91. Richard Weingroff, e-mail to author, December 3, 2002. The statistics are for the year 2000.

92. "Yearly Motor Vehicle Registration" (unpublished fact sheet, Division of Motor Vehicles, NCDOT, 2001). The cars-to-persons ratio includes people such as children and the elderly, who do not hold driver's licenses.

93. "Organization and Functional Overview," 4A-9; Paul Muschick, "N.C. Gains 13th Seat in Congress," *News and Record*, December 29, 2000.

Chapter 6

EXPLORING ALTERNATIVES
into the future

When the North Carolina Department of Transportation (NCDOT) was getting started in 1973 as part of a massive reorganization and consolidation of state agencies, it consisted of a dominant highway program, a growing ferry system, and the beginnings of multimodal programs to address bicycle, airport, and public transportation issues. The agency's first long-range plan, *North Carolina Highways: A Seven Year Highway Improvement Program, July 1973 thru June 1980,* was published that year. Also in 1973, the North Carolina Department of Administration released a study calling for a transportation infrastructure to boost economic development. The report concluded that if the state sought to create an adequately coordinated transportation system to underpin and help shape the direction of that development, then all transportation modes must receive equal treatment at all planning levels.[1] Consequently, the challenge faced by the NCDOT was not only to develop and fund appropriate multimodal programs but also to integrate them with the existing highway program.

In 1973-1974 Americans faced a recession and, as a result of turmoil in the Middle East, long lines to buy higher-priced gasoline—reminders that alternatives to the automobile were needed. Although the state's Highway Fund had long supported a ferry program, other multimodal activities had less secure funding. Bicycle and rail programs at first received modest support from the Highway Fund. Aviation and public transportation programs were tied to federal revenues designated for such programs. Moneys for public transportation programs (principally municipal bus systems) were supplemented by the state's Highway Fund, aviation programs by the General Fund.

Gas lines in North Carolina during oil crisis of 1973-1974. Courtesy James Barringer, *Salisbury Post.*

State and federal funding for multimodal programs began to grow by the late 1980s and 1990s. David King, NCDOT deputy secretary for transit, has been the single most important leader in patiently building those programs within the state, often working behind the scenes.[2] In order to support such new transportation-related initiatives, Congress created an enhancement (unrelated to highway construction) program as part of its 1991 highway and transportation legislation, the Intermodal Surface Transportation Efficiency Act (ISTEA). Enhancement funds helped underwrite bicycle and rail programs, and the General Assembly increased funding for other multimodal programs. Gov. James G. Martin's two administrations (1985-1993) aided the growth of these programs; NCDOT secretary Jim Harrington was especially helpful in finding more permanent funding for them. During his first term (1977-1981), Gov. James B. Hunt Jr. had boosted rural public transportation. During his third and fourth terms (1993-2001), he strongly advocated all multimodal programs, especially intercity rail service.

The escalating pace of highway construction in the 1990s created a more urgent need for multimodal programs. North Carolina was the nation's ninth-fastest-growing state during that decade. Although growth occurred throughout the state, it was especially dramatic in Charlotte, the Research Triangle (the Raleigh/Durham/Cary/Chapel Hill area), and the Triad (Greensboro/Winston-Salem/High Point) regions. According to a survey by the American Lung Association, Charlotte had the nation's eighth-worst ozone pollution, the Triangle had the eleventh, and the Triad the twenty-fifth. The main contributor to the air-pollution problem was the number of vehicles on the roads, which had doubled during the preceding thirty years.[3]

Brent McKinney, executive director of the Piedmont Authority for Regional Transportation, based in the Triad, sees an uphill battle for acceptance of public transportation. "The problem is our rural mentality, so closely attached to the automobile," McKinney surmises. "Even people in cities are usually only one generation removed from rural areas."[4] Nationally, the term "public transportation" often pertains to trains as well as buses, and, indeed, the Rail and Public Transportation Divisions of the NCDOT have the largest budgets of the multimodal programs. (The Division of Aviation is active in encouraging growth of passenger service at airports, and the Division of Bicycle and Pedestrian Transportation encourages walking and the use of bicycles.)

Nevertheless, 75 percent of the 2000-2001 NCDOT budget of approximately $3 billion was spent on highways. Although multimodal operations, like highways, attained division-level status within the NCDOT organization, such activities received only 6 percent of the agency's budget and accounted for but 3 percent of its staff. On the other hand, multimodal programs were imminently successful in attracting federal dollars to the NCDOT. As the table below indicates, fully 40 percent ($70 million) of the NCDOT's total funding for multimodal programs in 2000-2001 ($173.5 million) came from the federal government. The following table summarizes funding for the multimodal budgets in the 2000-2001 fiscal year.[5]

State senator Wib Gulley (left) and NCDOT deputy secretary David King discuss ways to strengthen multimodal transportation programs, such as services provided by buses, vans, rail, mass transit, and bicycles.

TABLE 3
Summary of 2000-2001 Budgets for NCDOT Multimodal Programs
(in Millions of Dollars)

DIVISION	HIGHWAY FUND	HIGHWAY TRUST FUND	GENERAL FUND	NCDOT RECEIPTS	FEDERAL FUNDS	TOTAL
Ferry	18.2			1.5	.75	20.5
Bicycle	5				3	8
Pedestrian						
Aviation			11.6		15.5	27.1
Public Transport.	42.7				21.8	64.5
Rail	19.5	5			28.9	53.4
TOTALS	85.4	5	11.6	1.5	70	173.5

Source: NCDOT

Ferry Division

When Hurricane Floyd hit eastern North Carolina in September 1999, Candice Boyd, a junior at East Carolina University in Greenville, knew she had to get home to her family in Bath. "The electricity was cut, the water was contaminated, and I'd lost everything in my apartment," she recalled. But she couldn't travel the usual route home, because the bridge over the Pamlico-Tar River and portions of U.S. 264 were closed. So she managed to drive down N.C. 33 on the south side of the Pamlico River and make her way to the Bayview-Aurora ferry. When she saw the long line of cars waiting to board, she parked her Ford and walked onto the ferry. "The crew was really nice," she said. Meeting emergencies during hurricanes is just one of the duties of the NCDOT's Ferry Division.[6]

Privately operated ferries have played a vital role in North Carolina since the colonial era, especially at river crossings where there were no bridges. As the State Highway Commission constructed bridges throughout the state in the 1920s and 1930s, many of those independent ferries disappeared. In the mid-1920s, Capt. J. B. "Toby" Tillett operated a private ferry on the Outer Banks at Oregon Inlet. The Highway Commission first became involved in ferry service in 1934 by subsidizing Tillett's business as a means of keeping tolls reasonable, then eliminated the tolls in 1942, and

Cars entering privately owned ferry in the 1920s.

Carteret ferry with Ocracoke Island and lighthouse in background.

finally acquired the business outright in 1950. In 1947 the commission purchased and operated the business of T. A. Baum, whose ferries traversed the Croatan Sound, linking Manns Harbor (U.S. Highway 64) to Roanoke Island and Manteo. That same year, the agency organized a new ferry service across the Alligator River, linking U.S. Highway 64 between Tyrrell and Dare Counties.[7]

In 1955 those three ferry operations, together employing nine ferryboats, accommodated 198,000 vehicles and 453,000 passengers at a cost of $215,000. All repair work and rebuilding of engines was done by workers at the commission's shipyard in Manns Harbor, which included a marine runway used to pull boats from the water. The biggest problems of the ferry service were shallow water, tides, winds, and shifting shoals at Oregon Inlet. Within a few years, bridges replaced all three ferries. The commission completed the paving of N.C. Highway 12 to the town of Hatteras by 1953, the same year Frazier Peele opened a ferry service connecting Hatteras and Ocracoke Island. Four years later, the state purchased Peele's ferry.[8]

In 1960 the State Highway Commission established a separate ferry office in Manteo, headed by D. W. Patrick. Prior to that time, highway division offices operated the state's ferries. In 1964 the commission moved the office to its present headquarters in Morehead City. During the 1960s, ferry services experienced their biggest expansion. In 1961 the commission began operating the ferry *Sea Level*, replacing a private ferry on a two-and-one-half hour run from the southern tip of Ocracoke Island to the mainland town of Atlantic. Soon thereafter, the port was switched from Atlantic to Cedar Island at N.C. Highway 12. This was the first toll ferry route, and the first lengthy one, operated by the State Highway Commission.

In 1961 the ferry program began operating ferries to link N.C. 58 across Bogue Sound in Carteret County, enabling motorists to reach

Emerald Isle and Atlantic Beach from the west end of Bogue Banks. Additional ferry service soon commenced to link Knotts Island with Currituck via Currituck Sound in the northeastern corner of the state (1962), Southport and Fort Fisher across the mouth of the Cape Fear River below Wilmington (1965), and Aurora and Bayview across the Pamlico River on N.C. Highway 306 in Beaufort County (1966). All of those ferries are still in operation. The Knotts Island-Currituck ferry carries 130 schoolchildren and county workers daily from Knotts Island to the mainland, allowing them to avoid a long commute through Virginia. The Aurora-Bayview ferry transports workers by way of N.C. 306 to a major phosphate mining and chemical company on the south side of the Pamlico River, which keeps the workers from driving sixty miles daily. By 1970 the ferry program was operating six ferries and attracting two million riders annually. Bogue Sound ferry, the state's busiest, was superseded by a bridge the following year. A ferry across the Neuse River, also on N.C. 306, between Minnesott Beach in Pamlico County and Cherry Branch, near Cherry Point Marine Corps Air Station, was added in 1972. By 1977 the ferry program (now the Ferry Division within the NCDOT), operating on a budget of $500,000, had added a ferry route between Swan Quarter in Hyde County and Ocracoke. For much of that trip across Pamlico Sound, passengers lose sight of land.[9]

When Jim Harrington became NCDOT secretary in 1985, he found that half of the department's ferries were obsolete.[10] He initiated the purchase of new, modern vessels, as well as a staff reorganization of Manns Harbor to allow better maintenance and repair of all the ferries. In the early 1990s Secretary Tommy Harrelson asked David King, who was already responsible for the public transportation and rail programs, to over-

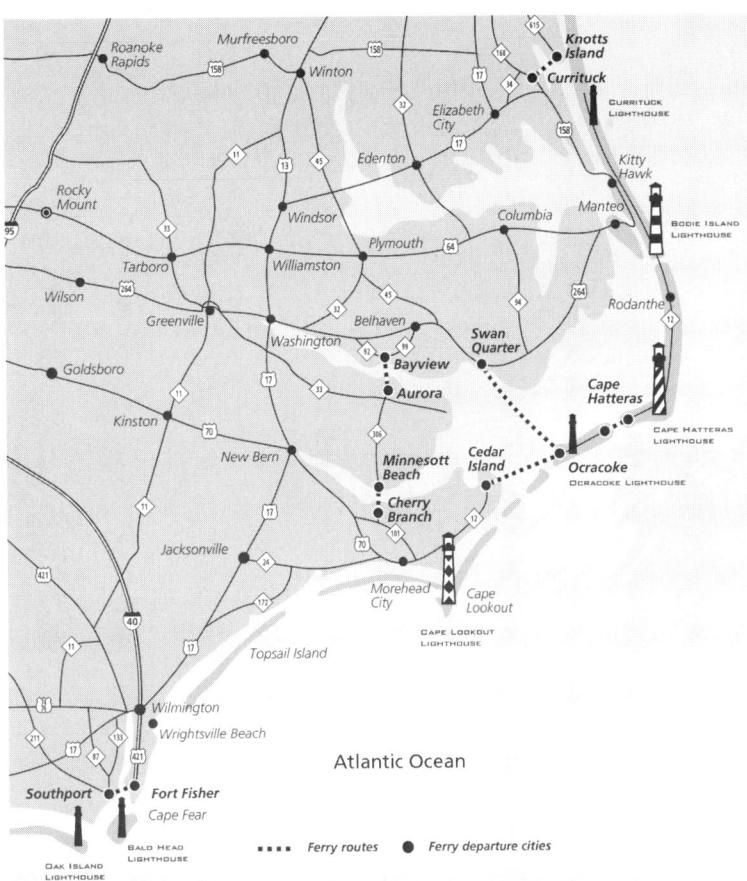

The NCDOT, with twenty-four ferries on seven routes in eastern N.C., operates the second-largest ferry system in the nation; the state of Washington has the largest. Map courtesy NCDOT; adapted by Jeffrey E. Plowman.

see ferries. At the time, ferry employees were too often hired because of political influence. After Governor Hunt began his third term, the NCDOT hired Jerry Gaskill in 1993 to reform the Ferry Division. Since becoming the division's director, Gaskill, who had been a managing partner in several businesses in eastern North Carolina, has expanded ferry services and improved employee morale. Gaskill soon set about to acknowledge the state's pride in its colleges. He arranged for each ferry to recognize a different North Carolina college by featuring that respective institution's logo and school colors prominently on the vessel's sides. Each of the sixteen colleges in the University of North Carolina system and eight private colleges is represented.[11]

In 2002 North Carolina operated twenty-four ferry vessels on seven routes, with an average speed of ten knots. The system, which transported 792,000 vehicles in 1993, now carries more than 1 million vehicles and 2.5 million passengers each year. For passenger convenience, Ocracoke, Cedar Island, and Hatteras include visitor centers. Passengers can make toll-free telephone reservations for ferries leaving Ocracoke, Cedar Island, and Swan Quarter. Several vessels and terminals sell ferry-related gift items. The Hatteras-Ocracoke ferry, which carries 40 percent of the system's overall traffic, often adds extra runs during the summer tourist season. The infrastructure at Hatteras includes three ferry landings and a football-field-size lot with eight lanes for waiting vehicles.[12]

Manns Harbor Shipyard, operated by the Ferry Division and renovated in 1989, is a fourteen-acre complex situated a few miles west of Manteo. The full-service facility maintains a dredge, tugboats, and various support equipment to ensure that thirteen ferry locations are dredged to at least eight feet deep; it also conducts contract work for towns and state government.

The state's Highway Fund is the main source of funding for the Ferry Division ($18.2 million in 2000-2001), with tolls bringing in about $1.5 million per year. The division has constructed seven new ferryboats in the 1990s with federal discretionary funding. Administratively, ferry services were part of the highway program until they became a separate NCDOT division in 1975. The Ferry Division has a year-round staff of 350 (fifty fewer than in 1993), which includes 15 at its Morehead City headquarters, 78 at Manns Harbor, and 257 with ferry operations. During the summer months, an additional 120 full-time employees are hired.[13]

The division operates the second-largest ferry system in the nation. Although the state of Washington maintains about the same number of vessels as does North Carolina, its ferryboats are substantially larger in order to carry greater numbers of commuters to Seattle and other locations. Whether accommodating commuters, schoolchildren, tourists, or those trapped by hurricanes, the NCDOT Ferry Division is safely transporting people where they need or want to go.[14]

Jerry Gaskill (right) talks with Bobby Hill, operations manager for the Ferry Division. Since becoming director of the ferry program in 1993, Gaskill has improved services and morale without increasing the staff's size.

Division of Bicycle and Pedestrian Transportation

Curtis Yates got to practice what he preached. While a planner for the North Carolina Department of Administration in the early 1970s, he wrote a forty-six-page paper, "Bikeways for North Carolina: Bicycle Program Requisites." The study not only documented the need for a state-sponsored bicycle program in North Carolina but also included a draft legislative bill to make selected roads safer for bicycle use. In January 1974 the study was published, and Yates came to the NCDOT as bicycle coordinator to initiate the program—in effect to implement a concept that he had helped to create.[15] With the assistance of state senator McNeill Smith, who regularly biked to his law office in Greensboro, the Bicycle and Bikeway Act passed the General Assembly that spring. The following year Yates hired as an assistant Mary Meletiou (now program manager), who had toured the nation on a bicycle.[16]

The main goals in that period were to promote safety for bicyclists and to develop bikeways, as well as practical and attractive bike-related facilities. The safety goal stemmed from North Carolina's having one of the highest bicycle accident and death rates in the U.S. The term "bikeways" in the second goal referred to specially built thoroughfares for bicyclists, which could be part of a highway or a separate trail. "Multi-use trails" are built for bicyclists, walkers, and skaters. The paved trails use relatively little space and respect the natural environment. They are called by different names, such as "greenways" (a system of paths near lakes, streams, or rivers) or "rail-trails" (trails comprised of former rail corridors).

At that time Greensboro, Winston-Salem, High Point, Burlington, Rocky Mount, and Chapel Hill, as well as Dare County, had local bicycle programs in the early stages of development. One of the NCDOT bicycle program's first projects was to designate a seven-hundred-mile "Mountains to the Sea" bicycle route along less traveled highways. It took a few more years, however, to add appropriate signage to designate these routes.[17]

By 1978 a North Carolina Bicycle Committee was appointed to advise and assist the program. Bicycle projects were first included in the department's long-range planning and funding program in *Transportation Improvement Program (TIP), 1979-1985*. It projected seven projects, including a series of bicycle highway maps. The first county bicycle map was published in 1983, and the first urban map appeared in 1991. When communities began requesting information on how to build multi-use trails for bicyclists, the bicycle program developed a guidebook on the development of bicycle facilities. The U.S. 401 bike path in Fayetteville, the first state-funded bikeway, opened in 1981.

In that same year, the NCDOT board adopted a policy "to consider and evaluate the need for bicycle facilities in conjunction with highway improvements, where sufficient existing and potential bicycle usage is evident."[18] Influencing the highway builders to include bike facilities as part of highways, a bigger challenge than building separate bikeways, was showing results by the mid-1980s. The board approved fourteen such projects for the 1986-1995 *TIP*—one for each highway division—using state and federal moneys from the Highway Fund. Those projects included bicycle lanes with re-striping, widened paved shoulders, off-road bicycle paths, widened curb lanes, and improvements to intersections. Several long bridges, especially along the coast, were built with wide shoulders and safety railings for bicyclists. By 2001 the Highway Fund furnished between five and fifteen million dollars each year through the *TIP*s for bicycle/pedestrian facilities related to highways.[19]

"Independent" bicycle projects (those not directly connected to construction of a specific highway), often locally initiated, provide a variety of opportunities, among them multi-use trails and improvements to bridges and roads. Beginning in 1987, the board approved a $250,000 annual budget from federal funds for such efforts. The first project was in Elizabeth City, where a paved shoulder was added to the road connecting Elizabeth City State University with the local U.S. Coast Guard base. Annual funding for independent bicycle projects was increased to $500,000 in 1988 and to $1 million two years later. The creation of the enhancement program in the ISTEA legislation of 1991 added stable funding and significantly boosted the independent projects. Annual enhancement funding for bicycle programs (80 percent federal and 20 percent state and local) increased from $2 million in 1992 to $6 million in 2002.[20]

In 1992 the NCDOT added a pedestrian component to the bicycle program to create the Office of Bicycle and Pedestrian Transportation. Within a few years $1.4 million was available every year for pedestrian projects ($100,000 for each of the fourteen highway divisions). Qualifying projects were usually sidewalks but could also be trails. In 1997 the Office of Bicycle and Pedestrian Transportation became a division of the NCDOT, adding prestige to the program. The small Division of Bicycle and Pedestrian Transportation (DBPT) currently has a staff of ten persons.[21] It has worked closely with the Rail Division to help create at least fourteen miles of rail-trails along former railroad corridors. The first ones were established in Carrboro, Greensboro, and Winston-Salem. In recent years rail-trails have been established in Lincolnton and Durham. Curtis Yates characterizes them as "urban trails, offering both recreation and transportation."[22]

Through cooperative projects with other groups, the DBPT took the leading role in design, funding, and implementation. The Lincolnton trail, a collaborative venture with the city, opened in 1998 and is a half-mile-long route through the heart of the town. Enhancement funds in the amount of $251,000, designated to the DBPT, provided the major funding.[23] In the Durham area, the American Tobacco Trail when completed will be a 23.5-mile rail-trail from downtown Durham southward into Chatham and Wake Counties. Its creation has involved a number of governments and private organizations. The DBPT has worked closely with the city of Durham in opening eight miles of the trail during 2000 and 2002. The DBPT relied upon $900,000 of enhancement funding; Durham expended both local and federal funds. More than fifty communities in the state are creating multi-use pedestrian and bicycle trails, many of which traverse unaltered natural terrain rather than former rail corridors.[24]

Each year, more than 35 bicyclists and 185 pedestrians are killed in North Carolina. Education is a key to overcoming this problem. Half of the state's school districts are already using the division's "Basics of Bicycling," a comprehensive curriculum for children in grades four and five. The 2001 General Assembly passed a law requiring helmets for all bicycle riders under sixteen years of age riding on public streets and roads. NCDOT secretary Lyndo Tippett was instrumental in securing funds to furnish helmets for safety-awareness programs throughout the state.[25]

At present, bicyclists can cover much of North Carolina by trails, highways, buses, trains, and ferries. Ten routes of bicycle highways in the state cover three thousand miles, most with appropriate signage. The Carolina Connection, which parallels U.S. 1, is part of a bicycle route that will connect Maine and Florida. The division to date has produced eight large urban maps and fifteen county maps to help riders find the best routes. For example, a recent map of High Point (which includes additional maps of surrounding towns) encompasses several regional bike routes, as well as information about signs, interaction with motorists, commuting, safety, and bicycle equipment.[26]

Winston-Salem was the first city in the state to place bicycle racks on the front of city buses for selected routes. Durham, Raleigh, Boone, Asheville, and the Triangle Transit Authority (serving Raleigh/Durham/Cary/Chapel Hill) likewise added this service. Aboard the state-owned Piedmont, a daily train operated by Amtrak between Raleigh and Charlotte, folding bikes can be stored in baggage shelves in each car at no charge. Boxed bikes, requiring removal of the front wheel and adjustment of the handlebar, are accepted on all Amtrak trains and can be checked along with other baggage. The NCDOT Ferry Division carries more than five thousand bikes each year. All seven ferry routes are connected to highways with bicycle facilities. A bicyclist can travel on historic N.C. Highway 12 from Whalebone (east of Manteo) southward to Cedar Island by completing two ferry rides.[27] Because of the Division of Bicycle and Pedestrian Transportation, North Carolina's bicyclists and pedestrians have better opportunities to move about the state in a safe and enjoyable manner.

Curtis Yates (left), who led the growth of the Division of Bicycle and Pedestrian Transportation for three decades, meets with NCDOT Secretary Tommy Harrelson.

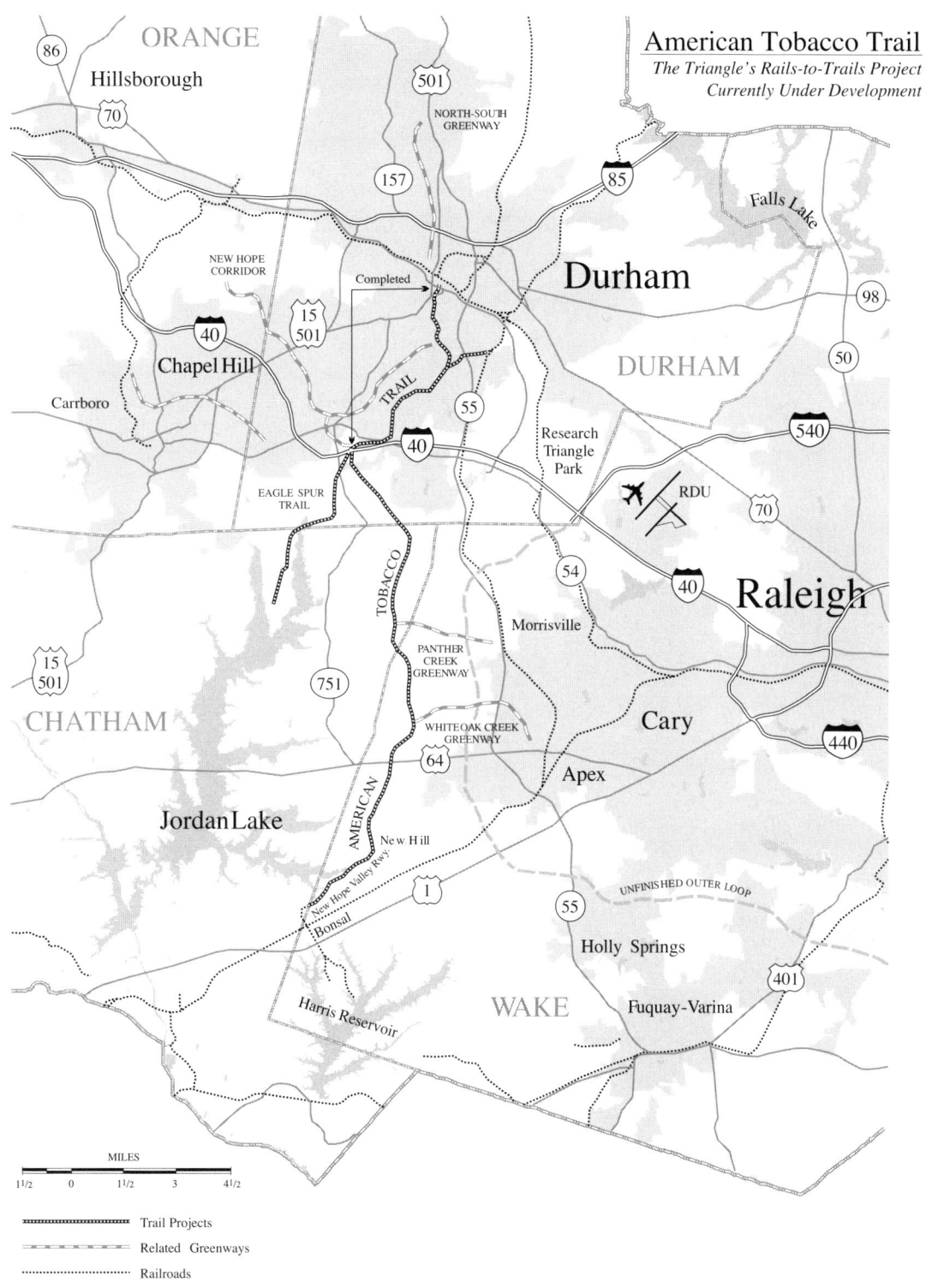

Eight miles of the American Tobacco Trail are open from downtown Durham southward. The trail will eventually cover twenty-three miles along a former railroad corridor. Map by Mark A. Moore, A&H.

Larry Sams, retired NCDOT official, rides on the American Tobacco Trail in Durham.

Division of Aviation

When Willard G. "Will" Plentl Jr. came to the NCDOT in 1973 to direct its new aviation program, he was a staff of one. When he left in 1997, the Division of Aviation staff of twenty-three had helped create new airports and expand existing ones.[28] The 1973 study "A Report on Transportation Needs in North Carolina" provided a summary of aviation at that time. There were then thirteen commercial airports in the state, providing regularly scheduled air service, and six military airports. The state had 154 significant general aviation facilities (42 publicly owned, 75 privately owned for public use, and 37 privately owned for private use).[29] Asheville, Charlotte, Fayetteville, Greensboro-High Point, and Raleigh-Durham airports accounted for 90 percent of passengers carried in the state. The report concluded that commercial airports and general aviation facilities would require capital improvements and expansions. Finally, the ground-breaking study recommended that the primary objective of long-range planning for airports should be "integration of the airport program into a coordinated, multimodal transportation system" to include municipal, regional, and state services.[30]

The NCDOT's aviation programs became the Division of Aeronautics in 1976; its name was later changed to the Division of Aviation. In 1978 aviation projects were included in the *TIP* for the first time. One of the major duties of the division was to administer the State Aid to Airports program, which began in 1967 to provide grants mostly to small airports. After consultation with the Aeronautics Council (eleven members appointed by the governor) and other groups, the division in 1979 approved grants totaling $1.9 million to forty-two airports. The money, some of which was matched with federal funds, was used for projects such as expansions of runways, terminal buildings, parking, and safety features. State grants of $3.4 million were made to fifty-one airports in 1984. Only nineteen of the grantees received federal aid, which went primarily to the large airports. In 1990 the Division of Aviation began administering the Federal Aviation Administration's (FAA) state bloc-grant program, which assured close coordination of funding for the state's general aviation airports.[31]

The Highway Division helped the Division of Aviation with safety features, such as tree clearing and runway markings, at selected airports. Additional projects of the Division of Aviation included educational programs for pilots and encouraging airports to offer instruction in approach capability and weather information. Congress passed the Airline Deregulation Act in 1978, allowing airlines more flexibility in setting their routes and fares. Piedmont Airlines responded to the resulting changes by growing faster, establishing a large hub at Charlotte/Douglas International Airport in the early 1980s. At the same time, the airline discontinued commercial service to Hickory, Winston-Salem, Rocky Mount, Elizabeth City, and Pinehurst; some of those cities were able to substitute commuter services. American Airlines established a hub at Raleigh-Durham in 1987.

The NCDOT worked with the Charlotte and Raleigh areas to plan "reliever" airports, designed to provide alternative airports nearby for personal and business aviation. New airports were built at Concord, Sanford, Louisburg, and Roxboro for that purpose. In a 1986 interview, Will Plentl cited the "excellent service" then being provided by smaller carriers such as Henson Airlines, CCAIR, Atlantic Southeast, Eastern Metro Express, and others as positive results of deregulation.[32] As an example, at Pitt-Greenville Airport the number of passengers carried by CCAIR, a regional carrier in the Piedmont Airlines system, more than doubled in one year. American Airlines began serving Fayetteville, and United added Wilmington flights, giving those airports a boost.

In the late 1980s NCDOT Secretary Harrington pushed for the Division of Aviation to have a dependable source of permanent funding. The 1987 General Assembly, with strong leadership from Rep. Robert C. Hunter of McDowell County and others, enacted landmark legislation tying state aid to airports to the annual tax revenues of aviation users. All aviation goods and services were made subject to the state sales tax. While reviewing revenues, the 1993 General Assembly implemented a formula under which aviation funding would grow at the same rate as the state's General Fund revenues. With that modification in place, the state began providing long-term growth in appropriations for airport development. For fiscal year 2000-2001, the Division of Aviation budget was $27.1 million ($15.5 from federal funds and $11.6 from the state's General Fund).[33]

In a 1986 interview, Plentl evinced a considerable degree of prescience by projecting a need for as many as twenty-four new airports in North Carolina to complete the state's general-aviation airport system.[34] When Plentl left office in 1997, precisely twenty-four new airports were completed or under construction. In assessing the progress of the division, Plentl gave credit to Bruce Matthews and the Aviation staff. Plentl recalled that Matthews, who died in 2000, "was a brilliant young man who loved aviation and airports."[35] Bill Williams was appointed director of the NCDOT Division of Aviation in 1998, bringing with him years of experience in strengthening national aviation standards at the FAA.[36]

Airports and aviation activity have grown at a rapid pace in the past three decades. The state's largest and busiest airport is still Charlotte/Douglas (US Airways has expanded the hub begun by its predecessor, Piedmont), followed by Raleigh-Durham (with a growing Southwest Airlines presence to replace the former American Airlines hub).[37] In 1993 and 1994 the NCDOT collaborated with the North Carolina Department of Commerce to encourage increased tourism between North Carolina and Europe. That initiative was one factor that ultimately led to expanded nonstop service from Raleigh-Durham and Charlotte to and from European destinations. Next in airport size is Piedmont Triad, serving the Greensboro/Winston-Salem/High Point area; a Federal Express sorting hub will open there by 2007. Asheville, Wilmington (which opened a new terminal in 1990), and Fayetteville form a second tier of airports. Still others that continue to receive passenger service include Greenville, Jacksonville, and New Bern. Several cities previously served by Piedmont Airlines—Winston-Salem, Hickory, Pinehurst, Kinston, Rocky

Under Will Plentl, the NCDOT's Division of Aviation helped create twenty-six airports.

Dare County Regional Airport in Manteo, one of several small airports that have received state and federal funds from the NCDOT.

Mount, Goldsboro, Morehead City, and Elizabeth City—no longer receive any passenger service.

There was another side to the growth of the state's largest airports, especially at Raleigh-Durham. A local business magazine predicted in early 2000 that the advent of passenger service provided by Southwest Airlines out of Raleigh-Durham, combined with faster and more efficient highways, would probably result in the demise of a number of small eastern North Carolina airports.[38] Indeed, since that time, passenger service has been discontinued at several such facilities. Nevertheless, the state's growth in air travel continues and currently includes increasing numbers of small aviation facilities, presently consisting of 67 public airports, 3 public heliports (including one at North Carolina State University), and about 300 private airfields.[39]

Public Transportation Division

During the 1889-1920 period, small electric utility companies or their subsidiaries built electric streetcar systems in several North Carolina towns and cities. As Charlotte-based Southern Power Company—which subsequently became Duke Power Company—and Raleigh-based Carolina Power and Light Company (CP&L—now Progress Energy) expanded in the early twentieth century, they purchased smaller utilities that included streetcar systems. Later, when operating streetcars became unprofitable in the 1920s and 1930s, the large utility companies replaced streetcars with buses. CP&L sold its bus systems in the mid-twentieth century, while Duke Power continued to operate its systems in the state for several more years.[40] The bus systems reached their peak during the 1950s. Between 1964 and 1969 the number of buses operating in the state's cities declined by 31 percent. After that time, increased car ownership, urban sprawl, rising operating costs, and cutbacks in service almost led to the demise of bus service in the state.[41]

To address such problems, the 1973 "Report on Transportation Needs in North Carolina" recommended establishing regional institutions with taxing authority; it further suggested that the state furnish funding and transit planning staff to assist local programs. The report concluded that the poor, the unemployed, the elderly, the handicapped, and especially the young needed bus or van transportation. Rather than declining services, the problem in rural areas was one of having little or no transportation services at all. Meeting rural needs would not be as financially feasible as responding to those of urban areas. Finally, the study recommended establishment of intermodal transfer facilities to maximize passenger transfers between modes, such as scheduled trains and buses.[42] In response, the NCDOT organized the Public Transportation Division (PTD) in 1974 with a mission "to provide technical assistance and state grant funds for the improvement of all forms of surface public transportation." David Robinson was appointed director.[43]

Governor Hunt in 1978 initiated an agreement between NCDOT and the Department of Human Resources. The Governor's Committee on

Rural Public Transportation began planning to meet rural needs. The PTD was included in the NCDOT's seven-year *TIP* for the first time. Two years later the PTD, working closely with large companies, organized 180 vanpools. That development helped commuters during peak traffic congestion in an energy-efficient way.[44]

In 1978 seventeen of the state's fifty-six "urban" areas (with populations greater than ten thousand) had bus systems, which transported 23 million riders each year. That year, the PTD administered state grants totaling $664 thousand for twenty-three projects, which provided part of the necessary non-federal share to attract $5.3 million in federal funds. The funds were used for planning and capital improvements, such as buying buses and contributing to building or renovating bus stations and maintenance facilities. By 2001 the state's eighteen urban and regional bus systems carried a total of 36 million passengers annually.

By the early 1990s, Duke Power Company sold its bus systems in Durham and Greensboro, completing the transition of city bus systems from private to public control. Although all of the urban bus systems in the state are now owned by city governments and/or public transportation authorities, eight cities currently contract management of their bus systems to private companies. The major reason is that much of the systems' labor force, primarily drivers, is unionized, and in some cases dispatchers and mechanics are unionized as well. State law prevents municipalities from engaging in collective bargaining.

In 1982 Congress passed the Bus Regulatory Reform Act, which deregulated the intercity bus industry and allowed Greyhound, Trailways, and smaller companies to discontinue unprofitable routes. At that time, intercity bus routes served 352 towns and cities in North Carolina, but that

Downtown Greensboro, showing three Duke Power Company buses in 1930 and the Jefferson Standard Building at left. During the 1920s and 1930s, buses replaced streetcars in many N.C. towns and cities. Photo courtesy Duke Energy Archives.

service declined to only 100 destinations by 2002. The PTD has provided financial assistance to enable transportation companies to provide bus service to selected rural areas. Those routes connected Manteo and Norfolk, Asheville and Charlotte, Boone and Charlotte, and Raleigh and coastal destinations. The division continues to evaluate potential bus routes to receive financial assistance.[45]

The PTD began receiving dedicated funding in 1987—50 cents from each vehicle registration. The sum amounted to at least $2.5 million for the division each year, allowing it to plan multi-year projects as part of the *TIP* process. From 1985 to 1990, total state funding for the Public Transportation Division grew from $1.6 million to $4.7 million.[46]

The 1989 General Assembly appropriated $2 million from the Highway Fund for a new transportation initiative for the elderly and disabled. The moneys were distributed to counties in a way that would add to rather than replace existing funds. By 1992 ninety-two counties were participating in the program.[47] In the late 1990s counties developed community transportation programs primarily for persons whose transportation needs were not already met by human service agencies. The counties also took measures to assist welfare recipients (or former welfare recipients) with transportation to employment and medical care.

David King was promoted from administrative coordinator to director of the Public Transportation Division in 1979 and continued as director in 1990, when the division's name was changed to Public Transportation and Rail Division. By 1994 the division split into the Public Transportation Division (directed by Sanford Cross until 2002, with twenty-one full-time positions) and the Rail Division (directed first by Bob Grabarek, then Pat Simmons, with six positions), and King became the NCDOT's deputy secretary for transit, rail, and aviation.[48]

Cross and Simmons realized that their programs needed increased funding in order to address public transportation needs. They discussed the matter with King and NCDOT secretary Sam Hunt. Secretary Hunt indicated that documentation was needed to justify more support and funding, similar to the way Secretary Harrington's booklet, *Planks, Pavement and Progress*, had justified the need for the Highway Trust Fund in the late 1980s. In 1995 Gov. Jim Hunt signed an executive order appointing twenty-three prominent North Carolinians, including six members of the General Assembly, to a committee to develop and implement a master plan for public transportation initiatives; Hunt appointed Thomas K. Hearn, president of Wake Forest University, to serve as committee chairman.[49]

That prestigious committee issued *Transit 2001*, a comprehensive 133-page booklet, in 1997. Chairman Hearn introduced the report with an urgency "born of the conviction that we must address transit issues now before this window of opportunity closes." He further made the point that North Carolina "must have a transportation system which embraces various modes and alternatives if we are to move goods and people safely and conveniently."[50] As a result of the study, the 1997 General Assembly appropriated $26 million in state highway funds and $10 million in federal "flexible" or "transfer" highway funds (those able to be transferred from one agency or program to another) for public transportation. The appropriation allowed both the Public Transportation and Rail Divisions to double their annual budgets.[51]

Transit 2001 also endorsed a significant increase in transit availability within all urbanized areas with a population of fifty thousand or more.[52] The report further recommended that the Research Triangle Park and Charlotte areas "expand transit service to optimal levels by 2010" to include expanded bus service and the implementation of regional rail service.[53] The recommendation for the Triad area was to improve bus transit service and "develop initial phases of regional rail or busways [separate bus lanes] by 2010."[54] As advocated by *Transit 2001*, planning for all the systems' regional rail or busway projects has assumed that funding would be shared among federal (50 percent), state (25 percent), and local/regional (25 percent) governments.

Both the Triangle Transit Authority (TTA) and the Piedmont Authority for Regional Transportation (PART) are public transportation regional authorities with powers of eminent domain. TTA covers Wake (Raleigh and Cary), Durham (Durham), and

David King in 1980, when he headed the NCDOT's Public Transportation Division.

Orange (Chapel Hill) Counties. Citizens in those counties support the TTA by paying five dollars from each vehicle registration and 5 percent of gross receipts on rental cars. The first phase of the TTA's regional mass-transit system is designed to be a thirty-five-mile-long regional rail system linking Durham, the Research Triangle Park, Cary, and Raleigh, using self-propelled diesel trains. The system, projected to open by 2008, will include new tracks (generally within existing railroad right-of-way) and sixteen stations. Studies are being done to determine ways to connect both Chapel Hill and Raleigh-Durham International Airport in a second phase. In addition, the TTA already operates regional buses and a vanpool program. Until early 2002, the general manager (since the TTA's inception) was James M. Ritchey Jr., who had worked for the NCDOT's Public Transportation Division and the Winston-Salem Department of Transportation; the current general manager is John Claflin, who held senior management positions with the mass-transit systems of Portland, Oregon, and Denver, Colorado. The TTA's thirteen-member board includes ten representatives appointed by municipalities and counties and three appointed by the NCDOT secretary.[55]

PART covers Guilford (Greensboro and High Point), Forsyth (Winston-Salem), Alamance (Burlington), Randolph (Asheboro), Davidson (Lexington and Thomasville), and Rockingham (Reidsville) Counties, and the legislature has granted it authority to expand into six additional counties. Brent McKinney, longtime transportation director for the city of Winston-Salem, is executive director. The organization took over operation of the region's vanpool program and in 2002 implemented a regional bus system while continuing to study rail alternatives. The commissioners of both Forsyth and Guilford Counties gave PART permission to impose a tax of 5 percent of gross receipts on rental cars.[56]

In 1999 the city of Charlotte hired Ronald J. Tober, formerly head of transit systems in Seattle and Cleveland, to be director of the Charlotte Area Transit System (CATS). Tober and his staff develop recommendations and work plans for approval by the Metropolitan Transit Commission (MTC). The MTC oversees transit services for Mecklenburg County and the use of revenues derived from a voter-approved one-half-percent local-option sales tax in the county, which funds the local/regional share of the system. The MTC currently consists of voting representatives from the six incorporated towns within Mecklenburg County, as well as the city of Charlotte and county of Mecklenburg, and nonvoting regional representatives of neighboring counties and both the North Carolina and South Carolina departments of transportation.

Light-rail service between "uptown" Charlotte (which now refers to its central business district as "uptown" instead of "downtown") and the suburban southside town of Pineville is scheduled to begin by 2006. Like nearby Matthews, Pineville is a town with its own government but is now functionally a part of greater Charlotte. CATS will begin constructing the line, one of five planned corridors for its regional mass-transit system, in late 2003. The system will also implement commuter rail service northward to Mooresville and light-rail service northeastward to the University of North Carolina at Charlotte. A streetcar service

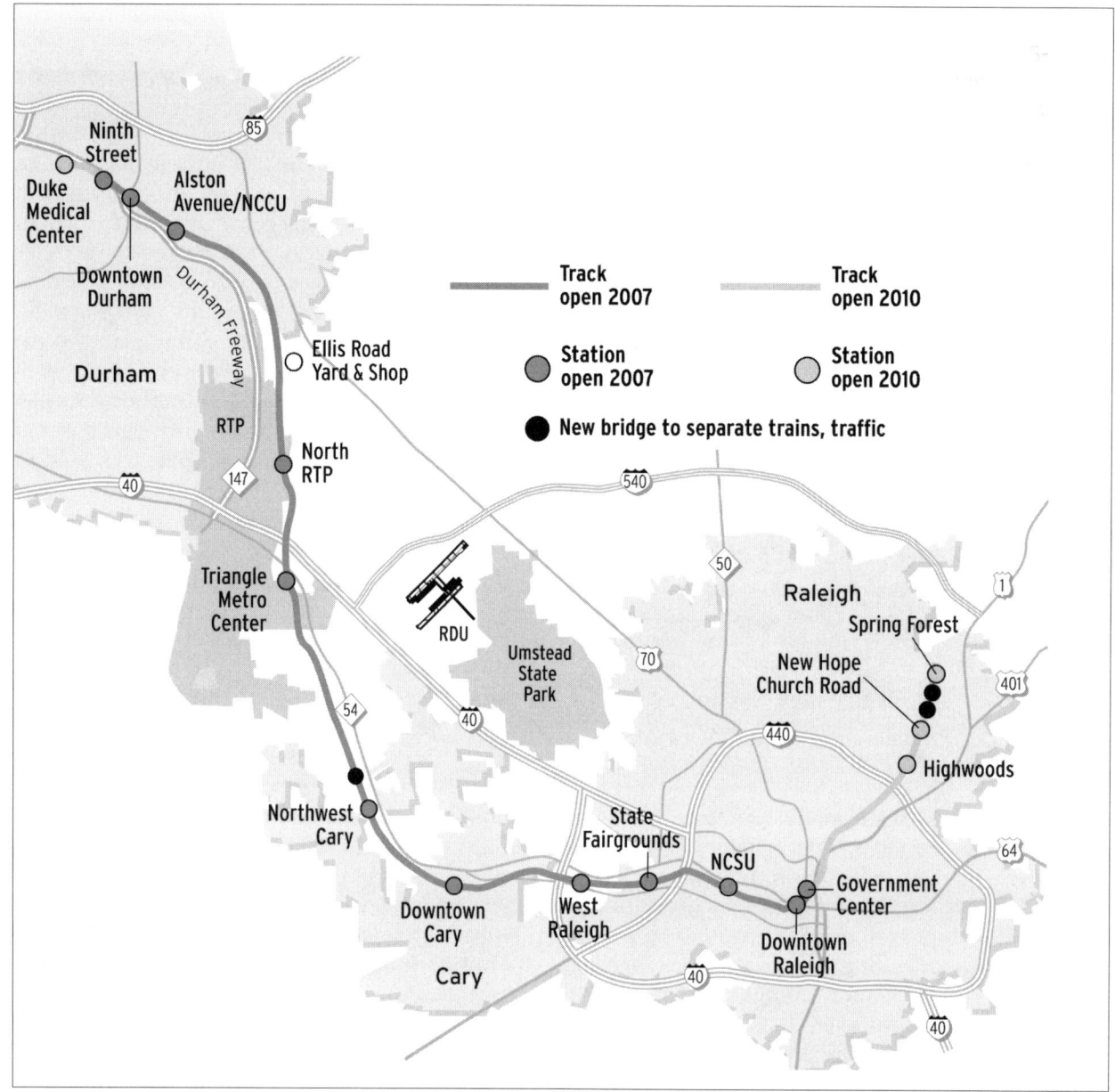

The Triangle Transit Authority (TTA) is close to final federal approval for a regional rail system to link Durham, Research Triangle Park, Cary, and Raleigh in the first phase. Map courtesy *News and Observer* (Raleigh).

will speed commuters through various uptown portions of the city and beyond. After CATS director Tober recommended the use of bus rapid transit southeastward via Independence Boulevard to Matthews and westward by way of Wilkinson Boulevard to the airport, leaders in Matthews, as well as in Charlotte's southeast and west-side neighborhoods, protested and lobbied for further consideration of light rail. Consequently, CATS will conduct additional studies, and final decisions concerning the type of service available via those two corridors will be delayed until 2005.[57]

Well-planned multimodal transportation centers are essential for mass-transit systems to succeed. In the late 1980s the PTD began to address the need for multimodal centers and mass transit.

The division assisted the city of Wilson in combining services provided by city buses, Greyhound, Trailways, and taxis and making them available in one location.[58] Both the NCDOT's Public Transportation Division and its Rail Division have been involved in planning multimodal transportation centers for Greensboro (where renovation and conversion of a railroad station into a center began in 2001), Charlotte and Durham (where sites have been chosen), and Raleigh. Each of those centers plans to connect at one site its city and regional bus systems, intercity buses (Greyhound/Trailways), Amtrak, and commuter/light rail. Wilmington is considering two adjacent sites for its transportation center that could accommodate both rail and bus services.

Mike Kozak, the PTD's assistant director for metropolitan transportation, says that the NCDOT's major role in the mass-transit systems is providing planning and funding assistance. For these systems to succeed, state government support is critical, especially in dealing with the high cost of implementation of facilities such as light rail, commuter rail, and busways. "It will be around 2003 or 2004 when the Charlotte and TTA projects move from planning and environmental documentation to buying right-of-way, construction, and purchase of equipment," Kozak concludes.[59]

When the 2001 General Assembly authorized the NCDOT to transfer funds from the Highway Trust Fund for major maintenance projects, it also authorized such funds for public transportation—$20 million in 2001-2002, $25 million in 2002-2003, and $75 million in 2003-2004. NCDOT deputy secretary David King credits state senator Wib Gulley of Durham, state representatives James W. Crawford Jr. of Granville County and E. Nelson Cole of Rockingham County, and NCDOT secretary Lyndo Tippett for what he terms a "bold initiative."[60] The combination of traditional highway funds with highway trust funds guaranteed the state's 25 percent share of mass-transit funding for the Raleigh-Durham and Charlotte systems over the ensuing two and one-half years.

The Public Transportation Division's budget for 2000-2001 came mostly from the NCDOT's Highway Fund ($42.7 million), along with federal funds totaling $21.8 million, making a total division budget of $64.5 million. The division employed a staff of thirty-one in 2002. The PTD, presently headed by Miriam Perry, continues to support and strengthen bus and van transportation services throughout the state while helping to create mass-transit systems to meet the needs of growing metropolitan areas.

Miriam Perry, new director of the Public Transportation Division (PTD), chats with Danny Bridgers. For several years Bridgers, who works at the NCDOT, has driven fourteen other state workers daily in a TTA van between the Smithfield/Johnston County area and Raleigh. The PTD supports the TTA with finances and consultation.

Charlotte Area Transit System

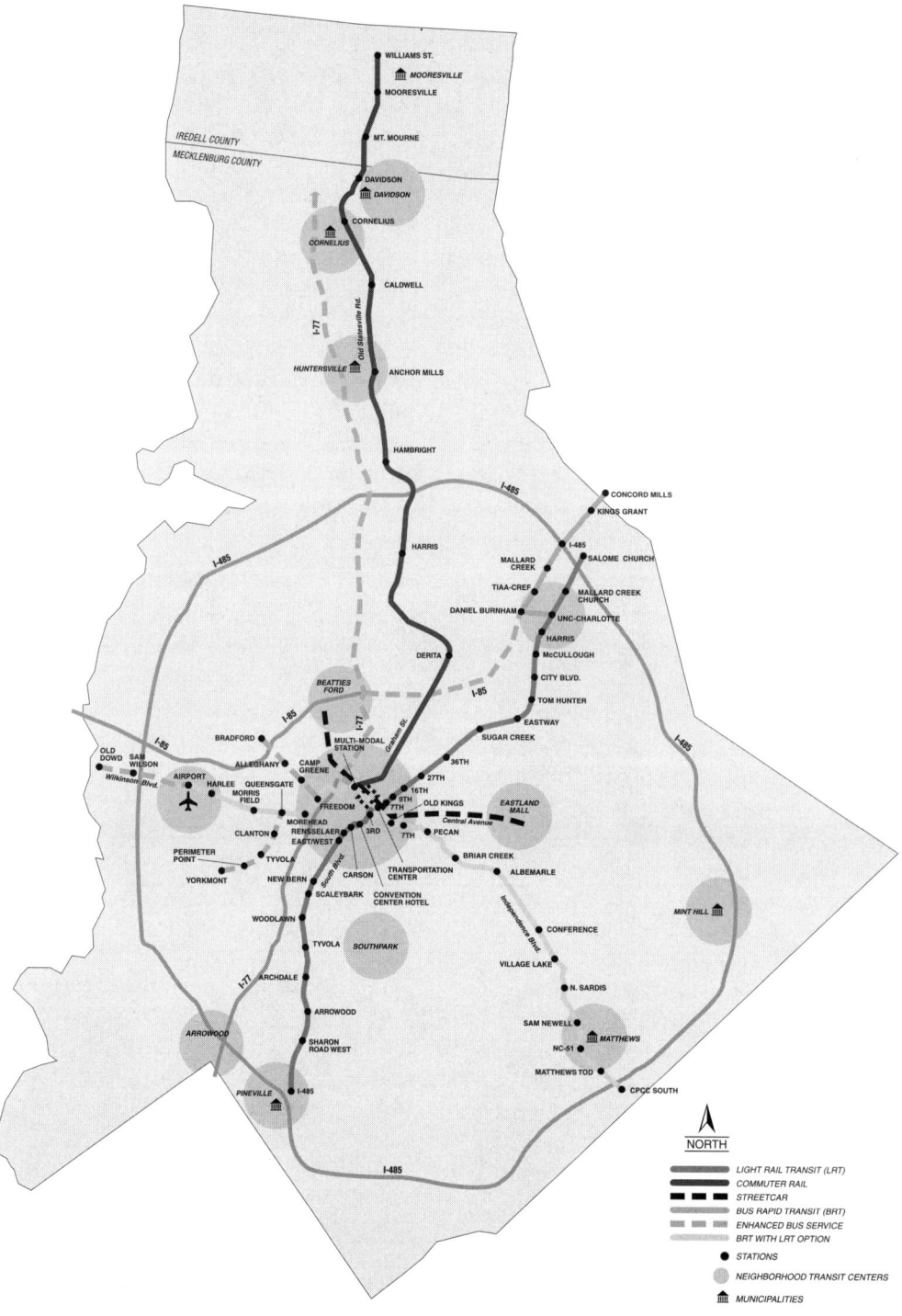

Charlotte is close to final federal approval for a mass-transit system that will utilize rail service, buses, and streetcars. Light-rail service on the eleven-mile corridor between Pineville and Charlotte's central business district is scheduled to open by 2006. Map courtesy Charlotte Area Transit System (CATS).

Rail Division

The nation's railroads experienced vast changes after World War II. Continuing rapid growth in the use of automobiles, trucks, buses, and aviation competed increasingly with railroads' passenger and freight services. By 1970, the railroads in the state were sustaining a loss of passenger patronage as a result of providing poor service and canceling services.[61] To address the problem of declining passenger service, President Richard Nixon initiated legislation, passed by Congress in 1970, establishing the National Railroad Passenger Corporation (Amtrak)—"a private corporation owned by the participating railroads but managed and funded, in part, by the Federal government."[62] The arrangement allowed railroads to abandon their money-losing long-distance passenger service. Congress subsequently passed the Staggers Act in 1980 to deregulate railroads. (Similar legislation had deregulated airlines in 1978). In 1982 the Norfolk & Western Railroad (based in Roanoke) and the Southern Railway (based in Washington, D.C.) merged to form Norfolk Southern Corporation, with headquarters in Norfolk. The Seaboard Air Line and the Atlantic Coast Line Railroads had merged in 1967 to form the Seaboard Coast Line Railroad. In subsequent mergers, the expanding company was known as Family Lines, the Seaboard System, and finally, in 1986, CSX.[63]

To further address the problem of railroads abandoning unprofitable passenger and freight lines, Congress passed the Rail Revitalization and Regulatory Reform Act in 1976. Three years later the NCDOT's Transportation Planning Division, which frequently dealt with multimodal issues, created the state's first comprehensive rail plan, which made North Carolina eligible for federal moneys to rehabilitate abandoned short lines. The NCDOT faced problems caused when private railroads, like the private companies that operated city bus systems, arbitrarily terminated or reduced important but unprofitable services to the state's communities. Since the mid-1970s, Norfolk Southern, CSX, and other merged railroads have continued to abandon rail lines that are unprofitable, adversely affecting industries and communities dependent on those lines.[64] The NCDOT has sought to reverse or at least slow the process. When a newly formed short line, the Aberdeen and Briar Patch Railroad, purchased the thirty-three-mile Star-Aberdeen rail line from Norfolk Southern, the NCDOT arranged about 1982 for state and federal funding to rehabilitate the tracks. The Aberdeen and Briar Patch was one of six short rail lines, serving eighteen communities, that the NCDOT helped save during the early 1980s.[65]

In 1988 the NCDOT purchased sixty-six miles of railroad tracks lying west of Asheville, between Dillsboro and Murphy, that Norfolk Southern had abandoned; the acquisition included the original station at Bryson City. The NCDOT leased the route to the Great Smoky Mountains Railroad (GSMR), a private firm, which began running popular excursion trains. (GSMR later returned to the

Greensboro's former Southern Railway station, built in 1927, is being renovated and converted into a multimodal transportation center to serve Amtrak, city and Greyhound/Trailways buses, and possibly mass transit. Photo courtesy Wingate Lassiter.

NCDOT the fourteen miles between Andrews and Murphy.) GSMR, purchased in 1999 by the operator of a scenic railroad in Colorado, attracts some 200,000 passengers annually and employs sixty full-time staff members.[66]

The NCDOT saw the need for additional passenger service in North Carolina and worked with Amtrak to plan a one-year trial of a new round-trip passenger train to connect Charlotte and New York City via Greensboro and Raleigh. The General Assembly appropriated $500,000 for that purpose, and the train, dubbed the Carolinian, began service in the fall of 1984. Although the train was drawing some nine thousand passengers a month, disagreements between Amtrak and the NCDOT led to the demise of the run after ten months. An additional factor in the demise of the Carolinian was competition from Piedmont Airlines and People Express, which offered cut-rate air fares to New York from both Greensboro and Raleigh.[67]

At that point, state officials nonetheless concluded that North Carolina had a clear need for increased passenger and freight rail services. But such services were costly. More than six hundred miles of tracks had been abandoned in the state between 1975 and 1985. By 1987 the NCDOT's railroad programs began receiving $100,000 in annual dedicated funding in the form of dividends from the state's ownership of the North Carolina Railroad. When the annual dividend was less than $100,000, General Fund moneys were added to bring the total up to that level. The General Assembly in 1989 created the Highway Trust Fund to expand funding for highways. The law included a provision that allowed the NCDOT to "use up to $5 million to develop economic transit alternatives to highway construction" each year. Also in 1989, Gov. Jim Martin's Governor's Rail Passenger Task Force recommended restoring train service between Charlotte, Raleigh, and New York. The available five million dollars from the Highway Trust Fund enabled the Carolinian service to be restored in 1990 and to continue since that time. The total number of passengers has increased from 124,000 in 1990-1991 to 185,000 in 2000-2001. The Carolinian has one of the best records among Amtrak trains for passenger fares meeting operating expenses.[68]

The Task Force recommended the establishment of daily passenger train service running east and west between Raleigh and Charlotte. Based on that recommendation, the NCDOT successfully collaborated with Amtrak to inaugurate the Piedmont, a new passenger train, in 1995. The train departs Raleigh each morning (as does the Carolinian, from Charlotte) with stops in Cary, Durham, Burlington, Greensboro, High Point, Salisbury, Kannapolis, and Charlotte. It then reverses its route for a return trip the same day. The trip currently takes about three hours and thirty minutes each way. The NCDOT owns the engines and rail cars of the Piedmont, although Amtrak operates the train. The Rail Division of the NCDOT also owns and operates a maintenance location in Raleigh, which provides cleaning, maintenance, and minor repairs. The number of passengers carried by the Piedmont increased from 25,000 in 1995-1996 to 53,000 in 2000-2001. In addition to the Carolinian and the Piedmont, the trains Amtrak operates through North Carolina include the Crescent (between New York City and New Orleans) and three New York-Florida trains (the Silver Meteor, the Palmetto, and the Silver Star). In 2000-2001 Amtrak carried 504,000 passengers to and from North Carolina. Of the sixteen Amtrak stations in the state, Charlotte is the busiest (115,000 passengers) with Raleigh (112,000) a close second.[69]

Adequate railroad stations are indispensable to improved rail service to the state. One of the responsibilities of the NCDOT Rail Division is to provide planning, project oversight, and funding for passenger railroad stations and multimodal transportation centers. The enhancement portions of the 1991 ISTEA and 1998 TEA-21 bills have provided $42 million in funding to restore several of the state's historic railroad stations. Those funds have been invaluable in providing attractive stations for passenger rail services. They also stimulate other restoration projects, reviving downtown areas in which the stations are located. (For additional details on station restorations, see the "Enhancement" section.)

The Rail Division worked with the town of Cary and the Triangle Transit Authority in planning the new Cary station, and the division furnished funds for the station's passenger platform alongside the tracks. The Cary station, opened in 1996, serves Amtrak, as well as regional buses sponsored by the TTA (and also houses a state driver license office). Large new multimodal transportation centers will be built in Charlotte and Raleigh; one will be created from a historic railroad station in Greensboro; one in Durham will be located in a former tobacco warehouse and in a new building. All will serve Amtrak and buses, and all (with the possible exception of Greensboro) will serve commuter rail. Charlotte, in consultation with the Rail Division, chose a downtown site between West Trade Street and Fourth Street for its center. In addition, new stations will be built in Gastonia (multimodal) and Kannapolis (rail). Burlington's historic enginehouse building, used by the North Carolina Railroad in the late 1800s, has been renovated for that city's rail station. Officials of the city of Winston-Salem and the Rail Division have recently discussed the possibility of establishing a multimodal facility at that city's former railroad station.[70]

The *Transit 2001* report declared that the state government needs to "establish clear responsibilities and authority for executing an aggressive, intercity rail passenger program."[71] To achieve that goal, the NCDOT and the state have overcome formidable challenges, including buying out minority stockholders of the North Carolina Railroad (NCRR); seeking the cooperation of Norfolk Southern and CSX; and finding the necessary funds for new technology, improved tracks, and elimination of grade crossings.

A century ago North Carolina agreed to a low-cost, ninety-nine-year lease to Southern Railway of the mainly state-owned North Carolina Railroad (which connected Goldsboro and Charlotte by way of Raleigh and Greensboro). When Norfolk and Western Railroad and Southern merged in 1982, the newly formed company, Norfolk Southern, assumed the lease. But there were still citizens—minority stockholders—who owned NCRR stock. The state bought out all of those minority stockholders for $71 million in 1998. The 2000 General Assembly then agreed that the NCRR, though wholly owned by the state, would remain a private corporation under the direction of former NCDOT secretary Sam Hunt

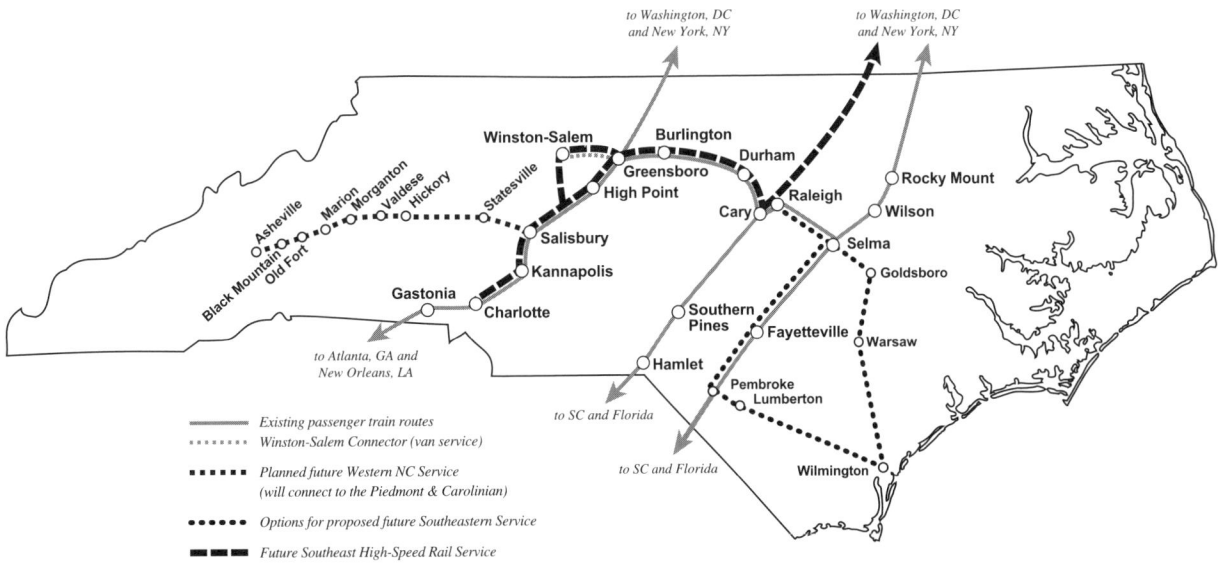

North Carolina Passenger Rail Service

This map shows present Amtrak routes, as well as a planned high-speed route and proposals to expand passenger service to Asheville and Wilmington. Map by Ellen Holding, NCDOT.

Governor Hunt, who supported increased passenger rail service, greets passengers on the inaugural run of the Piedmont in 1995. The NCDOT's funds and supportive services facilitate Amtrak's operation of this train between Raleigh and Charlotte.

rather than under the control of the NCDOT. In the meantime, the NCRR negotiated a new lease with Norfolk Southern.[72]

The NCDOT contracts with Amtrak to provide two trains—the Carolinian and the Piedmont—to travel a portion of the NCRR tracks, primarily between Raleigh and Charlotte. A trackage-rights agreement signed in 1999 allows Norfolk Southern to continue operating freight services on the NCRR. Since Norfolk Southern and CSX carry only freight, they often resist use of the same tracks by passenger trains—although that attitude could change as the state continues to fund track improvements. The state is spending $48 million for such renovation between Charlotte and Cary, which is expected to shorten passenger travel time between Raleigh and Charlotte by a half-hour.[73] The NCDOT has $24 million of this work under contract to be completed by 2004, including extending passing sidings, improving banking of curves, and realigning tracks at Greensboro's multimodal transportation station.[74]

Complicating improvement in rail service is North Carolina's large number of roads and streets that cross railroad tracks. When the state's roads were paved and expanded in the 1920s and 1930s, they often paralleled or crossed tracks. Although the main highways and urban expressways are now separated (bridged) to avoid tracks, a large number of grade crossings remain, even on the busy rail lines used by the freight railroads and Amtrak. In 2000 there were ninety-three collisions of vehicles with trains in the state, resulting in six deaths. The NCDOT eliminated thirty-three grade crossings between 1992 and 2001, despite resistance from towns and cities, and also made many other crossings safer.[75]

The NCDOT instituted the Rail Industrial Access Program in 1994 to create more jobs, especially in rural areas. In the first six years, the program assisted forty-five companies in financing railroad spurs to better transport raw materials or finished products. Those companies have invested $900 million in plant development or expansion, creating 5,600 jobs. Another benefit is reducing highway maintenance costs, inasmuch as the new freight can be transported by rail instead of truck.[76]

In 1992 the U.S. Department of Transportation designated five national high-speed rail corridors in the nation. The Southeast Corridor, originally linking Washington and Charlotte by way of Richmond and Raleigh, is considered the corridor with the greatest economic potential—one that would take in enough revenues to offset its expenses. After many public hearings, the USDOT chose a route that will connect Washington and Charlotte by way of Raleigh (but no longer via Rocky Mount or Wilson) and Greensboro, with a spur route to Winston-Salem. With the capability of handling train traffic at an average speed of eighty-five miles per hour and of enabling trains to complete a trip between Charlotte and Raleigh in only two hours and fifteen minutes, this segment is scheduled to be completed by 2010. USDOT extended planned routing for the Southeast Corridor by adding Charlotte-Atlanta and Raleigh-Jacksonville, Florida, segments. North

Carolina is the leading state in the Southeast in advocating and planning high-speed rail passenger service.

In 2001 the NCDOT completed a study of the feasibility of providing passenger rail service to western North Carolina. The study recommended restoring passenger trains between Salisbury and Asheville, a route discontinued in 1975. Amtrak receives more inquiries about service to Asheville than to any other city in the nation not presently served. Other factors favoring the plan are tracks that are in good condition and the need for only two new stations (Asheville and Valdese) out of eight potential stops. Federal TEA-21 enhancement (nonhighway) funds would pay for most of the renovations and related facilities required for historic stations at Statesville, Hickory, Morganton, Marion, Old Fort, and Black Mountain. Indeed, $2.4 million of the $5.87 million needed for initial station restoration is already earmarked in the *Transportation Improvement Program, 2002-2008*. In addition to development of rail service to Asheville, the NCDOT is also undertaking feasibility studies to determine routing and financing of possible Raleigh-Wilmington passenger service.[77]

The $53.4 million budget for the Rail Division in 2000-2001 is derived from nearly equal portions of state and federal revenues. It includes state moneys of $19.5 million from the Highway Fund and $5 million from the Highway Trust Fund, along with federal moneys in the amount of $17 million for grade crossings, $9.9 million in enhancement funds, and $2 million in flexible funds. The division has a staff of fifty. The efforts of the Rail Division are bringing a variety of new opportunities to the state, including expansion of intercity passenger service, preservation of freight service, and the creation of mass-transit options for urban areas.

Enhancement

Congress in 1991 passed the Intermodal Surface Transportation Efficiency Act (ISTEA), a comprehensive six-year highway/transportation bill that included enhancement funds for nontraditional transportation programs. Enhancement projects relate to environmental and quality-of-life issues, including "rail corridor preservation, historic preservation, bicycle and pedestrian facilities, scenic byways and landscaping."[78]

Kelly Fletcher, Miss North Carolina (with champagne bottle), and Scarlet Morgan, Miss Rocky Mount, dedicate Amtrak's Carolinian in Rocky Mount in 1990. The Carolinian, which runs between Charlotte and New York City, carried 185,000 passengers during the July 2000-June 2001 year.

Transportation officials in the individual states were authorized to administer the enhancement program in accordance with federal regulations. North Carolina was allocated $78 million for the 1991-1997 period. In North Carolina, ISTEA enhancement funded a total of $24 million in bicycle and pedestrian projects, $23 million in beautification and wildflower projects, $14 million for restoration of railroad stations serving Amtrak passengers, $12 million to preserve former railroad corridors for "rails to trails," and $4 million for scenic highways. The balance funded other departmental activities, such as the relocation and preservation of historic bridges, archaeological planning activities, and the acquisition of scenic vistas.[79]

Whit Webb, former NCDOT program development branch manager, recalls that one of the many problems he encountered in establishing the program was accurately estimating the cost of restoring train stations. It was likewise difficult to negotiate leases with the railroads for use of their stations. Such leases had to satisfy both the railroads and the contract terms required by the Federal Highway Administration. Acquiring right-of-way for bikeways and multi-use trails involved additional legal hurdles, especially in cases in which former rail corridors had reverted to adjoining landowners.[80]

One of the most important ISTEA-funded enhancement projects involved $5.8 million for renovation of the historic 1924 roundhouse and related improvements at the North Carolina Transportation Museum in Spencer, the former site of a Southern Railway maintenance and repair center. This project was a cooperative effort among the NCDOT, the North Carolina Department of Cultural Resources, and the museum's nonprofit support group, the North Carolina Transportation Museum Foundation. The 1996 opening of the roundhouse, the largest surviving example in the United States, placed the museum in the first tier of the nation's railroad-oriented museums. Since that time, the NCDOT has committed an additional $6 million of enhancement funds for the restoration of the museum's Back Shop, an enormous railroad building three stories high and the length of two football fields. The structure will be converted into an exhibit hall to tell the comprehensive story of the state's transportation development.[81]

Artist's drawing of future Back Shop exhibit hall at the North Carolina Transportation Museum at Spencer, N.C. Enhancement funds helped to fund initial renovation (to be completed in 2003) of a unique railroad building that is the length of two football fields and includes large windows and a skylight. Drawing courtesy N.C. Transportation Museum and N.C. Historic Sites.

The mission-style Salisbury depot was designed by architect Frank Milburn and constructed by Southern Railway in 1908. Its restoration was made possible by private funds provided by the Historic Salisbury Foundation and enhancement funds from the NCDOT.

In 1998 Congress passed a new six-year highway and transportation bill, the Transportation Equity Act for the 21st Century ("TEA-21"). The legislation strengthened the enhancement program, increasing North Carolina's allocation to $110 million for the 1998-2003 period. Laurie Smith, who took over the enhancement program in 1995, created an administrative structure to expand that program. The enhancement staff, which includes three project managers, designed an informative and colorful booklet titled *Transportation Enhancement Programs,* which offered examples of projects funded in the state in all eligible categories. By publicizing the availability of funds in 1999 and 2000 and organizing informational workshops throughout the state, the NCDOT provided additional opportunities for nonprofit organizations and local governments to apply for assistance. A citizens' enhancement advisory committee, representing a variety of the state's professions and groups, reviewed all applications, with the NCDOT Board of Transportation making the final selections. The $12 million in funding announced in 1999 (for implementation beginning in 2000) covered forty-seven projects. In 2000 the enhancement advisory structure was expanded to three regional committees (eastern, central, and western), as well as a statewide committee to consider the largest requests. The $22 million in assistance announced that year funded 114 projects (for implementation beginning in 2001 and 2002). In early 2003 the NCDOT designated additional moneys totaling $10 million to finance 104 projects.[82]

One of the initiatives announced in 2000 was for $259,000 to provide landscaping, sidewalks, a bike trail, and period streetlights at the Glencoe Mill Village near Burlington on the Haw River. A bicycle trail, located along a portion of the river, will connect an existing bike trail on N.C. 62 to downtown Burlington. Preservation North Carolina, a nonprofit organization, purchased the former textile mill and mill village (which operated from 1880 to 1954 and is listed on the National Register of Historic Places) and is now selling the houses to buyers who agree to restore them.

Among the most visible results of ISTEA and TEA-21 enhancement funding has been restoration of the state's historic railroad stations at a total cost of more than $22 million. The first such significant restoration project was the mission-style Salisbury depot, designed by renowned architect Frank Milburn and constructed by Southern Railway in 1908. The Historic Salisbury Foundation raised three million dollars, and the

The waiting room in the Rocky Mount train station, after renovation. Enhancement funds represented $7.3 million of the $9.5 million renovation project for the station, which opened in 2001.

NCDOT furnished an additional one million dollars in enhancement funds. The Wilson station, designed by A. M. Griffin and constructed by the Atlantic Coast Line Railroad in 1924, reopened in 1999. It features Flemish-style architecture with platform canopies, Spanish terra-cotta roof tiles, and a mural depicting the town's railroad history. The large Rocky Mount station, once a bustling hub for the Atlantic Coast Line Railroad, reopened to passenger traffic in 2001. Enhancement funds contributed $7.3 million to the $9.5 million project. The building includes an Amtrak ticket office on the ground level and new businesses on the second and third floors. The station, along with an adjacent landscaped square, is expected to help transform the city's historic downtown from an area of decline to one of economic activity.

During 2001, enhancement-funded restorations began at Selma ($2.7 million), High Point ($5.9 million), and Greensboro ($5.6 million). Greensboro's Southern Railway station will become the state's first urban multimodal transportation center and, as noted previously, will serve Amtrak, Greyhound, city buses, and possibly commuter rail. Alfred Fellheimer and Steward Wagner, nationally recognized New York City-based architects of urban railroad stations, designed the Neoclassical Revival Greensboro station in 1927. Hamlet's turn-of-the-century station, once a busy hub for the Seaboard Coast Line, features Queen Anne-style architecture. The station has been moved further from the tracks as a safety measure and is being restored with enhancement funding in the amount of $4.5 million.[83]

One of the Blue Ridge Parkway's long-range challenges is preserving its vistas by preventing inappropriate growth in adjacent areas. The enhancement program has funded four land purchases, totaling 553 acres, to protect the Parkway.[84] In addition, the program funded a one-mile scenic road connecting the Parkway to the North Carolina Arboretum, south of Asheville. (The road is named Frederick Law Olmsted Way in honor of the acclaimed landscape architect.)

"The enhancement program is creating and preserving treasures that can be enjoyed by future generations," concludes NCDOT official Laurie Smith.[85] Clearly, enhancement efforts and other alternatives to conventional highways are giving the NCDOT a wider range of options for transportation in a new century, which almost certainly will be characterized by increased population growth, environmental concerns, and energy shortages.

Notes

1. "A Report on Transportation Needs in North Carolina" (research report, Office of State Planning, North Carolina Department of Administration, 1973), 36.

2. King and his staff have received praise for their consistent advocacy and accomplishments in the face of relatively modest funding. *Transit 2001* (Raleigh: North Carolina Department of Transportation, 1997), foreword.

3. "Triad Air among Dirtiest in U.S.," *News and Record* (Greensboro), May 1, 2001.

4. Brent McKinney, telephone conversation with author, April 18, 2001.

5. "Organization and Functional Overview, North Carolina Department of Transportation," informational notebook for NCDOT board members (Raleigh: North Carolina Department of Transportation, January 2001), 2-1. Other portions of the NCDOT budget funded management and support, the Division of Motor Vehicles, and agencies also funded in part by the state's General Fund.

6. Candice Boyd, conversation with author, Spencer, N.C., April 10, 2001.

7. "The History of the N.C. Ferry Division, NC Department of Transportation" (unpublished report, NCDOT, 2001), 1, 2.

8. George K. Mack, "Highway Commission Maintains Vital Ferry Boat Operation," *North Carolina Roadways* 6 (May/June 1956): 1, 20; North Carolina State Highway Commission, *Biennial Report, 1955-1956* (Raleigh: State Printer, 1956), 17 (hereafter cited as *Biennial Report*, with appropriate dates); *Biennial Report, 1959-1960*, 7; John Harden, *North Carolina Roads and Their Builders*, vol. 2 (Raleigh: Superior Stone Company, Division of Martin Marietta Corporation, 1966), 26, 27; "History of the N.C. Ferry Division," 4. The Governor Umstead Bridge replaced the Croatan Sound Ferry in 1956, the Alligator River was bridged in 1962, and the Herbert C. Bonner Bridge opened across Oregon Inlet in 1963. "History of the N.C. Ferry Division," 3-5.

9. "History of the N.C. Ferry Division," 4-6; "'Sea Level' Joins Highway Commission Fleet," *North Carolina Roadways* 11 (March-April 1961): 2; *Biennial Report, 1965-1966*, 40-42; *Biennial Report, 1969-1970*, 21; *Biennial Report, 1971-1972*, 17.

10. James E. Harrington, telephone conversation with author, February 5, 2001.

11. David King, interview with author, Raleigh, March 21, 2001; Jerry Gaskill, telephone conversation with author, April 9, 2001. Gaskill is a lifelong resident of Cedar Island and is active in community activities in Carteret County and eastern North Carolina.

12. Reed Hellman, "Pamlico Ring," *Our State* 68 (May 2001): 76.

13. Jerry Gaskill, director, and Charles Utz, Ferry Division, NCDOT, telephone conversation with author, March 19, 2001; "Organization and Functional Overview," 4E-1, 4E-2; "North Carolina Ferry System Schedule 2000," published by the North Carolina Department of Transportation, January 2000.

14. Gaskill telephone conversation (April 9, 2001).

15. Curtis Yates, e-mail to author, March 28, 2001. Oregon was then the only other state with a bicycle coordinator.

16. Curtis Yates and Mary Meletiou, NCDOT, interview with author, Raleigh, March 13, 2001. Yates, who resided in several different communities in North Carolina while growing up, studied architectural design and earned a sociology degree from North Carolina State University; he retired in 2002.

17. *Biennial Report, 1977-1978*, 6; Cathy Handley, "One State's Pacesetter Program for Bicycles," *Bicycle Dealer Showcase*, February 1975, 33.

18. "Bicycle Program," *Transportation Improvement Program, 1987-1993* (hereafter cited as *TIP*, with appropriate dates).

19. "Bicycle Program," *TIP, 1985-1994*; *Bicycling and Walking in North Carolina* (Raleigh: North Carolina Department of Transportation, Division of Bicycle and Pedestrian Transportation, 1996), 13, 54; *TIP, 1988-1996*, 6; *Bicycling and Walking*, 29; Yates e-mail.

20. *TIP, 1987-1995*, 8; *TIP, 1990-1996*, 8; *Biennial Report, 1991-1992*, 22; *Bicycling and Walking*, 50, 54.

21. *Bicycling and Walking*, title page, 50, 63, 64; Ferry, Aviation, Public Transportation, and Rail are NCDOT multimodal programs that reached division status by the mid-1970s.

22. Curtis Yates, telephone conversation with author, April 10, 2001.

23. *Bicycling and Walking*, 60; "Lincolnton Rail Trail," in *Transportation Enhancement Programs* (Raleigh: North Carolina Department of Transportation, 1998); Yates and Meletiou interview.

24. "Durham, Wake Move ATT Development," *Little Toot* (newsletter of North Carolina Rail-Trails) 11 (winter 2001): 2; Yates telephone conversation; "ATT Construction Pushes through South Durham," *Little Toot* 12 (spring 2002): 1, 2.

25. Mary Meletiou, telephone conversation with author, October 30, 2001. The NCDOT awarded more than $300,000 in
federal safety funds through the Governor's Highway Safety Program to the State Highway Patrol and local police and sheriff's departments. "Child Bicycle Safety Act Takes Effect October 1," press release, NCDOT, September 24, 2001.

26. Yates e-mail, March 19, 2001; Winston-Salem/Forsyth County Bike Map, published by NCDOT Bicycle Program (March 1992).

27. *Bicycling and Walking*, 59; Mary Meletiou, telephone conversation with author, March 23, 2001; Rail Division, *www.ncdot.org* (NCDOT Web site).

28. Willard G. Plentl, telephone conversations with author, March 19, April 2, 2001; "Aviation Services and Growth are Spurred by Deregulation," *North Carolina* 38 (July 1980): 30. Plentl, now assistant director of Charlotte/Douglas International Airport, earned a degree in civil engineering at Virginia Military Institute, served in the U.S. Air Force, and was an airport engineer at the Florida Department of Transportation before coming to the NCDOT. He served as airport director at Wilmington International Airport from 1997 to 2000.

29. "A Report on Transportation Needs in North Carolina," 16.

30. "A Report on Transportation Needs in North Carolina," 16, 17.

31. "Aeronautics Element," in *TIP, 1979-1985*; *Biennial Report, 1983-1984*, 1; "A Report on Transportation Needs in North Carolina," 16.

32. "North Carolina Interview: Willard G. Plentl, Jr.," *North Carolina* 44 (July 1986): 34.

33. Plentl telephone conversations; *Biennial Report, 1989-1990*, 24.

34. "North Carolina Interview: Willard G. Plentl, Jr.," 52.

35. Plentl telephone conversations.

36. Williams, a native of Duplin County, spent eight years in the U.S. Air Force. His twenty-eight-year career with the FAA included senior executive service, executive managerial positions in various regions.

37. Midway Airlines operated an active hub at Raleigh-Durham between 1995 and 2001, filed for bankruptcy and discontinued operations in late 2001, briefly resumed a limited operation in 2002, and most recently announced a possible business combination with US Airways. "Midway to Join US Airways," *News and Record*, July 19, 2002.

38. "Shippers and Travelers Find Brand New Ways to Get There," *Business North Carolina* 20 (February 2000): 101.

39. *Biennial Report, 1989-1990*, 24; Organization and Functional Overview, 4F-1.

40. CP&L sold its Asheville bus business in 1942 and its Raleigh operation in 1950 to White Transportation Company. Jack Riley, *Carolina Power & Light Company, 1908-1958* (Raleigh: Edwards & Broughton Company, 1958), 233.

41. "A Report on Transportation Needs in North Carolina," 18.

42. "A Report on Transportation Needs in North Carolina," 18-21, 40, 41.

43. After stepping down as director in 1979, Robinson worked in the highway division and in private business.

44. "Public Transportation Division," *TIP, 1979-1985*, PT-1; *Biennial Report, 1977-1978*, 32, 33; *Biennial Report, 1979-1980*, 75; *TIP, 1994-2000*, PT-1, PT-2.

45. Frederic D. Fravel, e-mail to author, January 13, 2003; Charles Glover, telephone conversation with author, January 23, 2003.

46. *Biennial Report, 1977-1978*, 32; *Biennial Report, 1985-1986*, 16; *TIP, 1987-1995*, 9; *Biennial Report, 1987-1988*, 13; *Biennial Report, 1989-1990*, 22; McKinney interview.

47. *Biennial Report, 1989-1990*, 23; "The Public Transportation and Rail Program," *TIP, 1993-1999*, unpaged.

48. Sanford Cross of Wake County earned a B.A. in geography and an M.Ed. in education at East Carolina University and worked in transportation with the Wake County School System. He joined the Public Transportation Division of the NCDOT in 1981 and became its director in 1993. Sanford Cross, interview with author, Raleigh, March 13, 2001. Pat Simmons grew up in North Carolina, earning degrees in psychology and marine biology at the University of North Carolina at Wilmington. He joined the NCDOT in 1981, working in rural and urban programs, left the department between 1991 and 1994 to organize a computer software company, and returned to head the Rail Division in 1994. Pat Simmons, e-mail to author, April 5, 2001.

49. Cross interview.

50. *Transit 2001*, foreword.

51. Cross interview; "Report to the Transportation Oversight Committee, North Carolina General Assembly" (unpublished document, NCDOT, October 1, 1997); Public Transportation Division, *www.ncdot.org* (NCDOT website).

52. Since that 1997 study, Goldsboro and Jacksonville have instituted bus systems, and Concord/Kannapolis is in the planning process. Burlington does not have a bus system. Mike Kozak, assistant director, metropolitan transportation, PTD, NCDOT, telephone conversation with author, May 25, 2001.

53. *Transit 2001*, 64.

54. *Transit 2001*, 64.

55. *A Regional Transit Plan for the Triangle* [Research Triangle Park: Triangle Transit Authority, ca. 1999]; Kim Crawford, senior policy analyst, TTA, telephone conversation with author, August 31, 2001; *News and Observer* (Raleigh), January 7, 2002.

56. Paul Muschick, "Guilford Board Approves Rental Tax for Transit Aid," *News and Record*, January 18, 2002; Muschick, "Board Votes for Extension of PART's Tax," *News and Record*, February 21, 2003.

57. Jennifer A. Green, community relations specialist, Charlotte Area Transit System (CATS), telephone conversation with author, May 24, 2001; Sarah LaBelle, project manager, CATS, e-mail to author, May 24, 2001; Dianne Whitacre, "Panel Delays Decision on Rail to Matthews, Airport," *Charlotte Observer*, November 21, 2002. Light-rail service, a descendant of the trolley, uses passenger vehicles propelled by electric motors with propulsion power supplied by overhead electric distribution wires. Commuter rail, usually pulled by diesel locomotives, is used on routes with more widely spaced stops and employs a newer type of technology known as Diesel Multiple Units, with the engine located beneath the passenger car. Bus rapid transit (BRT) is a newer, growing technology that utilizes buses, which usually travel in specially designated lanes of traffic called "busways," "transitways," "runningways," or "bus lanes." BRT stations also feature conveniences usually associated with light rail, such as stations, benches, lighting, artwork, and competitive high-frequency all-day service at a fraction of the cost of other rapid-transit modes. Brad Schulz, community relations specialist, CATS, e-mail to author, February 4, 2003; *www.ridetransit.org* (CATS website).

58. *Biennial Report, 1987-1988*, 13.

59. Kozak telephone conversation.

60. David King, interview with author, Raleigh, December 18, 2001. Senator Gulley, chair of the Appropriations Subcommittee on Transportation in the state senate, was a founding member of the Triangle Transit Authority's board of trustees and a member of the Transit 2001 Commission. Representatives Crawford and Cole are co-chairs of the Appropriations Subcommittee on Transportation in the state House of Representatives.

61. "A Report on Transportation Needs in North Carolina," 15.

62. "A Report on Transportation Needs in North Carolina," 15.

63. Paul Faulk, *Atlantic Coast Line Color Guide to Freight and Passenger Equipment* (Scotch Plains, N.J.: Morning Sun Books, 2000), 3.

64. "A Report on Transportation Needs in North Carolina," 8, 9; "Transportation Planners Now Looking at Railroads," *North Carolina* 34 (July 1976): 36, 92.

65. Larry Sams, longtime assistant to Deputy Secretary David King, also served as assistant to Chief Deputy Secretary Gene Conti before retiring in September 2002. Larry Sams, interview with author, Raleigh, March 21, 2001; Chris McAdams, NCDOT, e-mail to author, September 26, 2002; "Rail Program," *TIP, 1984-1993*, RR-1; *Biennial Report, 1983-1984*, 31, 32; *TIP, 1987-1995*, 9.

66. Quintin Ellison and Sandy Wall, "Return to Glory," *Asheville Citizen-Times*, April 4, 2001; *Biennial Report, 1987-1988*, 12.

67. "This Hopeful Rail Experiment Seems Headed for Termination," *North Carolina* 43 (July 1985): 46, 47, 59, 60.

68. *TIP, 1987-1995*, 9; *TIP, 1988-1996*, 7; *Biennial Report, 1989-1990*, 23; "NC Passenger Trains Celebrate Birthdays," *North Carolina on Track* (semiannual newsletter of the Rail Division, NCDOT), summer 2000, 2; Julia Hegele, marketing manager, Rail Division, NCDOT, telephone conversations with author, April 12, 2001, July 9, 2002.

69. "NC Passenger Trains Celebrate Birthdays," 2; Hegele telephone conversations.

70. Rail Division, *www.ncdot.org* (NCDOT website); Craig Newton, Rail Division, NCDOT, e-mail to author, April 11, 2001.

71. *Transit 2001*, 77.

72. Jack Betts, "In the DOT Driver's Seat," *Charlotte Observer*, February 6, 2001. In 1895 North Carolina leased the North Carolina Railroad to Southern Railway for $266,000 a year for six years and afterward at a rate of $286,000 yearly. Hugh T. Lefler and Albert R. Newsome, *North Carolina: The History of a Southern State*, 3d ed. (Chapel Hill: University of North Carolina Press, 1973), 516.

73. Hegele telephone conversations.

74. "$48-million Project to Cut Travel Time for Trains between Raleigh and Greensboro," *North Carolina on Track*, summer 2000, 1; Allan Paul, Rail Division, NCDOT, e-mail to author, April 3, 2001; Pat Simmons, e-mail to author, April 11, 2001; Jim Schlosser, "Rail Line to Get Major Improvements," *News and Record*, December 21, 2001.

75. Paul Worley, Rail Division, NCDOT, e-mail to author, June 6, 2001.

76. Hegele telephone conversations; "45 Industries Able to Grow, Thanks to State's Rail Access Program," *North Carolina on Track*, summer 2000, 3.

77. Paul Muschick, "Train Route Gains Approval," *News and Record*, March 22, 2002; "High Speed Rail," *www.bytrain.org*; *Western North Carolina Passenger Rail Study* (Raleigh: North Carolina Department of Transportation, 2001); Craig Newton, Rail Division, NCDOT, e-mail to author, April 11, 2001.

78. "ISTEA," *Biennial Report, 1992*.

79. Laurie Smith, former enhancement administrator, NCDOT, e-mail and telephone conversation with author, June 4, 5, 2001, respectively. For additional examples of enhancement programs, see "Bicycle and Pedestrian Division" and "Rail Division" sections of this chapter.

80. Whit Webb, telephone conversation with author, April 17, 2001. Webb left the Department of Transportation in 1999 to join a Raleigh transportation consulting company.

81. Smith telephone conversation.

82. Laurie Smith, Dorene Creech, and Rob Ayers, members of the enhancement staff, NCDOT, interview with author, Raleigh, March 13, 2001; Creech and Ayers, interview with author, March 22, 2001; Smith, e-mail to author, April 9, 2001; I. Mei Chan, ed., *Building on the Past, Traveling to the Future* (Washington, D.C., Federal Highway Administration and National Trust for Historic Preservation, [ca. 1995]), 59. Laurie Smith, who grew up in Raleigh, earned undergraduate degrees in accounting, economics, and business administration at North Carolina State University. She began her career with the NCDOT in its Fiscal Section in 1982. Beginning in 1995, she served as enhancement administrator and also oversaw both the Powell Bill program and the agency's contractual agreements. In September 2002 she transferred to the NCDOT's Financial Management Division.

83. Rail Division, *www.ncdot.org* (NCDOT website); Newton e-mail; "Train Stations Are Making a Comeback across North Carolina," *North Carolina on Track*, summer 2000, 2; "Rocky Mount's Restored Station a Center of Regional Commerce," *North Carolina on Track*, winter 2001, 1, 2; "Charlotte, High Point, Greensboro, Selma Station Projects Begun," *North Carolina on Track*, fall 2001, 3; Smith telephone conversation.

84. The land acquisitions included 206 acres at Grandmother Mountain in Avery County, 132 acres at Altapass Apple Orchard in Mitchell and McDowell Counties, 203 acres at Bull Head Mountain in Alleghany County, and 12 acres in Watauga County. Smith telephone conversation.

85. Smith, e-mail to author, April 4, 2001.

EPILOGUE
Looking Back and Ahead

Tar Heel native son Thomas Wolfe once wrote: "I believe that we are lost here in America, but I believe we shall be found."[1] In order to become more "found" than "lost" in the twenty-first century, what transportation challenges must North Carolinians and the North Carolina Department of Transportation face? A new paradigm is needed: a new way of thinking—with an acknowledgment that paving more of the state will not necessarily solve transportation problems.

Insofar as roads were concerned, North Carolina clearly was lost and, moreover, often stuck in the mud during the early twentieth century. The popularity of automobiles, citizen pressure, and political circumstances led to the creation of the North Carolina State Highway Commission. It moved slowly at first, then picked up speed under extraordinary leadership in the 1920s to achieve national recognition. While adapting to different governors and political realities, the agency set a standard for high-quality work and service to all one hundred counties in a fair manner.

During the Great Depression, with much of the nation's economy in unprecedented decline and North Carolina's local governments struggling with finances, the General Assembly gave the Highway Commission responsibility for county roads in addition to state highways. During World War II, despite a slowdown in new construction, the commission upgraded and widened highways in the vicinity of military bases and installations. When service personnel came home after the war, the demand for cars and roads was unending. The department gained new recognition by paving a large number of secondary roads, which helped to unite the state and expand opportunities in less-populated areas. At the same time, however, the agency faltered in failing to anticipate the coming urbanization and need for interstate highways. In the late 1950s and 1960s, it began to modernize by better utilizing planning and technology.

In a progressive move, state government was reorganized in the early 1970s, creating the North Carolina Department of Transportation to bring together the major transportation modes. The department created a long-range planning process to coordinate a variety of programs and provide realistic timetables for construction projects. Especially during the 1990s, this process led to vigorous action with regard to paving secondary roads, expanding the network of four-lane and interstate highways, and strengthening multimodal programs. The 2001 General Assembly authorized a significant amount of funds, previously earmarked for new roads, to be used instead for needed highway maintenance and mass-transit programs.

Turning toward the future, what critical transportation issues do North Carolinians need to address? Writing a history of the department has provided this writer with thoughts and suggestions concerning complex issues the department faces. First, the NCDOT should continue assisting the three major urban regions to implement plans for mass-transit systems and multimodal transportation centers. In response to clear warnings about explosive growth and air pollution, the Raleigh-Durham and Charlotte metropolitan areas, with the Triad not far behind, have designed mass-transit systems and obtained approval for regional funding. The state needs to continue a consulting role and especially the financial commitment for its share of construction and equipment.

Second, the NCDOT should designate a larger percentage of its annual budget, only 6 percent in 2000-2001, to multimodal programs. While the planned urban highway loops and four-lane network should be completed, more available resources should be directed toward alternatives to the automobile. In order to encourage the increased use of bicycles, for example, the NCDOT, along with municipalities, needs to build more paved shoulders, wide outside lanes, and marked bicycle lanes on current and future roads. Doing so would create safer conditions for current bicyclists and encourage more people to use bikes instead of cars for short trips. It is also critical that North Carolina upgrade intercity passenger rail service. High-speed rail between Charlotte and Raleigh, however, needs to be assured before passenger service is extended to Asheville (via Salisbury) and to Wilmington (via Raleigh).

Third, the NCDOT should do its part to preserve the natural beauty of North Carolina. The Blue Ridge Parkway, for example, has provided delights for generations of visitors, yet its integrity and spectacular vistas are now threatened (despite assistance from the NCDOT) by air pollution and inappropriate development on adjoining land. Adequate funds need to be earmarked for proper maintenance of all highways and any other transportation structures the state builds. As early as 1931, Prof. Cecil Brown commented in his book, *The State Highway System of North Carolina*: "Far and wide, over the state highway system, the landscape is marred with ugly blots, usually in the form of unsightly billboards."[2] State legislators in recent sessions debated whether billboards should be allowed on the state's "main street"—I-40—but took no action.

At the turn of the twentieth century, the challenge was to build roads. At the turn of the twenty-first, the challenge is both to improve and maintain the state highway system and to create practical alternatives to traditional highways. For the moment, we may be somewhat lost in North Carolina, but we shall be found. Wolfe, who apparently never drove a car, would be proud.

Notes

1. Thomas Wolfe, *You Can't Go Home Again* (New York and London: Harper and Brothers, 1940), 741.

2. Cecil K. Brown, *The State Highway System of North Carolina: Its Evolution and Status* (Chapel Hill: University of North Carolina Press, 1931), 250.

Appendix A

Highway Fund Revenues
Fiscal Years 1922-2002
Dollars in Millions

FISCAL YEAR	GASOLINE TAX	VEHICLE REVENUE	FEDERAL AID	TOTAL REVENUE
1922	.7	2.1	1.7	4.5
1923	1.3	2.9	1.1	5.3
1924	4.0	4.0	1.5	9.5
1925	5.3	4.7	3.8	13.8
1926	6.9	5.3	1.7	13.9
1927	8.1	5.9	1.7	15.7
1928	9.4	10.2	1.7	21.3
1929	10.1	7.0	1.7	18.8
1930	12.9	7.0	2.9	22.8
1931	12.4	6.3	3.0	21.7
1932	14.9	5.6	1.8	22.3
1933	14.2	5.1	5.5	24.8
1934	15.2	6.8	9.5	31.5
1935	17.3	7.6	4.8	29.8
1936	18.9	7.0	12.5	38.4
1937	21.7	6.8	3.1	31.6
1938	22.7	7.5	4.9	35.1
1939	23.8	9.4	4.9	38.1
1940	25.3	8.7	3.2	37.2
1941	28.7	9.9	4.3	42.9
1942	29.1	10.3	6.2	45.6
1943	20.6	10.3	5.0	35.9
1944	21.3	11.0	1.0	33.3
1945	22.3	11.2	.3	33.8
1946	31.4	12.8	11.5	55.7
1947	32.1	12.9	11.4	56.4
1948	40.7	16.8	11.0	68.5
1949	44.5	18.2	.5	63.2
1950	52.8	20.3	10.2	83.3
1951	64.6	23.1	10.6	98.3
1952	69.7	24.6	11.9	106.2
1953	73.8	25.9	11.9	111.6
1954	75.9	26.4	13.8	116.1
1955	80.4	28.2	14.1	122.7
1956	87.5	30.0	21.9	139.4
1957	91.2	30.8	50.0	172.0
1958	78.4	30.1	153.4	261.9
1959	82.0	32.3	35.3	149.6
1960	85.1	34.1	29.6	148.8
1961	89.2	34.7	32.3	156.2
1962	92.5	36.1	41.0	169.6
1963	98.2	38.5	43.9	180.6
1964	101.1	45.0	45.9	192.0
1965	110.7	43.2	44.4	198.3
1966	117.6	46.7	61.2	225.5

Appendix A (continued)

1967	146.5	55.0	60.4	261.9
1968	153.3	61.2	60.2	274.7
1969	141.5	55.3	92.4	289.2
1970	196.0	71.0	91.3	358.3
1971	208.2	76.5	114.8	399.5
1972	225.7	81.8	112.2	419.7
1973	264.5	96.9	14.2	375.6
1974	268.6	97.3	106.2	472.1
1975	265.8	95.2	277.9	638.9
1976	286.4	103.8	51.7	441.9
1977	298.3	106.5	254.4	659.2
1978	312.0	114.2	159.7	585.9
1979	322.8	120.5	218.7	662.0
1980	304.0	125.7	231.6	661.3
1981	291.2	130.0	209.1	630.3
1982	380.8	151.7	176.5	709.0
1983	388.6	161.1	275.5	825.2
1984	411.8	200.0	362.3	974.1
1985	421.7	212.7	312.9	947.3
1986	438.7	219.7	305.2	963.6
1987	569.3	234.3	289.2	1,092.8
1988	612.2	250.5	297.9	1,160.6
1989	625.8	257.2	340.1	1,223.1
1990	619.7	257.9	230.8	1,108.4
1991	629.4	252.6	336.8	1,218.8
1992	650.6	273.6	454.6	1,378.8
1993	648.8	275.9	493.5	1,418.2
1994	677.6	283.8	495.1	1,456.5
1995	681.1	295.6	528.2	1,504.9
1996	709.2	320.4	444.6	1,474.2
1997	742.8	320.2	559.1	1,622.1
1998	774.5	328.4	659.4	1,762.3
1999	775.5	340.0	741.2	1,856.7
2000	793.3	351.8	787.9	1,933.0
2001	880.6	363.5	854.2	2,098.4
2002	901.0	379.0	870.3	2,150.3

Sources: *Biennial Reports* of the State Highway Commission, 1921-1922 to 1971-1972; *Biennial Reports* of the NCDOT, 1973-1974 to 1991-1992; *We the People of North Carolina* 10 (January 1953): 26; information provided by Crissty Martin, NCDOT.

Appendix B

Highway Trust Fund Revenues
Fiscal Years 1990-2002
Dollars in Millions

FISCAL YEAR	GASOLINE TAX	VEHICLE REVENUE	NET HIGHWAY USE TAX	TOTAL REVENUE
1990	184.9	51.5		236.4
1991	206.6	55.4		262.0
1992	213.4	58.5	72.3	344.2
1993	212.4	62.2	103.3	377.9
1994	222.0	68.1	160.5	450.6
1995	223.0	77.1	194.6	494.7
1996	232.7	77.0	227.3	537.0
1997	243.7	85.6	237.6	566.9
1998	254.6	87.0	283.2	624.8
1999	254.7	90.3	319.5	664.5
2000	260.7	93.3	375.3	729.3
2001	289.6	90.6	375.2	755.4
2002	296.3	90.7	303.6	690.6

*In 1990 $164.7 million was transferred to the General Fund, and in 1991 $231.4 million was transferred to the General Fund; $170 million was transferred each year thereafter until 2002, when the amount was increased to $251.7 million as a result of a budget shortfall.

Source: Information provided by Crissty Martin, NCDOT.

Selected Bibliography

Documents and Publications from the North Carolina State Highway Commission/North Carolina Department of Transportation (NCDOT)

Bicycling and Walking in North Carolina: A Long-range Transportation Plan. Raleigh: North Carolina Department of Transportation (NCDOT), Division of Bicycle and Pedestrian Transportation, 1996.

Burch, James S. "Historical Outline of Road Administration in North Carolina." Unpublished paper written for the North Carolina State Highway Commission, Raleigh, April 1940.

Harrington, James E. *Planks, Pavement and Progress.* Raleigh: NCDOT, 1989.

"The History of the N.C. Ferry Division, NC Department of Transportation." Unpublished report, NCDOT, 2001.

North Carolina Department of Transportation. *Biennial Reports*, 1973-1974 through 1991-1992.

_____. *Highway Improvement Program*, 1973-1980 through 1978-1984.

_____. *Transportation Improvement Program*, 1979-1985 through 2002-2008.

North Carolina State Highway Commission. *Biennial Reports*, 1915-1916 through 1971-1972 (agency existed as North Carolina State Highway and Public Works Commission, 1933-1957).

"Organization and Functional Overview, North Carolina Department of Transportation." Informational notebook for NCDOT board members. Raleigh: NCDOT, January 2001.

Transit 2001 Executive Summary and Technical Report. Raleigh: NCDOT, 1997.

Western North Carolina Passenger Rail Study. Raleigh: NCDOT, 2001.

Wilbur Smith and Associates, "Report of Governor's Blue Ribbon Commission on Transportation Needs and Financing," December 16, 1980.

Additional Public Documents and Publications

General Location of National System of Interstate Highways, Including All Additional Routes at Urban Areas Designated in September 1955. Washington, D.C.: U.S. Department of Commerce, Bureau of Public Roads, 1955.

North Carolina Department of Administration. "A Report on Transportation Needs in North Carolina." Research report, Office of State Planning, North Carolina Department of Administration, 1973.

Sniker, Janice L. "Roadside Architecture in Twentieth-Century North Carolina." Unpublished research report, Historic Sites Section, Division of Archives and History, North Carolina Department of Cultural Resources, 2001.

"Summary of Mileage of State Highway Systems, State Highway Mileage, 1925-1975," *Highway Statistics Summary to 1975* (Washington: Federal Highway Administration, 1975).

U.S. House. *Interregional Highways, A Report of the National Interregional Highway Committee, Outlining and Recommending a National System of Interregional Highways*, 78th Cong., 2d sess., January 12, 1944, H. Doc. 379.

Interviews with Author

Creech, Dorene, and Rob Ayers. Raleigh, March 22, 2001.

Cross, Sanford. Raleigh, March 13, 2001.

Hegele, Julia. Raleigh, March 21, 2001.

King, David. Raleigh, March 21, December 18, 2001.

Murdock, Jack. Raleigh, January 5, 2001.

Rankin, Edward L., Jr. Concord, August 2, 2000.

Rose, Billy. Raleigh, January 9, 2001.

Sams, Larry. Raleigh, March 21, 2001.

Sanders, John. Raleigh, July 13, 2001.

Smith, Laurie, Dorene Creech, and Rob Ayers. Raleigh, March 13, 2001.

Tippett, Lyndo. August 20, 2001.

Yates, Curtis, and Mary Meletiou. Raleigh, March 13, 2001.

Telephone Conversations with Author

Avant, Al. March 21, 2001.

Bradshaw, Thomas W., Jr., April 11, 2001.

Cashion, Jerry C., Frank D. Gatton, and Roger C. Jones. November 2, 9, 2000.

Church, Barbara. October 3, 2000.

Crawford, Kim. August 31, 2001.

Crosby, Tom. November 2, 2000.

DeLaughter, Eric. January 23, 2003.

Fulmer, Myra. January 12, 2001.

Gaskill, Jerry. April 9, 2001.

Gaskill, Jerry, and Charles Utz. March 19, 2001.

Glover, Charles. January 23, 2003.

Graf, Nicholas L. January 30, March 7, 2001.

Green, Jennifer A. May 24, 2001.

Harrington, James E. February 5, July 27, 2001.

Hegele, Julia. April 12, 2001, July 9, 2002.

Hill, Len. May 14, 2001.

Hughett, Jacquie. September 6, 2001.

Hutchinson, Kelly. January 22, 2003.

Hyatt, Stan. November 14, 2001.

Johnson, Kathi. January 3, February 14, 2001.

Jones, Charlie. March 23, 2001, October 22, 2002.

Kozak, Mike. May 25, 2001.

Lane, Doug. March 27, 2001.

Leggett, Carroll. August 5, 2002.

McAdams, Chris J. October 10, 2002, January 24, 2003.

McKinney, Brent. April 18, 2001.

Marley, William G. January 30, February 12, August 30, 2001.

Martin, Crissty. January 12, February 20, 2001.

Medford, Houck. November 22, 2000.

Meletiou, Mary. March 23, October 30, 2001.

Murdock, Jack. October 3, 2002.

Plentl, Willard G., Jr. March 19, April 2, 2001.

Rankin, Edward L., Jr. October 5, 2000.

Rose, Billy. October 5, November 22, 2000.

Sanders, John. May 14, 2001.

Smith, Laurie. June 5, 2001.

Stankiewicz, Paul. January 29, 2003.

Vann, Andre D. October 22, 2002.

Wadelington, Charles. August 23, 2001.

Warrick, Kirby. March 2, 2001.

Watkins, John. February 9, 12, 2001.

Webb, Whit. April 17, 2001.

Yates, Curtis. April 10, 2001.

E-mails to Author

Burns, Nicole. July 15, 2002.

Clemmons, Cary. January 2, 2003.

Fravel, Frederic D. January 13, 2003.

LaBelle, Sarah. May 24, 2001.

McAdams, Chris. September 26, 2002.

Newton, Craig. April 11, 2001.

Paul, Allan. April 3, 2001.

Schulz, Brad. February 4, 2003.

Simmons, Pat. April 5, 11, 2001.

Smith, Laurie. April 4, 9, June 4, 2001.

Weingroff, Richard F. June 5, 2001, August 9, 19, December 3, 2002.

Worley, Paul. June 6, 2001.

Yates, Curtis. March 19, 28, 2001.

Books

American Association of Passenger Traffic Officers. *Official Guide of the Railways and Steam Navigation Lines of the United States*. New York: National Railway Publication Company, 1916, 1930.

BIBLIOGRAPHY

America's Highways, 1776-1976: A History of the Federal-Aid Program. Washington: Federal Highway Administration, U.S. Department of Transportation, 1976.

Badger, Anthony J. *North Carolina and the New Deal.* Raleigh: North Carolina Department of Cultural Resources, Division of Archives and History, 1981.

Bell, John L., Jr. *Hard Times: Beginnings of the Great Depression in North Carolina, 1929-1933.* Raleigh: Division of Archives and History, North Carolina Department of Cultural Resources, 1982.

Bowman, Gary M. *Highway Politics in Virginia.* Fairfax: George Mason University Press, 1993.

Brown, Cecil K. *The State Highway System of North Carolina, Its Evolution and Status.* Chapel Hill: University of North Carolina Press, 1931.

Chan, I. Mei, ed. *Building on the Past, Traveling to the Future.* Washington: Federal Highway Administration and the National Trust for Historic Preservation, [ca. 1995].

Corbitt, David Leroy, ed. *Public Addresses, Letters, and Papers of William Kerr Scott, Governor of North Carolina, 1949-1953.* Raleigh: Council of State, State of North Carolina, 1957.

_____. *Public Papers and Letters of Oliver Max Gardner, Governor of North Carolina, 1929-1933.* Raleigh: North Carolina Council of State, 1937.

Costello, Dan, and Lisa Schamess, eds. *Building on the Past, Traveling to the Future*, 2d ed. Washington: Federal Highway Administration and National Trust for Historic Preservation, 2001.

Covington, Howard E., Jr., and Marion A. Ellis, eds. *The North Carolina Century: Tar Heels Who Made a Difference, 1900-2000.* Charlotte: Levine Museum of the New South, 2002.

Crabtree, Beth G. *North Carolina Governors, 1585-1974.* Raleigh: Division of Archives and History, Department of Cultural Resources, 1974.

Faulk, Paul. *Atlantic Coast Line Color Guide to Freight and Passenger Equipment.* Scotch Plains, N.J.: Morning Sun Books, 2000.

Hanchett, Thomas H. *Sorting Out the New South City.* Chapel Hill: University of North Carolina Press, 1998.

Harden, John. *North Carolina Roads and Their Builders.* Vol. 2. Raleigh: Superior Stone Company, Division of Martin Marietta Corporation, 1966.

Hodges, Luther H. *Businessman in the Statehouse.* Chapel Hill: University of North Carolina Press, 1962.

Ireland, Robert E. *Entering the Auto Age: The Early Automobile in North Carolina, 1900-1930.* Raleigh: Division of Archives and History, North Carolina Department of Cultural Resources, 1990.

Jolley, Harley E. *The Blue Ridge Parkway.* Knoxville: University of Tennessee Press, 1969.

Kirby, Peggy Jo D. *North Carolina Museum of Art: The First Fifty Years, 1947-1997.* Richmond, Va.: Carter Press, 1997.

Lefler, Hugh T., and Albert R. Newsome. *North Carolina: The History of a Southern State.* 3d ed. Chapel Hill: University of North Carolina Press, 1973.

Lemmon, Sarah McCulloh. *North Carolina's Role in World War II*. Raleigh: North Carolina Department of Archives and History, 1964.

Lewis, Tom. *Divided Highways: Building the Interstate Highways, Transforming American Life*. New York: Penguin Group, 1997.

Morrison, Joseph L. *Governor O. Max Gardner*. Chapel Hill: University of North Carolina Press, 1971.

Morton, Hugh M., and Edward L. Rankin Jr. *Making a Difference in North Carolina*. Raleigh: Lightworks, 1988.

Guide to Research Materials in the North Carolina State Archives: State Agency Records. Raleigh: Department of Cultural Resources, Division of Archives and History, Archives and Records Section, 1995.

1990 Census of Population and Housing Unit Counts, North Carolina. Washington: U.S. Department of Commerce, 1992.

Orr, Douglas M., Jr., and Alfred W. Stuart, eds. *The North Carolina Atlas: Portrait for a New Century*. Chapel Hill: University of North Carolina Press, 2000.

Powell, William S., ed. *Dictionary of North Carolina Biography*. 6 vols. Chapel Hill: University of North Carolina Press, 1979-1996.

———. *North Carolina through Four Centuries*. Chapel Hill: University of North Carolina Press, 1989.

Rose, Mark H. *Interstate Express Highway Politics, 1939-1989*. Rev. ed. Knoxville: University of Tennessee Press, 1990.

Seely, Bruce E. *Building the American Highway System: Engineers as Policy Makers*. Philadelphia: Temple University Press, 1987.

Shank, William H. *Vanderbilt's Folly: A History of the Pennsylvania Turnpike*. York, Pa.: American Canal and Transportation Center, 1993.

Snee, Julie W., ed. "James Grubbs Martin, Governor," in *North Carolina Manual, 1991-1992*. Raleigh: Department of the Secretary of State, 1992.

Teer, Dillard, Robert D. Teer Jr., and Anna Daugird. *Courage Ever: An American Success Story—Nello L. Teer Sr. and His Company*. Durham: Teer Associates, 2001.

Tursi, Frank V. *Winston-Salem: A History*. Winston-Salem: John F. Blair, 1994.

Waynick, Capus. *North Carolina Roads and Their Builders*, Vol. 1. Raleigh: Superior Stone Company, 1952.

Articles

"ATT Construction Pushes through South Durham." *Little Toot* (newsletter of North Carolina Rail-Trails) 12 (spring 2002): 1, 2.

"About Highways." *North Carolina* 39 (July 1981): 20.

Bibliography

"Across Town in 15 Minutes." *Greensboro Daily News*, August 15, 1972.

"Advanced Planning." *North Carolina Roadways* 13 (September-October 1966): 1.

"Albemarle Prepared to Open New Bridge." *News and Observer* (Raleigh), August 14, 1938.

"Are Our Primary Highways Neglected?" *North Carolina Roadways* 1 (August 1950): 21.

Arthur, Billy. "The Mother of Good Roads." *The State* 57 (January 1990): 12, 13, 14.

"Aviation Services and Growth are Spurred by Deregulation." *North Carolina* 38 (July 1980): 30.

Baker, C. V. "Building Concrete Road on a Large Scale." *North Carolina Highway Bulletin* 4 (September 1923): 4, 23.

Barron, Andrew. "Congress OKs Interstate 73/74 through N.C." *News and Record* (Greensboro), November 21, 1995.

Betts, Jack. "In the DOT Driver's Seat." *Charlotte Observer*, February 6, 2001.

"Bid Collusion." *North Carolina* 38 (July 1980): 10.

Bonner, Lynn. "DOT Contracts Protested." *News and Observer*, February 8, 2002.

Boyd, C. O. "Raleigh-Durham Highway Completed." *North Carolina Highway Bulletin* 4 (July 1923): 4.

Brant, F. H. "New Emphasis on Highway Beauty." *North Carolina Roadways* 13 (March-April 1966): 1, 2, 3.

"Bypasses Give Major Traffic Relief to Cities and Towns." *North Carolina Roadways* 5 (May-June 1955): 1, 2, 4.

"Chairman Graham Announces the First Links in the New Road Program." *We the People* 14 (November 1956): 40, 42.

"Charlotte, High Point, Greensboro, Selma Station Projects Begun." *North Carolina on Track* (semiannual newsletter of the Rail Division, NCDOT), fall 2001, 3.

Cherry, R. Gregg. "Some Problems Facing the State," *We the People* 4 (December 1946): 5.

Christensen, Rob. "New Jersey Sprawl Is Here, Y'all." *News and Observer*, May 6, 2001.

Claiborne, Jack. "Airport Memorializes Former Mayor Ben Douglas." *Charlotte Observer*, April 25, 1982.

"Commission's First Bridge." *North Carolina Roadways* 1 (January-February 1951): 20.

"Conference on Beautification." *North Carolina Roadways* 13 (March-April 1966): 11.

"Contract Let for 4.3 Mile Beltline Link." *Raleigh Times*, August 12, 1977.

Cooper, David. "N.C. Gearing Up Campaign for More Interstate Roads." *News and Observer*, December 8, 1963.

BIBLIOGRAPHY

———. "N.C. Interstate Limits Set in 1945." *News and Observer*, March 18, 1962.

Davis, Chester. "A Progress Report." *North Carolina Roadways* 1 (September 1950): 2.

"Department of Transportation—Four Stormy, Controversial Years." *North Carolina* 34 (July 1976): 29-32.

"Downtown Boulevard Opened to Traffic." *North Carolina Roadways* 6 (November-December 1955): 3.

"Durham, Wake Move ATT Development." *Little Toot* 11 (winter 2001): 2.

Ellison, Quintin, and Tonya Maxwell. "DMV Officers Appear before Grand Jury." *Asheville Citizen-Times*, June 5, 2002.

Ellison, Quintin, and Sandy Wall. "Return to Glory." *Asheville Citizen-Times*, April 4, 2001.

"Eyes on Highway Surplus." *News and Observer*, May 22, 2001.

"Financial History of N.C. Highways." *We the People* 10 (January 1953): 26.

"The First Birthday of the State Highway Commission." *North Carolina Highway Bulletin* 3 (April 1922): 5, 7.

FitzSimon, Chris. "Real Problem Remains at State DOT." *Triangle Business Journal*, March 6, 1998, 47.

"$48-million Project to Cut Travel Time for Trains between Raleigh and Greensboro." *North Carolina on Track*, summer 2000, 1.

"45 Industries Able to Grow, Thanks to State's Rail Access Program." *North Carolina on Track*, summer 2000, 3.

"Frank Page, Gentleman, Banker, Soldier, Road Builder." *North Carolina Highway Bulletin* 4 (June 1923): 5.

"Frank Page, North Carolina's Pioneer Road Builder." *North Carolina Roadways* 1 (July 1950): 8, 9, 29.

"Getting the Land Where Highways Go." *North Carolina* 28 (July 1970): 50.

Gomlak, Norman, and Ames Alexander. "Official's Role Questioned in Road Projects." *Charlotte Observer*, September 8, 1997.

"Governor Seeks Public Support." *News and Observer*, February 10, 1931.

Gray, Tim. "Now He Wants to Make Agriculture His Business." *Business North Carolina* 20 (April 2000): 17.

Griffin, Anna. "New N.C. Bridge Is Poetry for Motion." *Charlotte Observer*, August 11, 2002.

"Group Continues Highway Efforts." *News and Observer*, August 5, 1947.

Hanchett, Tom. "When Wilkinson Made History." *Charlotte Observer*, November 20, 2000.

Handley, Cathy. "One State's Pacesetter Program for Bicycles." *Bicycle Dealer Showcase*, February 1975, 33.

"The Hard Choices." *North Carolina* 39 (February 1981): 10.

Harrington, James E. "North Carolina Highways in the Near and Far Terms." *North Carolina* 46 (July 1988): 14.

"Has Been Acting Chief Since Tolson's Resignation; Hunt Names David McCoy DOT Secretary." *Wilmington Morning Star*, June 23, 1999.

Hawkins, W. E. "Developments in the Construction of Concrete Roads." *North Carolina Highway Bulletin* 3 (March 1922): 8-10, 14-15.

Hellman, Reed. "Pamlico Ring," *Our State* 68 (May 2001): 76.

"Here's the First View of Our New Highway Building." *North Carolina Roadways* 1 (July 1950): 23.

"Highway Approves N.C. Toll Road." *North Carolina Roadways* 13 (September-November 1964): 3.

"Highway Summary 1969." *North Carolina Roadways* 16 (January-February 1970): 2, 3.

Hoover, Daniel C. "Light at the End of the Beltline." *News and Observer*, July 5, 1978.

"How the Carolinas' Traffic Safety Laws Measure Up." *Go* (newsletter of AAA Carolinas), March-April 2001.

Hyman, Vicki. "DOT Presses for Toll Roads." *News and Observer*, March 3, 2001.

"Interview: D. M. Faircloth." *North Carolina* 30 (July 1972): 27.

Ireland, Robert E. "Consolidation, Transportation and Educational Opportunity: The Paradox of the Early School Bus in North Carolina." *North Carolina Humanities* 3 (fall/winter 1995): 77-90.

_____. "Prison Reform, Road Building, and Southern Progressivism: Joseph Hyde Pratt and the Campaign for 'Good Roads and Good Men.'" *North Carolina Historical Review* 68 (April 1991): 125-128.

Jackson, Roger R., Jr. "Our Highway System Today." *We the People* 22 (July 1964): 73.

Lamm, Lester P. "The Early Days of Parkway Construction," in *Blue Ridge Parkway: Agent of Transition*, ed. Barry M. Buxton and Steven M. Beatty. Boone: Appalachian Consortium Press, 1986, 119-128.

McDowell, Robert W. "Getting Educated about Highways." *North Carolina* 49 (July 1991): 24, 25.

Mack, George K. "Highway Commission Maintains Vital Ferry Boat Operation." *North Carolina Roadways* 6 (May/June 1956): 1, 20.

May, A. L. "Hunt to Try to Show Woes of Highways." *News and Observer*, December 17, 1980.

"Midway to join US Airways." *News and Record*, July 19, 2002.

"Money Problems Are Nothing New in State's Roadbuilding History." *North Carolina* 39 (July 1981): 22, 23, 24, 26, 91.

Morrill, Dan. "The Road that Split Charlotte." *Parade*, May 2, 1982, 12, 15, 19.

Morris, John D. "Eisenhower Signs Road Bill; Weeks Allocates 1.1. Billion." *New York Times*, June 30, 1956.

———. "Roads Bill Sent to White House." *New York Times*, June 27, 1956.

Muschick, Paul. "Board Votes for Extension of PART's Tax." *News and Record*, February 21, 2003.

———. "Guilford Board Approves Rental Tax for Transit Aid." *News and Record*, January 18, 2002.

———. "N.C. Gains 13th Seat in Congress." *News and Record*, December 29, 2000.

———. "Train Route Gains Approval." *News and Record*, March 22, 2002.

"NC Passenger Trains Celebrate Birthdays." *North Carolina on Track*, summer 2000, 2.

"National Interstate System Long-range Goal." *Better Roads* 17 (September 1947): 20, 48.

"The National System of Interstate and Defense Highways." *We the People* 14 (November 1956): 12-83.

"New Connection." *North Carolina Roadways* 13 (December 1964): 21.

"New Proposal for I-73 Stirs Triad Rivalry." *News and Record*, April 14, 1995.

"New Transportation Secretary Is Young but Experienced Leader." *North Carolina* 35 (July 1977): 34.

"The 1981 Good Roads Package Just Bought Some Extra Time." *North Carolina* 40 (July 1982): 22.

"No Parkway Tolls This Year." *North Carolina Roadways* 5 (May-June 1955): inside front cover.

"North Carolina Interview: Willard G. Plentl Jr." *North Carolina* 44 (July 1986): 34.

"North Carolina Road Builders." *We the People of North Carolina* 14 (November 1956): 76, 78, 80.

"North Carolina Road System is a Billion Dollar Investment." *We the People* 6 (January 1949): 15.

"North Carolina's Gasoline Taxes No Longer Highest in the Nation." *North Carolina* 30 (July 1972): 39.

"Now It's a Full Powell Penny Going to Those City Streets." *North Carolina* 29 (July 1971): 46, 105.

O'Toole, Thomas. "Everyone Got a Piece of the Paving Job; Justice Department Unearths Bid-Rigging in 14 States." *Washington Post*, October 15, 1981.

"An Overview of North Carolina Transportation Policy and Recommendations for Policy Planning." Research report, State Planning Division, North Carolina Department of Administration, April 1973, 12.

Page, Frank. "What North Carolina is Doing." *North Carolina Highway Bulletin* 4 (March 1923): 3.

"A Paved Road Opens a 'Lost Province,'" *North Carolina Roadways* 1 (August 1950): 12.

Paxson, Frederic L. "The Highway Movement, 1916-1935." *American Historical Review* 51 (January 1946): 246, 249.

Porter, Alan L., and Thomas D. Larson. "State Departments of Transportation: A Perspective," in *Management of Transportation and Environmental Review Functions*. Washington, D.C.: National Academy of Sciences, 1976, 12.

"Primary Road Needs in North Carolina." *We the People* 9 (March 1952): 4, 5, 28.

"Problems at DOT." *Charlotte Observer*, March 3, 1998.

"Protest Parkway Toll." *North Carolina Roadways* 5 (March-April 1955): inside front cover.

Raferty, Heidi Russell. "Open Road." *North Carolina* 60 (July 2002): 46, 48-53.

"Raleigh Beltline Nears Completion." *North Carolina Roadways* 13 (May-June 1964): 1.

Rawlings, Wade. "'Transit Guy' Gets Broad Power at DOT." *News and Observer*, March 8, 1998.

Rawls, Wendell, Jr. "Scandal Builds in Southeast." *New York Times*, July 6, 1980.

"A Report on Transportation Needs in North Carolina." Research report, Office of State Planning, North Carolina Department of Administration, 1973, 24, 25.

Reynolds, Jane. "Plans for Highway Picking Up Speed." *News and Record*, August 19, 1996.

"Roads Are Bustin' Out All Over!" *North Carolina Roadways* 1 (July 1950): 10.

"Rocky Mount's Restored Station a Center of Regional Commerce." *North Carolina on Track*, winter 2001, 1, 2.

Rogoski, Richard. "Still the Good Roads State?" *North Carolina* 58 (July 2000): 21, 23.

Rondthaler, Mrs. Theodore. "Paved Roads Come to Ocracoke." *North Carolina Roadways* 1 (January-February 1951): 2, 3.

Sack, Kevin. "A Road-Building Scandal Forces a Governor's Hand." *New York Times*, January 14, 1998.

Schlosser, Jim. "Leader Plagued by Work, Injury." *News and Record*, May 26, 2002.

_____. "Rail Line to Get Major Improvements." *News and Record*, December 21, 2001.

Schreiner, Mark. "I-40, Road Changed How Southeastern N.C. Gets Around." *Wilmington Morning Star*, June 28, 2000.

"'Sea Level' Joins Highway Commission Fleet." *North Carolina Roadways* 11 (March-April 1961): 2.

"Shippers and Travelers Find Brand New Ways to Get There." *Business North Carolina* 20 (February 2000): 101.

"$6-Million Expressway Will Be Opened Today." *Asheville Citizen*, December 15, 1960.

Snider, William D. "The Precious Nature of North Carolina." *News and Record*, January 14, 2001.

"Solid Accomplishment." *News and Observer*, October 27, 1952.

"State Boasts Longest Expressway in South." *North Carolina Roadways* 6 (January-February 1956): 1.

"The State of Bridges in the Carolinas." *Go*, March-April 2001, 6.

"State Government Roundup." *North Carolina* 27 (October 1969): 6, 7.

"State Short-Changed on Interstate Roads." *Wilmington Morning Star*, June 17, 1967.

"State's Roadbuilding Efforts Beefed Up by New Tax Revenues." *North Carolina* 45 (July 1987): 24-52.

Swofford, Stan. "Building a Power Base." *News and Record*, January 1, 2001.

―――――. "A History-Making Comeback." *News and Record*, January 2, 2001.

"The System and Its Future Needs." *North Carolina* 29 (July 1971): 35.

"Thinking about Primary Roads." *We the People* 21 (July 1963): 24.

"This Hopeful Rail Experiment Seems Headed for Termination." *North Carolina* 43 (July 1985): 46, 47, 59, 60.

Thornton, Mary. "Bid-Rigging Probe Has Grown to Largest U.S. Antitrust Case." *Washington Post*, August 10, 1982.

"$300 Million Post-War Road Building Plan." *We the People of North Carolina* 1 (October 1943): 8, 9.

"Toll-Road Era Coming to an End." *U.S. News & World Report* 41 (July 13, 1956): 54, 55.

"Traffic Engineer Is First N.C. Woman to Become Licensed." *North Carolina Roadways* 10 (November-December 1960): 9.

"Train Stations Are Making a Comeback across North Carolina." *North Carolina on Track*, summer 2000, 2.

"Transportation Highways." *We the People* 12 (November 1955): 40.

"Transportation Planners Now Looking at Railroads." *North Carolina* 34 (July 1976): 36, 92.

"Transportation Secretary; Wilmington's Garrett Leads Roads Office; Hunt Rewards Longtime Ally." *Wilmington Morning Star*, September 1, 1995.

"Transportation Secretary Thomas W. Bradshaw, Jr." *North Carolina* 36 (August 1978): 22.

Trent, Lisa. "One Thousand N.C. Businesses 'Adopt-a-Highway' to Clean Roads." *North Carolina* 47 (July 1989): 50.

"Triad Air among Dirtiest in U.S." *News and Record*, May 1, 2001.

Turner, Walter R. "The Good Roads State." *Our State* 68 (August 2000): 62-63.

"Two N.C. Cities Open Up Million Dollar By-passes." *North Carolina Roadways* 2 (November-December 1951): 20.

Upham, Charles M. "Recent Developments in Road Construction." *North Carolina Highway Bulletin* 3 (March 1922): 11-12, 15.

"W. F. Babcock Named Director of Highways." *North Carolina Roadways* 8 (July-August 1957): 1.

Warren, Jule B. "Thumb-Nail History of the Highway System." *We the People of North Carolina* 9 (March 1952): 6-8, 27.

Weigl, Andrea. "Judge Finds Bias at DMV." *News and Observer*, October 2, 2002.

"What Goes into a Mile of Concrete Road." *North Carolina Highway Bulletin* 4 (June 1923): 1.

Whitacre, Dianne. "Panel Delays Decision on Rail to Matthews, Airport." *Charlotte Observer*, November 21, 2002.

"William L. Craven, Bridge Engineer." *North Carolina Highway Bulletin* 2 (January 1922): 9.

Theses

Coon, John William. "Kerr Scott, The 'Go Forward' Governor: His Origins, His Program, and the North Carolina General Assembly." Master's thesis, University of North Carolina at Chapel Hill, 1968.

McKown, Harry Wilson, Jr. "Roads and Reform: The Good Roads Movement in North Carolina, 1885-1921." Master's thesis, University of North Carolina at Chapel Hill, 1972.

Index

A

Abandoned rail lines, 131
Aberdeen and Briar Patch Railroad, 131
Aberdeen-Star rail line, 131
Adopt-a-Highway program, 90
Advanced Planning Department, State Highway Commission, 59
Aeronautics, Division of. *See* Division of Aeronautics
Aeronautics Council, 122
African American students. *See* Black students
Airfields, 124
Airline Deregulation Act (1978), 122
Airports, 122-124
Alamance County: and projected regional rail line, 127
Albemarle Sound: bridges across, 21, 41, 89
Albemarle Sound Bridge, 41; visitors at opening of, pictured, 43
Alexander, Jake F., 82
Alligator River: ferry service, bridge across, 116
All-weather roads. *See* Hard-surface roads
American Airlines, 122, 123
American Association of State Highway Officials, 13, 16, 22, 41
American Automobile Association, 20, 68; report of, on condition of bridges in N.C., cited, 102
American Lung Association: survey by, cited, 114
American Tobacco Trail (rails-to-trails), 120; map of, 121; rider on, pictured, 122
Ames, Leslie, 40
Amtrak, 72, 129, 131, 132, 134, 135, 138; present routes of, in N.C., shown on map, 133; railroad stations of, in N.C., 133
Appalachian Regional Development Act (1965), 59
Asheboro, N.C.: bypasses of, 62, 68
Asheville, N.C.: and airline service, 122, 123; and bus service to Charlotte, 126; and projected interstate connector, 101; and rail service, 135
Asheville Expressway, 63, 65, 85; portion of, pictured, 66
Atlantic Beach, N.C.: and ferry service across Bogue Sound, 116-117
Atlantic Beach-Morehead City bridge, 40, 89
Atlantic Coast Line Railroad, 1, 131, 138
Atlantic, N.C.: and ferry service, 116
Atlantic Southeast Airlines, 123
Aurora, N.C.: and ferry service, 115, 117

Automobile registration fees. *See* Vehicle registration fees
Automobile registration taxes, 5, 6
Automobile registrations. *See* Vehicle registrations
Automobiles: growing popularity of, 3, 7, 17, 45, 71, 106
Aviation, Division of. *See* Division of Aviation
Aviation programs, 113, 122

B

Babcock, W. F., 58-59, 66, 68, 101; brief biographical sketch of, 58-59; pictured, 58, 73
Back Shop exhibit hall, North Carolina Transportation Museum: artist's depiction of, 136; restoration of, 136
Bailey, Josiah W., 38
Bailey, Wayne D., 92
Baise, W. Vance, 40; quoted, concerning N.C.'s lack of interest in interstate highways, 60-61
Bank panic: pictured, 30
"Basics of Bicycling" (safety curriculum for children), 120
Battleground Avenue (U.S. 220, Greensboro), 103
Baum, T. A., 116
Bayview, N.C.: and ferry service, 115, 116, 117
Beal Brothers (private construction contractor), 17
Beaucatcher Mountain (Asheville), 85
Beaucatcher Tunnel (Asheville), 65; pictured, 34
Beautification, 92, 135
Benjamin, J. C. *See* J. C. Benjamin Company
Berry, Harriet Morehead, 5-6, 18; pictured, 5, 12; reinvigorates N.C. Good Roads Association, 11-12
Better Roads (magazine): article in, quoted, 60-61
Betz, Don: pictured, 89
Bickett, Thomas W., 6; quoted, concerning his decision to hire Frank Page as chairman of Highway Commission, 6-7
Bicycle and Bikeway Act (1974), 118
Bicycle helmets, 120
Bicycle and Pedestrian Transportation, Division of. *See* Division of Bicycle and Pedestrian Transportation, NCDOT
Bicycle programs, 92, 99, 113, 114, 118, 119, 135. *See also* Division of Bicycle and Pedestrian Transportation, NCDOT
Bicycle racks (on buses, trains), 120

Bicycle-related highway improvements, 119, 120
Bicycle routes: map of, 121
Bid-rigging scandal, 85-86
"Bikeways," 118, 119, 136
"Bikeways for North Carolina: Bicycle Program Requisites" (research study), 118
Billy Graham Parkway (Charlotte): dedication ceremony for, pictured, 87
Black Mountain, N.C.: railroad station at, 135
Black students: and relative lack of school buses, 20
Blount, Emily, 55
Blue Ridge Parkway, 39, 61, 89-90, 139; bridge along, pictured, 40; pictured under construction, 39
Blythe, F. J. (Joe), 17
Blythe, Joseph (Jack) L., 17
Blythe Brothers Construction Company, 17
Board of Transportation (NCDOT), 81, 83, 87; members of, pictured with Governor Easley (2001), 100; undergoes major reorganization, 97
Bogue Sound: bridge across, 69; ferries across, 116, 117
Bonner Bridge. *See* Herbert C. Bonner Bridge
Bonsal Company, 17
Boone, N.C.: and bus service to Charlotte, 126
Boyd, Candice: quoted, concerning her experiences with hurricane, 115
Bradshaw, Thomas W., Jr., 83, 84, 85; pictured, 84
Bragg Boulevard (Cumberland County), 42
Bragtown (Durham County), 42
Bridgers, Danny: pictured, 129
Bridges, 3, 7, 15, 40-41, 87, 96; across Albemarle Sound, 21, 41, 89, pictured, 43; across Bogue Sound, 69; across Cape Fear River, 69, pictured, 73; across Croatan Sound, 96; dangerous conditions of, reported, 102; durability of, 22; across French Broad River at Asheville, 69; at Lee-Chatham County line, pictured, 53; major expense in N.C., 21; across Neuse River at New Bern, 96, pictured, 98; across Oregon Inlet, pictured, 69; replace ferry service to Outer Banks, 115; across Yadkin River, pictured, 21
Brookings Institution, 30
Broughton, J. Melville, 44; pictured, 52
Broughton, J. Melville, Jr., 59
Brown, C. E., 55
Brown, Cecil K.: quoted, concerning inability of counties to construct roads, 2, concerning unsightliness of billboards, 148
Browning, R. Getty, 38, 39; pictured, 39
Brutality: and chain gangs, 35
Bryan, Joseph, 96
Bryan Boulevard (urban expressway, Greensboro), 96

Buffalo-Springfield Rollers: advertisement for, reproduced, 19
Burch, James S., 40
Burlington, N.C.: rail station for, 133
Burnley, Jim, 89
Burrell, Conrad: pictured, 100
Bus Regulatory Reform Act (1982), 125
Bus service, 124, 125, 126, 129
Bus station, Elizabeth City: pictured, 44
Busways, 126
Bypasses (of cities and towns), 55, 61, 62, 65, 68, 94, 96, 101, 102
Byrd, Harry F., 38
Byron, Hannah, 89

C

CCAIR (small airline), 123
CSX (railroad company), 131, 133
Caledonia prison farm (Halifax County), 35
Cameron, J. E.: pictured, 14
Camp Butner, 42
Camp Davis, 42
Camp Lejeune marine base, 42
Camp Polk (Raleigh), 35
Campbell, D. M., Jr.: pictured, 100
Campbell, Ralph, 96
Cape Fear River, 21; bridge across, 22; ferry service across, 21, 117
Cape Fear River Bridge (Wilmington), 69; pictured, 73
Capital Boulevard (urban expressway, Raleigh), 63
Carolina Coach Company, 41; intercity bus of, pictured, 42
Carolina Connection (N.C. bicycle highway), 120
Carolina Freight Carriers, 41
Carolina Motor Club, 20, 68
Carolina Power and Light Company, 22, 124
Carolinian (passenger train connecting Charlotte and New York City), 132, 134; dedication ceremony for, pictured, 135
Carteret ferry: pictured, 116
Cary, N.C.: and projected regional rail line, 127; railroad station at, 133
Cedar Island: and ferry service, 116, 118
"Central Highway" (authorized by 1911 General Assembly), 3, 7, 22
Central Motor Lines, 41
Central Prison (Raleigh), 35
"Chain gangs," 1, 18, 35; pictured, 35
Chapel Hill, N.C.: and projected regional rail system, 127
"Chapel Hill Plan," 6, 11

Charlotte, N.C.: and air pollution, 114; and airline service, 122; and bus service to Asheville, Boone, 126; bypass of, 62; and need for expanded transit service, 126; and projected multimodal transportation center, 129, 133; projected outer loop around, 99-100, 101

Charlotte Area Transit System, 127-129; map of projected routes of, reproduced, 130

Charlotte Coliseum, 63

Charlotte/Douglas International Airport, 122, 123

Charlotte-Gastonia highway, 23, 42. *See also* U.S. Highway 74

Charlotte-Gastonia route: possible venue for toll road, 98

Cherokee, N.C., 39

Cherokee Indian reservation, 39

Cherry, R. Gregg, 44, 52; pictured, 52; quoted, concerning plans to accelerate paving of rural secondary roads, 45

Cherry Branch: and ferry service, 117

Cherry Point marine air base, 42

Chowan River Bridge, 34

Church Street (Burlington), 68

City expressways. *See* Urban expressways

Civilian Conservation Corps, 39

Claflin, John, 127

Clinton, N.C.: bypass of, 62

Cole, E. Nelson, 129

Coleman, R. Frank, 83

Commercial vehicles, 41, 45

Community transportation programs, 126

Concord, N.C.: and airline service, 123

Concrete roads, 18-19

Cone, Ben, 54

Cone Boulevard (urban expressway, Greensboro), 63

Consolidated public schools, 20, 36

Conti, Eugene A., Jr., 97

Contractors: and highway construction, 17

Controlled-access highways, 60, 96

County finances, 29, 31

County roads, 1, 2, 12, 18, 29, 31

Cox, J. Elwood: pictured, 14

Cox, Tyrone Y. (Ty) 105; pictured, 100

Craig, Locke, 2

Craven, William L., 5, 41

Crawford, James W., Jr., 129

Crescent (train connecting New York City and New Orleans), 132

Crime Control and Public Safety, Department of. *See* Department of Crime Control and Public Safety

Croatan Sound: bridge spanning, 96; ferry service across, 116

Cross, Sanford, 126

Currie, Claude, 57

Currie committee: recommendations of, summarized, 57-58

Currituck, N.C.: and ferry service, 117

Currituck Sound: bridge spanning, 40; and ferry service, 117

D

Dan River: bridge spanning, 40

Daniels, Josephus, 38

Dare County Regional Airport (Manteo): pictured, 124

Davidson County: and projected regional rail line, 127

"Death Valley" (junction of I-40 and I-85, Greensboro), 101

Defense access roads, 41, 42

Defense Highway Act (1941), 41

Democratic Party, 11, 82

Department of Crime Control and Public Safety, 83, 105

Department of Motor Vehicles. *See* Division of Motor Vehicles

Department of Transportation Act (1966), 67

D'Ignazio, Janet, 96

Disabled persons: special transportation program for, 126

Division of Aeronautics, NCDOT, 83, 122

Division of Aviation, NCDOT, 83, 114, 122-124

Division of Bicycle and Pedestrian Transportation, NCDOT, 114, 118-120. *See also* Bicycle programs

Division of Highway Safety, 105

Division of Motor Vehicles, 70, 73, 81, 83, 105

Division of Purchase and Contract, 31

Division of Statistics and Planning (N.C. Highway Department), 40

Dixie Culvert and Metal Company, 17

Doby, Troy, 82

Dodd, Jean H., 90

Doughton, Robert L., 32, 38

Doughton, Rufus A., 32; pictured, 14

Douglas, Ben, 63

Downtown Boulevard (urban expressway, Raleigh), 63

Drawbridges, 21

Driver education, 20, 68, 91, 92, 105

Driver's license fees, 36

Driver's licenses, 36, 105

Duke Power Company: and buses, 124, 125; buses operated by (Greensboro), pictured, 125

Dunlap, Frank, 39
Dunn, Nancy W.: pictured, 100
Durham County: and projected regional rail line, 127
Durham, N.C.: and airline service, 122, 124; and buses, 125; and projected multimodal transportation center, 129, 133; projected outer loop around portion of, 101; and projected regional rail line, 127
Durham Freeway, 68
Durham-Oxford road (old), 42
Durham-Raleigh highway, 15-16

E

Easley, Michael F., 97, 98, 99; pictured, 100
East-West Expressway (Winston-Salem), 63; portion of, pictured, 65
Eastern Metro Express (small airline), 123
Ehringhaus, J. C. B., 38, 44; brief biographical sketch of, 33-34; pictured, 52
Eisenhower, Dwight, 61
Elderly people: special transportation program for, 126
Elizabeth City, N.C.: and airline service, 122, 124; bypass of, 62
Emerald Isle, N.C.: and ferry service across Bogue Sound, 116-117; and new bridge, 69
Emergency fund transfers, 98
Emergency Relief and Construction Act (1932), 37
Energy crisis of 1973-1974, 82
Enforcement Section (DMV; now part of Department of Crime Control and Public Safety), 105
"Enhancement" activities (initiatives not directly connected with highway construction), 92, 114, 137-139; scope of, 135
Erby, Samuel L., Jr.: pictured, 100
Evans, Merrill, 66
Excise taxes: help finance proposed interstate highway system, 62
Executive Organization Act (1971), 72
Exhaust emissions, 105
Expressways, 60, 62. *See also* Urban expressways; Four-lane hard-surface highways

F

Faircloth, Duncan M. ("Lauch"), 68, 93; pictured, 73, 84; quoted, concerning decision by Governor Scott to reorganize Highway Commission, 68
Fallis, W. S., 3, 14
Fallon, George: quoted, concerning significance of proposed interstate highway system, 62
Family Lines (railroad company), 131
"Farm-to-market" secondary roads, 45, 51. *See also* Secondary roads

Fayetteville, N.C.: and airline service, 122, 123; central business loop in, 68
Federal-Aid Highway Act (1944), 60; and urban roads, 62-63
Federal-Aid Highway Act (1956), 61, 85
Federal-Aid Highway Act (1973), 83
Federal-Aid Road Act (1916), 4; shortcomings of, 13
Federal-aid road funding, 3, 4, 7, 13, 23, 29, 36, 37, 38, 42, 45, 70, 85, 87, 99. *See also* Federal funding
Federal Emergency Relief Administration, 38
Federal Express, 123
Federal funding: of bicycle programs, 119; of enhancement programs, 135, 136, 137; of public transportation projects, 131; of rail projects, 135. *See also* Federal-aid road funding
Federal Highway Act of 1921: provisions of, 13
Federal Highway Administration, U.S. Department of Transportation, 72, 94, 136
Fellheimer, Alfred, 139
Ferries (privately owned), 115; example of, pictured (1920s), 115
Ferry Division, NCDOT, 83, 115-118; present system of, shown on map, 117
Ferry programs, 99, 116-117
First Citizens Bank, 90
Fletcher, Kelly: pictured, 135
Forestry roads, 38
Forsyth County: and projected regional rail line, 127
Fort Bragg, 42
Fort Fisher: and ferry service, 117
Four-lane bypass road (first in state), 55
Four-lane hard-surface highways, 23, 42, 62. *See also* Urban expressways; Expressways
Frederick Law Olmsted Way, 139
Freeman Mill Road (Greensboro), 104
French Broad River: bridge across, 69
Friendly Avenue (Greensboro), 104
Fund transfers, 98

G

Galyon, J. Douglas (Doug), 98; pictured, 100
Gardner, Jim, 92
Gardner, O. Max, 11, 39; accepts resignation of Frank Page as chairman of Highway Commission, 23; brief biographical sketch of, 29; commissions study of state's finances, 30; and gubernatorial election of 1920, 11; newspaper headline announcing passage by N.C. House of Representatives of road bill proposed by, reproduced, 33; pictured, 32; proposes sweeping changes in responsibilities, makeup of

Highway Commission, 31; quoted, concerning his proposal to expand authority of Highway Commission, 31, concerning need for frugality on part of Highway Commission, 33

Garrett, Garland, 93, 96

Garrison Boulevard (Gastonia), 68

Gaskill, Jerry, 117; pictured, 118

Gasoline lines, 113; pictured, 113

Gasoline tax (federal), 87, 88, 98, 99

Gasoline tax (state), 23, 29, 42, 45, 52, 85, 99; authorized for first time (1921), 12; increased, 30, 91, 98; increased to help finance proposed interstate highway system, 61; increased at suggestion of Governor Gardner, 31, at suggestion of Governor Hunt, 86, at suggestion of Governor McLean, 17, at suggestion of Governor Morrison, 16, at suggestion of Gov. Robert W. Scott, 68, and at suggestion of Gov. W. Kerr Scott, 51; and municipalities, 54-55; proposed for N.C., 12; revenues from (1930s), 36

Gastonia-Charlotte highway, 23, 42. *See also* U.S. Highway 74

Gastonia-Charlotte route: possible venue for toll road, 98

Gastonia, N.C.: projected multimodal station for, 133

General Assembly. *See* North Carolina General Assembly

General Fund, 6, 92, 98; and funding for aviation programs, 113, 123; and funding for rail programs, 132; and prison-related programs, 58, 66; receives transfer of highway funds during depression, 36

Georgia: interstate highway mileage initially allotted to, 60

Gilbert, John N., 17

Gilbert Engineering Company, 17

Gilbert Southern Corporation, 94

Glencoe Mill Village, 137

"Go Forward" program, 51

Goins, J. Don, 93

Gold, John, 63

Goldsboro, N.C.: and airline service, 124; bypass of, 62

"Good roads" bill (1919), 6

"Good Roads State" (reputation acquired by N.C.), 11

Goode, Larry R., 93, 96

Gore, Albert, Sr.: quoted, concerning significance of proposed interstate highway system, 62

"Governor's Blue Ribbon Commission on Transportation Needs and Financing" (Moore commission): findings, recommendations of, summarized, 86

Governor's Committee on Rural Public Transportation, 124-125

Governor's Rail Passenger Task Force (Martin administration), 132

Grabarek, Bob, 126

Grade crossings, 133, 134

Graf, Nicholas L., 94

Graham, Alexander H. ("Sandy"), 44, 45, 52, 53, 55; pictured, 60; requests Governor Hodges's support for bond issue, 56

Graham, Rev. and Mrs. Billy: pictured, 87

Grandfather Mountain, 89

Gravel roads, 1, 12

Great Depression: effects of, 32, 36

Great Smoky Mountains National Park, 38, 90; brochure on, pictured, 41

Great Smoky Mountains Railroad, 131

Green River Bridge, 67; pictured, 70

Greene, G. Perry, 82

Greensboro, N.C.: and airline service, 122, 123; downtown intersection in, pictured (1930), 125; and enhancement-funded restorations, 138; and high-speed rail corridor, 134; and projected multimodal transportation center, 129, 133, 134, 138; projected outer loop around, 101

Greensboro-High Point road, 2

Greensboro loop: projected route of, shown on map, 104

Greensboro-Thomasville highway, 23. *See also* U.S. Highway 29

Greenville, N.C.: and airline service, 123

"Greenways," 119

Greyhound (intercity bus line), 125, 129, 138

Griffin, A. M., 138

Grimsley, Joseph W.: pictured, 84

Guilford County: constructs road linking Greensboro and High Point, 2; and projected regional rail line, 127

Gulf States Creosoting Company, 41

Gulley, Wib, 129; pictured, 114

H

Hackney school bus: pictured, 36

Hamlet railroad station, 138

Harden, John: quoted, concerning effectiveness of State Highway Commission under W. F. Babcock, 58

Hard-surface roads, 12; constructed by Highway Commission during 1920s, 23; construction of by the state, authorized for the first time (1921), 13

Harrelson, Thomas (Tommy) J., 92, 117; pictured, 120; quoted, concerning ongoing need for highway funding during recession, 92

Harrington, James (Jim) E., 88, 89, 114, 117, 123, 126; pictured, 88; quoted, concerning need for permanent revenue sources, 91

Hart, W. A.: pictured, 14
Harvey's Neck Seaplane Base, 42
Hatteras, N.C.: and ferry service, 116, 118
"Hawthorne Curve" (on East-West Expressway, Winston-Salem), 63, 65; pictured, 65
Hayti (inner-city neighborhood, Durham), 68
Hearn, Thomas K.: his introduction to report on public transportation, quoted, 126
Heliports, 124
Helms, Larry S.: pictured, 100
Henderson, N.C.: bypass of, 62
Hennis Freight Lines, 41
Henson Airlines, 123
Herbert C. Bonner Bridge, 66; aerial view of, 69
Hertford, N.C., 42
Hickory, N.C.: and airline service, 123; railroad station at, 135
High Point, N.C.: and airline service, 122, 123; and enhancement-funded restorations, 138
High Point-Greensboro road, 2
High-speed passenger rail routes (proposed for N.C.): shown on map, 133
High-speed rail corridors, 134
Highway Act of 1921: newspaper headline concerning passage of, reproduced, 13; provisions of, 12-13
Highway Beautification Act (1965), 68
Highway bonds, 68, 91, 99; authorized for first time (1921), 12; and N.C. Constitution, 51; payments on, accelerated during Cherry administration, 45; proposed by Governor Moore, 67; proposed for N.C., 12; referendum on, proposed by Governor Scott, 51-52; series of, issued during 1920s, 16, 17, 23; sought for construction of primary roads (1955), 56; sought by 1977 General Assembly, 85
Highway construction costs, 70, 85
Highway construction methods, 18-20
Highway Division, NCDOT, 122
Highway Fund, 6, 83, 92, 98, 99, 104, 126; and bicycle programs, 113, 119; and ferry programs, 113, 118; and prison-related programs, 58, 66; and public transportation programs, 113; and rail programs, 135
Highway Improvement Program, 83, 84
Highway laborers: pictured wearing shoes made from discarded auto tires, 20
Highway mileage in N.C., 23
Highway numbering, 22
Highway Patrol. *See* North Carolina State Highway Patrol
Highway Safety, Division of. *See* Division of Highway Safety
Highway Safety Act (1966), 68

Highway signs, 15; pictured, 24
Highway Study Commission, 91
Highway Trust Fund, 92, 93, 98, 99, 101, 103, 104, 129; and alternatives to highway construction, 132; long-term goals of, summarized, 91; and rail programs, 135
Highways. *See* Roads and highways
Hill, Bobby: pictured, 118
Hill, John Sprunt: pictured, 14
Historic preservation, 92
Historic Salisbury Foundation, 137
Hitch, Arthur, 17
Hodges, Luther H., 56-57; brief biographical sketch of, 56; leads effort to separate state prison system from highway commission, 58; leads opposition to proposal to charge tolls for use of Blue Ridge Parkway, 61; pictured, 58; quoted, on W. F. Babcock's qualifications to serve as state highway administrator, 58
Hodgkins, Sara W.: pictured, 84
Hoey, Clyde R., 39; pictured, 52
Holshouser, James E., Jr., 81; pictured, 82
Hopkins, Harry, 38
Hunt, James B., Jr., 81, 86, 92, 96, 97, 104, 114, 117, 124, 126; admits to problems in NCDOT, 96; brief biographical sketch of, 83; pictured, 82, 84, 87, 94, 134; quoted, on political difficulty of raising highway taxes, 86
Hunt, Joseph M., 66
Hunt, Sam, 92, 126, 133; pictured, 94
Hunter, Robert C., 123
Hyatt, Stan, 94; pictured, 97

I
Ickes, Harold L., 38
Inadequate funding, 91
Incident Management Assistance Patrol: employee of, pictured, 101
Independence Boulevard (urban expressway, Charlotte), 63, 66, 128; route of, shown on map (1949), 64
"Independent" bicycle projects, 119
Inflation, 82-83
Inmate labor. *See* Prison labor
Insurance Institute for Highway Safety: study by, cited, 104
Intercity bus lines, 125, 129
Intermodal Surface Transportation Efficiency Act (ISTEA), 92, 93, 114, 132; enhancement projects funded by, 135-136, 137-138; and independent bicycle projects, 119-120
Intermodal transfer, 124

Interstate highway extensions, 66, 85
Interstate highway mileage: comparisons among N.C. and its neighboring states, 60; increases in, sought by N.C. leaders, 65-66
Interstate Highway System: authorized by Congress (1956), 61; construction of, slowed by environmentalists, historic preservationists, financial problems, 67-68; financing of, supported by wide array of new taxes, 62; map of (1956-1957), 63; N.C. portions of, completed during 1980s, 85; original allocation to N.C. (1956), original projection (1947) of, remains largely unchanged, 61; projected in Federal-Aid Highway Act (1944), 60; specifications concerning, 62; urban additions to, 61; well under way in N.C. by mid-1960s, 67
Interstate highways: maintenance of, 103-104
Interstate 26, 62, 67, 85, 94; recommended routing of, 61
Interstate 40, 62, 69, 85, 94, 101; completed between Raleigh and Wilmington, 88; extension of, approved for N.C. (1968), 66, sought for N.C., 85; Pigeon River Gorge section of, 67; recommended routing of, 61; unfinished portion of, 67; Winston-Salem bypass portion of, 65; Winston-Salem portion of, 88
Interstate 40 Business, 65
Interstate 40/85, 62, 103
Interstate 66, 94
Interstate 73 (future), 93; proposed route of, shown on map, 95
"Interstate 73/Interstate 74," 94
Interstate 74 (future), 93, 94; proposed route of, shown on map, 95
Interstate 77, 61, 62, 85, 88, 89, 93, 94; and inner-city neighborhood in Charlotte, 68; southward extension of, approved, 66
Interstate 85, 62, 85, 88, 94; Greensboro bypass portion of, 101; recommended routing of, 61; unfinished portion of, 67
Interstate 85 Business, 62
Interstate 95, 62, 85, 96; eastward extension of, approved, 66; recommended routing of, 61
Interstate 240 (loop through Asheville), 65, 85, 88
Interstate 277 (Charlotte), 88, 89
Interstate 440 (loop around Raleigh), 100
Interstate 485 (projected outer loop around Charlotte), 99-100, 101
Interstate 540 (projected outer loop around Raleigh), 100-101; bridge construction connected with, pictured, 103
Interstate 785: proposed, 94
Interstate 840 (projected outer loop around Greensboro), 101

"Intrastate Highway System" (proposed), 91
Ireland, Robert: quoted, concerning need to build roads in response to popularity of automobiles, 7

J
J. C. Benjamin Company, 17
Jacksonville, N.C.: and airline service, 123
Jacksonville bypass (U.S. 17), 96
Jeffress, E. B., 32, 35
Johnson, Charles, 51
Johnson, Frank L: pictured, 100
Jolley, Harley: quoted, concerning naming of Blue Ridge Parkway, 39
Jordan, Everett, 52
Jordan, Henry, 52, 55
Jordan, Michael, 88

K
Kannapolis, N.C.: projected rail station for, 133
Keep North Carolina Clean and Beautiful, 90
Kindley, G. R.: pictured, 100
King, David, 96, 97, 114, 117, 126, 129; pictured, 114, 127
King, Martin Luther. *See* Martin Luther King Parkway
Kinston, N.C.: and airline service, 123
Kirkpatrick, T. L., 31
Kitty Hawk-Point Harbor bridge, 40
Kluttz, Margaret: pictured, 100
Knotts Island: and ferry service, 117
Kozak, Mike: quoted, concerning projected mass-transit systems, 129

L
Lake, I. Beverly, Jr., 86
Latham, Robert, 38
Laurinburg, N.C.: bypass of, 62
Lee, Cameron W., 59, 66; pictured, 59, 73
Lee, Howard N.: pictured, 84
Lee Street/N.C. 6 (urban expressway, Greensboro), 63, 103
Lentz, Bruce A., 81, 82
Lexington, N.C.: bypass of, 55
Liability insurance, 105
Light-rail service, 127
Limited-access highways, 56
Linn Cove Viaduct (Blue Ridge Parkway), 89; pictured (under construction), 90
Louisburg, N.C.: and airline service, 123
Loving, T. A. *See* T. A. Loving Company
Lumberton, N.C.: bypass of, 62
Lynch, Mark: pictured, 84

M

Macadam roads, 1, 2, 12, 18
McBee, J. C.: pictured, 14
McCoy, David, 97
McCracken, Frank W.: pictured, 59
McCrary, D. B., 44
McCrorey Heights (inner-city neighborhood, Charlotte), 68
MacDonald, Thomas, 5, 13, 41, 60, 61; pictured, 14; quoted, concerning pent-up desire to travel by car at end of World War II, 45
McDonald's restaurant (Greensboro): pictured, 71
McEntire, Earl H., 88
McGee, Chris, 93
McGirt, W. A.: pictured, 14
McKinney, Brent, 127; quoted, concerning public resistance to public transportation, 114
McLean, Angus Wilton: requests additional funding for highway construction, maintenance, 16
McLean Trucking Company, 41
McRae, Cameron W.: pictured, 100
Makepeace, Harold, 59
Manns Harbor: and ferry service, 117
Manns Harbor Shipyard, 116, 118
Manteo, N.C.: and bus service to Norfolk, Va., 126; and ferry service, 116
Manteo bypass (U.S. 64/264), 96
Marion, N.C.: railroad station at, 135
Market Street (Greensboro), 104
Market Street (Wilmington), 96
Marley, William G., 92
Martin, James G., 89, 90, 91, 114, 132; brief biographical sketch of, 88; pictured, 82, 89
Martin Luther King Jr. Parkway (urban expressway, Fayetteville), 96
Martin Luther King Jr. Parkway (urban expressway, Wilmington), 96
Mass transit, 98, 99
Matthews, Bruce, 123
Matthews, N.C., 127
Meletiou, Mary, 118
Merrimon (village), 53
Metropolitan Transit Commission (Mecklenburg County), 127
Milburn, Frank, 137
Military installations in N.C. (during World War II): shown on map, 46
Mills, Fred, 73
Milton, N.C.: bridge at, 40
Minnesott Beach: and ferry service, 117
Minority construction contractors, 105
Moore, Collice C.: pictured, 100
Moore, Dan K., 65, 68, 86; brief biographical sketch of, 66-67
Mooresville, N.C.: and commuter rail service to and from Charlotte, 127
Morehead City, N.C.: and airline service, 124
Morehead City-Atlantic Beach bridge, 40, 89
Morgan, Bob, 100: quoted, concerning absence of outer loop in Charlotte, 100
Morgan, Scarlet: pictured, 135
Morganton, N.C.: bypass of, 62; railroad station at, 135
Morrison, Cameron: activities of, on behalf of good roads, 12, 16; brief biographical sketch of, 11; pictured with members of N.C. State Highway Commission (1921), 14; quoted, concerning his commitment to better roads, 11
Morrow, Sarah T.: pictured, 84
Morton, Hugh, 89
Motor & Equipment Company, 17
Motor Vehicle Bureau, state Department of Revenue, 36
Motor vehicle taxes, 36
Motor Vehicles, Division of. *See* Division of Motor Vehicles
Motor vehicles: and roads, 1
Motorists: create better driving conditions, 20
"Mountains to the Sea Bicycle Route," 119
Multimodal programs, 113-114, 129, 132, 133, 138; and state, federal funding, 114-115
Multimodal transportation centers (projected) 128, 129, 133
"Multi-use trails," 119, 120, 136
Municipalities: and gasoline-tax revenues, 54-55
Murdock, Jack, 68, 81, 83, 88, 93; pictured, 72

N

National Environmental Policy Act (1969), 67
National Highway System Designation Act (1995), 93
National Historic Preservation Act (1966), 67
National Industrial Recovery Act (1933), 38
National Park Service, 38
National Railroad Passenger Corporation. *See* Amtrak
National Register of Historic Places, 67
"National System of Interstate Highways" (draft proposal), 60
Nello L. Teer Company, 17, 39; road-building equipment of, pictured, 39
Nelson, R. B.: pictured, 91
Neuse River: bridge spanning (at New Bern), 96

INDEX

New Bern, N.C.: and airline service, 123
New Deal programs, 33, 36, 38, 60
New Jersey Turnpike, 61
News and Observer (Raleigh): editorial praising Frank Page, quoted, 23; endorses new spending on mass transit, 98; praises Scott administration's efforts at paving secondary roads, 53-54; quoted, concerning Frank Page's toughness as a negotiator, 17-18; quoted concerning speech delivered by Governor Morrison, 12; supports Governor Gardner's efforts to expand responsibilities of Highway Commission, 31
Nixon, Richard, 131
"Non-highway" activities, 66
Norfolk, Va.: and bus service to Manteo, N.C., 126
Norfolk Southern Corporation, 131, 133, 134
Norfolk & Western Railroad, 131, 133
North Carolina: fails to apply for urban additions to its allotted interstate highway mileage, 61; interstate highway mileage initially allotted to, 60, 62; population of, increases dramatically after 1945, 71
North Carolina (magazine): cited, 86
North Carolina Arboretum, 139
North Carolina Bicycle Committee, 119
North Carolina Department of Cultural Resources, 136
North Carolina Department of Transportation, 70, 85; attempts to encourage intercity rail passenger service, 132, 134; and awarding of construction projects, 105; new divisions of, created, 83; recent budget allocations by, 114; revenues of, increase during 1970s, 1980s, 98-99; staff size of, 105-106; tainted by charges of improper procedures in setting construction priorities, 96; workers for, pictured repairing bridge, 105
"North Carolina Department of Transportation and Highway Safety," 81, 83
North Carolina Equipment Company, 41
North Carolina General Assembly: addresses bid-rigging scandal, 86; appropriates funds for public transportation, 126; authorizes "Central Highway" (1911), 3; authorizes special bonds to finance construction of drawbridges, 21; combines Highway Commission and state prison system, 35; creates North Carolina State Highway Commission, 2; enacts compromise bill to help fund highway construction (1919), 6; establishes State Highway Patrol, 30; expands authority of Highway Commission, 5; fails to match federal-aid highway funding (1917), 5; increases gasoline taxes, 86, 91; makes share of gasoline-tax revenues available to municipalities, 55; modifies revenue-sharing provisions of Powell Bill, 86, 89; proposes bond issue (1977), 85; provides dependable funding for aviation programs, 123; refuses to authorize bond issue, 91; reorganizes executive branch of state government, 72-73; reorganizes Highway Commission, 6; transfers highway funds to General Fund, 36
North Carolina Geological and Economic Survey, 2
North Carolina Good Roads Association, 2-3, 5-6, 11-12; members of, pictured, 3
North Carolina Highway Bulletin, 15, 17
North Carolina highway system: shown on map (1924), 18
N.C. Highway 6, 63, 103
N.C. Highway 10 (now largely U.S. Highway 70) 22, 23; portion of route of, shown on map (1931), 20; proposed routing of, provokes controversy, 21
N.C. Highway 10-A: route of, shown on map (1931), 20
N.C. Highway 12, 66, 116, 120
N.C. Highway 20 (now U.S. 74), 23; construction of portion of, described, 19
N.C. Highway 24, 42
N.C. Highway 26 (now U.S. 21), 23
N.C. Highway 30 (now largely U.S. 17), 23
N.C. Highway 32, 41, 89
N.C. Highway 37, 89
N.C. Highway 50 (old designation), 22
N.C. Highway 58, 116
N.C. Highway 87, 42
N.C. Highway 90 (now an extended U.S. 64), 23
N.C. Highway 130, 42
N.C. Highway 210, 42
N.C. Highway 306, 117
N.C. Highway 342 (now U.S. 17), 21
North Carolina Highway Trust Fund. *See* Highway Trust Fund
North Carolina Highways, a Seven Year Highway Improvement Program, July 1973 thru June 1980, 83, 113
North Carolina League of Municipalities, 54
North Carolina Railroad, 61, 132, 133, 134
North Carolina Roads and Their Builders (1952), 36; cited, 58
North Carolina Roadways (magazine of State Highway Commission): quoted, concerning expressway built by Highway Commission, 62
North Carolina State Highway Commission: adds substantial road mileage between 1949 and 1971, 71; assumes responsibility for care, custody of prisoners, prison camps, 33, 35, for secondary roads in N.C., 31, 33; authority of, expands, 5; begins period of important accomplishments, 13-16; and Blue Ridge

Parkway, 38-39; combined with state prison system, 35; concentrates on building expressways during 1950s, 62; early duties of, 2, 3; enlarged under administration of Gov. Robert W. Scott, 68; erects bridges, 21, 22; and ferry service, 116-117; first major project of, 5; geographic divisions of (1953), shown on map, 56; growth in number of employees of, summarized, 69-70; headquarters of (Raleigh), described, 69-70, pictured, 15; increasingly works directly with private construction contractors, 17; maintenance center of (outside Raleigh), pictured, 15; makes modest recommendations concerning proposed interstate highway system, 60; members of, pictured with Governor Morrison (1921), 14; progress made by, in constructing highways during 1920s, summarized, 23; prospers under leadership of W. F. Babcock, 59; provides guidance in constructing bridge, 3; and recommendations of Currie committee (1955), 57; refines organizational structure of NCDOT, 83; reorganized by General Assembly, 6; revenues of, enjoy steady growth, 70; separated from state prison system, 58, 70; subsumed into new N.C. Department of Transportation, 70, 73, 81; survives after being reestablished in 1915, 3; transforms state's highway system in 1949-1972 period, 71; truck operated by, pictured, 6

North Carolina State Highway Patrol, 20, 30, 68, 81, 83, 105

North Carolina Transportation Museum: Back Shop exhibit hall of, 136, shown in artist's depiction, 136; renovation of roundhouse at, 136

North Carolina Transportation Museum Foundation, 136

North Carolina Turnpike Authority, 98

Northeast Cape Fear River: bridge across, 22

O

Ocracoke, N.C.: and ferry service, 117, 118

Ocracoke Island: and ferry service, 116; paving of dirt road in, described, 53

Office of Bicycle and Pedestrian Transportation, NCDOT. *See* Division of Bicycle and Pedestrian Transportation, NCDOT

Old Fort, N.C.: railroad station at, 135

Olmsted, Frederick Law, 139

Orange County: and projected regional rail line, 127

Oregon Inlet: bridges, ferries across, 66, 116

Oregon Inlet Bridge: aerial view of, 69

Outer Banks: ferry service, bridges to, 115

Overman, Don, 83

Oxford, N.C.: bypass of, 62

Oxford-Durham road (old), 42

P

Page, Allison Francis, 7

Page, Frank, 6, 12, 13, 17, 31, 38; accomplishments of, praised by editorial, 23; brief biographical sketch of, 7; pictured, 14, 16; quoted, concerning his hiring of Charles Upham as chief engineer of Highway Commission, 14; resigns as chairman of Highway Commission, 23; widely recognized for his accomplishments, 16

Page, Robert, 7, 11

Page, Walter Hines, 7

Painter Boulevard (projected outer loop around Greensboro), 101; shown on map, 104

Palmetto (train connecting New York City and Florida), 132

Pamlico Sound: ferries across, 117

Paroles Commission: funding of, removed from Highway Fund, 66

Parsons, David E.: quoted, concerning pressing need to upgrade bridges, roads in N.C., 102

Parsons, Brinkerhoff, Hall & Macdonald (engineering firm): conclusions of special study (Parsons report) conducted by, summarized, 56

Patrick, D. W., 83, 116

Pedestrian programs, 92, 120, 135. *See also* Division of Bicycle and Pedestrian Transportation, NCDOT

Peele, Frazier, 116

Pennsylvania Turnpike, 60, 61

People Express (small airline), 132

Percentage-of-price gasoline tax, 86, 91

Perry, Miriam: pictured, 129

Peters, Larry, 93

Petroleum industry: opposes bond issue, 52

Piedmont (Amtrak train connecting Charlotte and Raleigh), 120, 132, 134

Piedmont Airlines, 122, 123, 132

Piedmont Authority for Regional Transportation (Guilford, Forsyth, Alamance, Randolph, Davidson, and Rockingham Counties), 127

Piedmont Triad International Airport, 123

Pinehurst, N.C.: and airline service, 122, 123

Pineville, N.C.: and projected light-rail service, 127

Pitt-Greenville Airport, 123

Planks, Pavement and Progress (booklet by James E. Harrington), 126

Planning and Environment Division, NCDOT, 96, 97

Plentl, Willard G. ("Will"), 122, 123; pictured, 123; praises service being provided by smaller airlines, 123

Point Harbor-Kitty Hawk bridge, 40

Pope, Bill: pictured, 89

INDEX

Population (N.C.): growth of, 1970-2000, 106; increases dramatically after 1945, 71
Ports Authority Division, NCDOT. *See* State Ports Authority
Powell, Junius K., 55
Powell, William S.: cited, concerning public opinion of Cameron Morrison as governor, 11
Powell Bill, 55, 86, 89, 91
Pratt, Joseph Hyde, 3, 5, 6, 18; pictured, 4
Prescott, George R., 65
Preservation North Carolina, 137
Primary roads/highways, 41, 45, 71; benefit from passage of 1949 bond issue, 55; construction of, languishes in mid-1960s, 66; focus of comprehensive study, 55-56
Prince, L. B., 44
Prison labor, 1, 18, 92
Prisoners. *See* State prisoners
Private airfields, 124
Private companies: and highway construction, 17
Probation Commission: funding of, removed from Highway Fund, 66
Progress Energy, 124
Proposed high-speed passenger rail routes (for N.C.): shown on map, 133. *See also* Railroad passenger service
Public schools, 20
Public transportation, 98, 99, 113, 114
Public Transportation Division, NCDOT, 83, 114, 124-129, 131
Public Transportation and Rail Division, NCDOT, 126
Public transportation regional authorities, 127
Public Works Administration, 38
Purchase and Contract, Division of. *See* Division of Purchase and Contract

Q
Queen City Trailways, 41

R
Racism: and chain gangs, 35
Ragland, William Trent, 41
Rail Division, NCDOT, 114, 126, 127, 129, 131-135
Rail Industrial Access Program, 134
Rail programs, 99, 113, 114
Rail Revitalization and Regulatory Reform Act (1976), 131
Railroad passenger service, 131, 132. *See also* Proposed high-speed passenger rail routes
Railroad stations, 1, 131, 132; renovations of, 135; restorations of, 136, 137, 138
Railroads (in N.C., ca. 1925), 1; shown on map, 2
Rail-trails, 119, 120
"Rails-to-trails" project, 135; pictured, 121
Raleigh Banking and Trust Company: crowd at, pictured, 30
Raleigh Beltline (urban expressway), 65, 85; aerial view of route of (under construction), 67
Raleigh Chamber of Commerce, 60
Raleigh, N.C.: and airline service, 122, 124; and bus service to coastal destinations, 126; and high-speed rail corridor, 134; and possible passenger rail service to Wilmington, 135; and projected multimodal transportation center, 129, 133; projected outer loop around, 100-101, 101; and projected regional rail line, 127
Raleigh-Durham highway, 15-16
Raleigh-Durham International Airport, 122, 123, 124; and projected regional rail system, 127
Ralph Whitehead Associates (engineering firm), 96
Rand, Jim, 93
Randolph County: and projected regional rail line, 127
Rankin, Edward L., Jr.: quoted, concerning leadership of W. F. Babcock, 59, concerning significance of 1931 road bill, 31, concerning inability of state to satisfy demand for new highways, 45
Ratios of cars to people, 71, 106
Reagan, Ronald, 89
Regional rail systems, 127
Registration fees. *See* Vehicle registration fees
Reidsville, N.C.: bypass of, 62
Reinforced concrete bridge: pictured, 53
"Report on Transportation Needs in North Carolina, A" (research report, 1973): cited, 103, 122, 124
Research Triangle (Raleigh/Durham/Cary/Chapel Hill area): and air pollution, 114; and need for expanded transit service, 126
Research Triangle Park: and projected regional rail line, 127
Reynolds, Robert R., 38
Right-of-way: escalating costs of, 70-71, 99
Ritchey, James M., Jr., 127
Road paving: pictured, 7, 54, 57; of secondary roads, 53, 103
Road traffic, 36, 70
Roads and highways (N.C.): conditions of, in early twentieth century, 1, during Great Depression, 36, in 1954, 56, during World War II, 42; construction, maintenance of, 1-2, 33, 42, 86-87, 93, 99, 103-104; subject of intensive study by committee, 30-31

Roanoke Island: and ferry service, 116
Roanoke Sound: bridge spanning, 40
Roberson, William R., Jr.: quoted, concerning need for retrenchment in highway building, 87
Roberts, Coleman, 20
Robeson Construction Company, 19
Robinson, David, 124
Rockingham County: and projected regional rail line, 127
Rocky Mount, N.C., 134; and airline service, 122, 123-124; bypass of, 62
Rocky Mount railroad station: restoration of, 138; waiting room of, pictured, 138
Rogers, William H., Jr. (Bill), 53, 55, 59
Roney, Ben, 66
Roosevelt, Franklin D., 38
Rose, Billy, 68, 81, 83, 88; cited, concerning most important urban expressways in N.C., 63; credits Winston-Salem city manager for construction of expressway, 63; pictured, 73; quoted, concerning W. F. Babcock's capabilities, 59
Ross, Charles, 44
Roxboro, N.C.: and airline service, 123
Rural transportation problems, 124

S

Safety issues, 68, 92, 104-105
Salisbury, N.C., 135
Salisbury railroad depot: pictured, 137; restoration of, 137-138
Sams, Larry: pictured, 122
Sand-clay roads, 1, 12, 19
Sanderson, Len, 96
Sanford, Terry, 65; pictured, 82
Sanford, N.C.: and airline service, 123; bypass of, 62
Scenic Byways, 90
Scenic highways, 135
School buses, 20-21, 36; pictured, 36
School crossing guards, 20
Scott, Robert W., 68, 86; pictured, 82
Scott, W. Kerr, 45, 54, 55; brief biographical sketch, 51; campaigns on behalf of bond referendum, 51-52; pictured, 52
Sea Level (ferryboat), 116
Seaboard Air Line Railway, 1, 17, 19, 131
Seaboard Coast Line Railroad, 131, 138
Seaboard System (railroad company), 131
Secondary Roads Council, 81, 83
Secondary roads/highways, 31, 41, 45, 51, 71; focus of ambitious paving programs, 53, 103, of comprehensive study, 55-56; focus on, in N.C., diverts attention from interstate highway system, 60; and recommendations of Currie committee (1955), 57. *See also* "Farm-to-market" secondary roads
Seely, Bruce: quoted, concerning federal spending on highways during New Deal, 38
Selma, N.C.: and enhancement-funded restorations, 138
Senate Bill 1005 (2001), 98
Sewell, Louis W., Jr.: pictured, 100
"Shelby Dynasty," 39
Shenandoah National Park, 38, 90
Signage. *See* Highway signs
Silver Meteor (train connecting New York City and Florida), 132
Silver Star (train connecting New York City and Florida), 132
Simmons, Furnifold, 11
Simmons, Pat, 126
Skyline Drive (parkway), 38
Slater, Rodney, 93
Smith, Laurie, 137; quoted, concerning goals of NCDOT's enhancement projects, 139
Smith, McNeill, 118
Smith, Wilbur. *See* Wilbur Smith and Associates
Smith Creek Parkway (urban expressway, Wilmington), 96
Snider, William D.: quoted, concerning benefits derived from 1949 bond issue, 54
South Carolina: interstate highway mileage initially allotted to, 60
Southeast Corridor (high-speed rail), 134
Southern Pines, N.C.: bypass of, 62
Southern Power Company, 124
Southern Railway, 1, 131, 133, 137, 138
Southern Railway station (former), Greensboro: pictured, 131; to become multimodal transportation center, 131, 133, 138
Southport, N.C.: and ferry service, 117
Southwest Airlines, 124
Staggers Act (1980), 131
Stallings, Wayne, 97
Star-Aberdeen rail line, 131
State Aid to Airports program, 122
State Highway Commission. *See* North Carolina State Highway Commission
"State Highway Fund" (1919). *See* Highway Fund
State Highway Patrol. *See* North Carolina State Highway Patrol
State Highway and Public Works Commission, 35, 58
State Highway System of North Carolina, Its Evolution and Status, The: quoted, 2, 148

State indebtedness, 16, 29, 45
State Ports Authority, 70, 73, 81, 83
State Prison Department: combined with State Highway Commission, 35; funding of, removed from Highway Fund, 66; separated from State Highway Commission, 58
State prisoners, 35
Statesville, N.C.: railroad station at, 135
Statistics and Planning, Division of. *See* Division of Statistics and Planning
Stikeleather, J. G.: pictured, 14
Stock-market crash of 1929, 29
Stranded motorist: pictured, 4
Streetcars, 124
Suburban development, 54
Superior Stone Company, 41
Surface Transportation Act (1982), 87
Swan Quarter, N.C.: and ferry service, 117, 118
Swift Island Bridge, 22
Szlosberg, Nina: pictured, 100

T
T. A. Loving Company, 41
Taxes: help finance proposed interstate highway system, 62
Teenagers: pictured at first McDonald's restaurant in N.C., 71
Teer, Nello L., 17
"Temporary I-85," 85
Tennessee: interstate highway mileage initially allotted to, 60
Tennessee Valley Authority, 38
Thomasville, N.C.: bypass of, 55
Thomasville-Greensboro highway, 23. *See also* U.S. Highway 29
Thornburg, Alan Z.: pictured, 100
Three-lane hard-surface highway, 23
Thurston Motor Lines, 41
Tidewater Construction Company, 41
Tillett, J. B. ("Toby"), 115
Tippett, Lyndo, 97, 98, 120, 129; pictured, 100
Tires: taxes on, help finance proposed interstate highway system, 62
Tober, Ronald J., 127
Toll booth (for twin bridges, Wilmington): pictured, 22
Toll bridges, 21, 22, 40-41
Toll ferries, 116
Toll roads/highways, 60, 61, 62, 98
Tolson, Norris, 96; proposed plan to reorganize Board of Transportation, summarized, 97

Topsoil roads, 1
Tourism, 39, 123
Traffic. *See* Road traffic
Traffic Engineering Section, State Highway Commission, 68
Trailways (intercity bus line), 125, 129
Train-related accidents, 134
Transit 2001 (report by special blue-ribbon study commission, 1997), 96, 126, 133
Transportation Enhancement Programs (booklet), 137
Transportation Equity Act for the 21st Century ("TEA-21"), 92, 132, 135, 137-138
Transportation Improvement Program (TIP), 84, 87
Transportation Improvement Program (TIP), 1979-1985, 84, 125; cited, 118, 119
Transportation Improvement Program, 1986-1995, 90
Transportation Improvement Program, 2000-2006, 84-85
Transportation Planning Division, NCDOT, 131
Traylor Brothers (contractor), 96
Triad (Greensboro/Winston-Salem/High Point area): and air pollution, 114; and need for expanded transit service, 126, 127
Triangle Transit Authority (Wake, Durham, Orange Counties), 120, 132, 133; map of proposed regional rail system, reproduced, 128
Trucking companies, 41
Tufts, Leonard, 6
Tunnels (on interstate highways), 67
Turner, Reginald, 3-4
Turner, Rupert, 3-4
Turnpikes, 60, 61

U
Umstead, William B., 56; brief biographical sketch of, 55
Uniform Driver's License Act, 36
United Airlines, 123
US Airways, 123
U.S. Bureau of Public Roads, 5, 22, 31, 38, 60, 61, 72
U.S. Department of Transportation, 72, 134
U.S. 401 bike path (Fayetteville), 119
U.S. Highway 1, 22, 55, 63, 65, 100
U.S. Highway 13, 91
U.S. Highway 17, 23, 42, 69, 96; projected Wilmington bypass portion of, 102; shown on map (World War II era), 46;
U.S. Highway 19/23, 65, 94

U.S. Highway 21, 23
U.S. Highway 25, 65
U.S. Highway 29, 17, 55, 62, 69, 94; four-lane segments of, bypassing Thomasville, Lexington, 55; portion of, upgraded as expressway, 62
U.S. Highway 29/70, 62
U.S. Highway 52, 93, 94
U.S. Highway 58: and ferry service across Bogue Sound, 116
U.S. Highway 64, 23, 55, 62, 65, 96, 100, 116; Asheboro bypass portion of, 68; four-laning of, extended eastward to Tarboro, 89
U.S. Highway 64/264 (Manteo bypass portion), 96
U.S. Highway 70, 22, 23, 53, 55, 62, 65, 85, 96; four-laning of, east from Raleigh, 67; portion of, upgraded as expressway, 62
U.S. Highway 74, 23, 63, 69, 93; bypass around Rockingham, Hamlet, 94; receives extensive upgrades, 55, 67
U.S. Highway 76, 69
U.S. Highway 220, 93
U.S. Highway 264, 96
U.S. Highway 301, 55
U.S. Highway 311, 93
U.S. Highway 401, 96
U.S. Office of Public Roads, 3
University of North Carolina at Charlotte: and light-rail service to and from Charlotte, 127, 128
University system: consolidation of, proposed, 30
Upchurch, Avery: pictured, 89
Upham, Charles, 14
Urban expressways, 62-63, 68-69, 96. *See also* Expressways; Four-lane hard-surface highways
Urban loops, connectors, 91, 99; cost of, 101; map of, reproduced, 102; projected for Asheville (proposed connector), 102, for Durham (proposed only), 101-102, for Wilmington, 102, for Winston-Salem (proposed only), 101; projected to surround Charlotte, 99-100, to surround Greensboro, 101, to surround Raleigh, 100-101
Urban sprawl, 101
Use tax, 92

V
Valdese, N.C., 135
Vanpools, 125
Varner, Henry, 6
Vehicle inspections, 105
Vehicle registration fees, 6, 12, 13, 23, 85, 98
Vehicle registrations, 7, 17, 45
Vehicle tax. *See* Use tax

Virginia: interstate highway mileage initially allotted to, 60
Virginia Dare Memorial Bridge, 96; pictured, 99

W
W. E. Graham & Sons (highway contractor), 62
Waff, Paul: pictured, 100
Wagner, Steward, 138
Wake County: and projected regional rail line, 127
Wakefield Plantation (residential development near Wake Forest), 101
Waldrop, John D., 39
Walnut Mountain range, 94
Ward Boulevard (Wilson), 68
Waynick, Capus, 36, 51
Webb, Whit, 136
Weigh stations, 105
Welcome centers, 68; first one in N.C., pictured, 70
Welfare recipients: community transportation programs for, 126
Wells, George W., 88
Wendover Avenue (U.S. 70, Greensboro), 68-69, 103
West Virginia Turnpike, 61
Western North Carolina: and passenger rail service, 135
Whitehead, Ralph. *See* Ralph Whitehead Associates
Wilbur Smith and Associates (highway contractor), 65, 86
Wil-Cox Bridge (across Yadkin River), 21; opening of, pictured, 21
Wildflower projects, 135
Wilkinson Boulevard (urban expressway, Charlotte, and part of U.S/29/74), 63, 128
Williams, Bill, 123
Willoughby, George S., Jr., 66, 68; pictured, 73
Wilmington, N.C.: and airline service, 123; and possible passenger rail service to Raleigh, 135; and projected multimodal transportation center, 129; and projected U.S. 17 bypass, 101; shipyard at, 42; toll bridge across Cape Fear River at, pictured, 22; and toll bridges, 21
Wilson, Lanny T.: pictured, 100
Wilson, N.C., 134; bypasses of, 62, 96; and projected multimodal transportation center, 129
Wilson railroad station: restoration of, 138
Winston-Salem, N.C.: and airline service, 122, 123; and high-speed rail corridor, 134; possible multimodal station for, 133; projected outer loop around portion of, 101
Wolfe, Thomas: quoted, 147
Wood, Word H.: pictured, 14
Works Progress Administration, 38, 42
World War II: effects of, 42, 44-45

180

Wrightsville Beach: bridge near, 40

Y

Yadkin River: bridge over, pictured, 21

Yates, Curtis, 118; characterizes rail-trails, 119; pictured, 120

"Yellow Book" (U.S. Bureau of Public Roads), 61

Young, Lloyd: pictured, 87

Yount, O. F., 3

Walter R. Turner serves as historian at the North Carolina Transportation Museum at Spencer. A fifth-generation North Carolinian, he grew up in Winston-Salem. He earned his undergraduate degree in history at Methodist College, Fayetteville, and a master's degree in social work at the University of North Carolina at Chapel Hill. He served with the Peace Corps in the Philippines and later became a social worker and travel agent. His articles on transportation history have appeared in *Our State*, *Business North Carolina*, and the state's major newspapers. He and his wife Pamela live in Greensboro with their Yorkshire terriers.

388.1097 Turner   c.2
Turner, Walter R.
Paving tobacco road : a century
of progress by the North Carolin

PROPERTY OF
HIGH POINT PUBLIC LIBRARY
HIGH POINT, NORTH CAROLINA